Y0-CKN-994

THE CHICANO HERITAGE

This is a volume in the Arno Press collection

THE CHICANO HERITAGE

Advisory Editor
Carlos E. Cortés

Editorial Board
Rodolfo Acuña
Juan Gómez-Quiñones
George F. Rivera, Jr.

See last pages of this volume for a complete list of titles.

MEXICANS IN CALIFORNIA AFTER THE U.S. CONQUEST

*With an Introduction
by Carlos E. Cortés*

ARNO PRESS
A New York Times Company
New York — 1976

155135

Editorial Supervision: LESLIE PARR

Reprint Edition 1976 by Arno Press Inc.

Copyright © 1976 by Arno Press Inc.

El Quacheno and Los Angeles in 1849 were
  reprinted from copies in the State
  Historical Society of Wisconsin Library

THE CHICANO HERITAGE
ISBN for complete set: 0-405-09480-9
See last pages of this volume for titles.

Manufactured in the United States of America

Library of Congress Cataloging in Publication Data
Main entry under title:
California after the U. S. conquest.

  (The Chicano heritage)
  CONTENTS: Griffin, J. S. Los Angeles in 1849.--
Foster, S. C. El quacheno.--Brent, J. L. The Lugo case.
--Robinson, W. W. People versus Lugo. [etc.]
  1. Mexican Americans--California--Addresses, essays,
lectures. 2. California--Politics and government--1846-
1850--Addresses, essays, lectures. 3. Lugo, Francisco--
Addresses, essays, lectures. 4. Lugo, Menito--Addresses,
essays, lectures. I. Series.
F870.M5C2   979.4'04   76-5225
ISBN 0-405-09535-X

MEXICANS IN CALIFORNIA AFTER THE U.S. CONQUEST

Introduction

In 1846, United States troops invaded and occupied Mexican California. By the 1848 Treaty of Guadalupe Hidalgo, Mexico officially ceded California to the United States. These two events and the many changes brought by the United States and by Anglo-Americans who migrated to California had a traumatic impact on Californios — California Mexicans who almost overnight became Mexican Americans. The eight selections in this anthology provide perspectives on this impact and the reaction of Californios to new and sometimes overwhelming pressures.

The first two selections are eye-witness reports by two of the earliest Anglo-American commentators on post-conquest California. Dr. John S. Griffin served as Assistant Surgeon in the U.S. invasion force of General Stephen Watts Kearny in 1846 and remained in Los Angeles following the conquest. His March 11, 1849, letter is filled with interesting comments on Los Angeles and California politics.

Stephen Clark Foster, another veteran of the U.S. conquest, settled in California and married into the Lugo family, one of the most powerful Mexican families in southern California. First as Alcalde (mayor) of Los Angeles, later as state senator, a member of the Los Angeles Board of Health and the Los Angeles Board of Education, and first Los Angeles Superintendent of Schools, he had considerable opportunity to observe California during its early U.S. decades. First published in the *Los Angeles Evening Express* in 1878, his recollections reflect a sensitivity to the problems faced by conquered Californios.

One critical Californio problem was that of obtaining justice. A salient example of this dilemma was the Lugo case, one of the most dramatic incidents of early U.S. California history. On January 27, 1851, two men — one Irish and one a Creek Indian — were murdered in the Cajon Pass connecting the Mojave Desert with the San Bernardino Valley in southern California. Murder charges were brought against a group of young Mexican Americans, including two sons of José María Lugo, owner of Rancho San Bernardino. Although the defendants were ultimately acquitted and the case was dismissed in late 1852, the incident set off explosive ethnic tensions, led to the attempted lynching of the Lugos by an Anglo-American gang, and resulted in the wiping out of the lynch gang by Cahuilla Indians who worked for the Lugos.

The next two selections deal with the Lugo case. In the first, Joseph L. Brent, the lawyer who defended the Lugos, presents a compelling eye-witness account, emphasizing the events preceding the trial and the climactic trial itself. The second, by historian W. W. Robinson, provides a retrospective look at the Lugo case.

Two perspectives on another event — the tribulations of Mexican Americans in the early years of post-conquest San Diego — comprise the next two selections. Historians Mario T. García and Charles Hughes analyze San Diego Chicano history of that era and compare it to the history of Mexican Americans in other parts of southern California at that time. Their studies reflect the diversity both of the Chicano experience and of interpretations of that experience.

In addition to suffering from changes brought by the U.S. conquest, the impact of U.S. institutions, and the arrival of masses of Anglo-Americans, California Chicanos also had to contend with the tragedy of natural calamities. One of these was the January 22, 1862, Santa Ana River flood in southern California. The next selection discusses the effect of the flood on one community, ironically named Agua Mansa.

The final entry in the anthology is a biography of Bernardo Yorba, a San Diego-born Californio and ranch owner of the Mexican and early U.S. periods. This biography describes not only Yorba's development of his own ranch, but also his post-war struggle to legitimize his land grant and provide for his family. Beyond giving a biography of Yorba, this book discusses the larger issues of the legal battle of Mexican Americans to defend their land and water rights.

The struggle of Mexican Californians for political, economic, social, and cultural survival in the early decades following the U.S. conquest is a complex and often controversial subject. The documents in this collection provide insight into some of the facets of this struggle.

>CARLOS E. CORTÉS
>Professor of History
>Chairman, Chicano Studies
>University of California, Riverside
>June, 1976

CONTENTS

Griffin, John S[trother]
LOS ANGELES IN 1849: A Letter from John S. Griffin, M. D.
To Col. J. D. Stevenson, March 11, 1849. Los Angeles, 1949

Foster, Stephen Clark
EL QUACHENO: How I Want to Help Make the Constitution of
California — Stirring Historical Incidents. Los Angeles, 1949

Brent, Joseph Lancaster
THE LUGO CASE: A Personal Experience. New Orleans, 1926

Robinson, W. W.
PEOPLE VERSUS LUGO: Story of a Famous Los Angeles
Murder Case and Its Amazing Aftermath. Los Angeles, 1962

Garcia, Mario T.
MERCHANTS AND DONS: San Diego's Attempt at
Modernization, 1850-1860. (Reprinted from *The Journal of San
Diego History,* Volume XXI, No. 1.) Winter, 1975

Hughes, Charles
THE DECLINE OF THE CALIFORNIOS: The Case of San
Diego, 1846-1856. (Reprinted from *The Journal of San Diego
History,* Volume XXI, No. 3), Summer, 1975

San Bernardino County Flood Control District
AGUA MANSA AND THE FLOOD OF JANUARY 22, 1862:
Santa Ana River. San Bernardino, March, 1968

Stephenson, Terry E.
DON BERNARDO YORBA. Los Angeles, 1963

LOS ANGELES IN 1849

A LETTER

FROM

JOHN S. GRIFFIN, M.D.

TO

COL. J. D. STEVENSON

MARCH 11, 1849

PRIVATELY PRINTED
LOS ANGELES, CALIFORNIA
1949

J OHN STROTHER GRIFFIN *was a surgeon who came overland with Kearney's Dragoons. His diary of 1846-47 has been published as* A Doctor Comes to California. *Griffin left Los Angeles in May of 1849 and served three years at Benicia. In 1854 he resigned his commission and returned to Los Angeles to become a noted pioneer doctor and civic leader. It was Dr. Griffin who sold the 4000 acres to the founders of Pasadena. He died in 1898 at the age of eighty-two.*

The original of the letter printed here was formerly owned by Robert Ernest Cowan and is now in the collection of Glen Dawson.

Los Angeles, California
March 11th, 1849

Col. J. D. Stevenson
　Monterey
　　California

My Dear Colonel:[1]

I owe you many thanks for your many interesting letters, and many apologies for not having answered them. When the last mail left I was not in town, which will explain to you the cause of my silence. Your supposition as to the number of letters I receive from San Francisco, I assure you is groundless.

[1] Colonel Jonathan Drake Stevenson came to California in command of the "First New York Volunteers." From May 1847 to September 1848 he was military commandant of Los Angeles.

Smith[2] is too damned lazy to write, Stoneman[3] ditto, Davy[4] the same, but Smith's silence is perfectly outrageous. I have written to him three times since he left, asking him to give me the necessary information for my movements, but damned the line he has sent me; so as they say at poker, I shall go it blind.

I will with pleasure make every effort to get possession of your animals on my way up. If I am at any expense in doing so, I shall keep an account; if not, I suppose the grass they will eat on the route will not

[2] Captain Andrew J. Smith, the officer who mustered out the Mormon Battalion and part of the New York Volunteers.

[3] Lieutenant George Stoneman, later a pioneer resident of Pasadena and from 1883 to 1887 Governor of California.

[4] Lieutenant John W. Davidson came overland with Kearny and was at the battle of San Pascual.

be very expensive to me. Your black horse was here in the Quartermaster's Corral. I requested Smith to deliver him to me before he left, but he was so much engaged in turning over property, &c., that he did not do so. The day after he left, I looked for the horse but he was not to be found. The Quartermaster's men are a sharp set of fellows; they saw at once that the horse did not belong to Uncle Sam, and of course appropriated him to their own purposes. I have made every effort to find him, but up to this time without success. I am fearful that it will be very hard to find any of the animals you have lost. Horses down this way bring a high price: an animal that you could have purchased when you left here for 25 dolls. will now readily bring from 100 to 150, according to the amount of money a man may have, and it is impossible to get them at that price. Mules are higher. If I can find the oxen, I will sell them for you: it would be impossible to drive them. I shall write to Don Carlos Carrillo,[5] Callaghan—or his father-in-law, and Capt. Dana[6] and Streeter[7] in Santa Barbara. I shall request the Don, &c., if they have the animals in their possession to have them ready in Santa Barbara by the 2 of April, as I expect to be

[5] Carlos Carrillo, governor of California in the south in 1837 and 1838 and author of the EXPOSICION, the first book written by a native Californian.

[6] William Goodwin Dana, who had been in California since 1826 and was one of the most influential pioneers of Santa Barbara.

[7] David Streeter was severely wounded at the Battle of San Pascual, was treated by Dr. Griffin and later was a barber at Santa Barbara.

there, and lest they should not be inclined to comply I shall write to Streeter to make all necessary enquiries on the subject; but with every effort, I must confess I have very small hopes of getting any of them.

The Pueblo has changed much since you left. It is now thronged with Soldiers, Quartermaster's men, Sonoranians, &c., the most vicious and idle set you ever beheld. Gambling, drinking, and whoring are the only occupations, and they seem to be followed with great industry, particularly the first and second. Monte banks, cock fights, and liquor shops are to be seen in all directions, and the only question that is asked is whether a man has been successful at monte. A fellow who breaks a bank or so is looked upon as a considerable character; I don't know but that he is looked upon with more admiration than if he had stormed a battery, and yet with all this drinking and gambling there are but few rows. Our men seem inclined to keep the peace among themselves, and the Sonoranians and Californians seem very much afraid of them. A Californian is a rare sight now in the streets. You never see them parading about on their fine horses as formerly. They seem to look upon me as a *pisano* [*paisano*] and tell me everything, particularly the women. They all profess to like the old crowd much better than the new, but *quién sabe*. Mrs. Segura[8] and Doña Susana are

[8] Jose Maria Segura was a Mexican captain

well, or at least were so the last time I saw them. They told me they had sold their house to Ocampo's wife for $4000 and that they were only waiting Miguel's arrival and an opportunity to leave for Mexico. Since that I have heard they have given up the trip. The old lady I believe has some trouble about some money affairs with Vincente. She sent for me one day to request me to get the Commandante to go to Foster[9] and be her advocate. I proffered to do anything in my power, but explained to her that the commanding officer had no right to interfere in civil affairs, and that the probability

[9] Stephen Clark Foster, Yale graduate, 1840, interpreter with the Mormon Battalion and first American Alcalde of Los Angeles. who acted as commandant of Los Angeles in 1846 and had departed for Mexico.

was that his presence as a friend of hers would be an injury rather than a benefit, as the case was to come before a jury. The affair did come to a trial and I believe Vincente got rather the best of it. I think it well for the peace of the Pueblo that Bonny[10] is not here. The old lady has a hopeful son, called Pepe, who she believes to be a perfect hero. This young gentleman is extremely attentive to Doña Dolores and it is said does all her small work; at all events he is extremely attentive.

Now it is my opinion that if Bonny was here he would lick the said Pepe certainly, as he wanted to shoot, poison, or whip Dolores Sepúlveda for much less.

[10] Lieutenant John C. Bonnycastle of the New York Volunteers.

Doña Louisa is living with her mother and has made Garfias a happy man by giving birth to a fine boy. Doña Francesca and the old negro are as usual and speak of all with great love, particularly Davidson. At Stearns'[11] they are all as usual. Isadora the belle, Dolores leading the rest of the crowd and likely within a year to lead Isadora, Chata growing very fast and looking very pretty. The old lady gave birth to a fine boy some two weeks since, and it looks so much like old Don Juan that I think there can be little doubt of its being legitimate. Doña Arcadia is well, and old Stearns as

[11] Abel Stearns. His biography appears in the DICTIONARY OF AMERICAN BIOGRAPHY, as do those of Smith, Stoneman, Mason, and Davidson, but not Stevenson or Griffin. See H. H. Bancroft's PIONEER REGISTER for details on others mentioned.

usual a complete Sir Oracle. Now he is engaged in getting up meetings —or, as they call them here, juntas —to answer to committees of Monterey and San Francisco on the subject of a provisional government. I don't think, however, anything will be done. The Californians don't seem to understand it; they are evidently afraid. They seem to think that it is a movement against the government, and they evidently don't like the idea of falling under Uncle Sam's clutches. Several have asked me what it all means, and I have tried to explain it as well as I could. The other night at the junta at Don Abel's old Carrillo got up and wished to know what the devil they meant by calling him to such a treasonable meeting; what Colonel

Richard B. Mason[12] had done that they wished to kick him out of office. And it was his opinion, the said José Antonio,[13] that el Governador was a *muy buen sujeto*; that he would not give his countenance or support to any such movements. And thereupon he left the meeting in high dudgeon. If they wish any movement in this part of the country, the thing ought to be explained to the Californians. Stearns told me that the meeting had come to the conclusion to write a letter to Col. Mason, asking him whether he considered himself Civil Governor or not, and I suppose his views upon

[12] Richard Barnes Mason, first American military and civil governor of California. His account of the discovery of gold was widely copied throughout the world.

[13] Jose Antonio Carrillo signed the treaty of Cahuenga as Mexican commissioner. A brother of Carlos Carrillo.

matters and things in general. The Americans don't seem to take any interest in the affair one way or the other ; they all seem inclined to wait the action of Congress or the President.

I have given you this little touch of politics, thinking it might be interesting to you to know how they would commence anything like a political move among such a set of people. I have moved down to my old quarters and have the whole house to myself. I only wish you were here to share it with me. As messing was rather expensive—as Pete had large notions of hospitality to the fair sex, I quit keeping house and board up at old Temple's.[14]

[14] John Temple came to California in 1827 from Massachusetts, builder of Temple Block, died in 1866.

The old lady and all hands are the greatest friends to me you ever saw. As for the *Abaha Gente*,[15] they go it strong—money in abundance. Last night there was a ball given by some of the Quartermaster's men at the Theater, and I heard the carriages running over town nearly all night loaded with the fair sex. To think of sending a carriage for a California woman to go to a dance! That goes ahead of Davy and Bonny all hollow —don't you think so? By the by, if you see Holly,[16] tell him Luz is in a most thriving condition, and that he ought not to leave California

---

[15] Lower class.

[16] Lieut. John McHenry Hollingsworth, whose Los Angeles JOURNAL has been published. It is interesting to note that four persons mentioned in this letter were signers of the California Constitution: Carrillo, Foster, Hollingsworth, and Stearns.

without sending some few mementoes of his affection, as well as a little dinero. The canana, cut face, won't look at less than an ounce these days; so there would be no chance for Holly there. The old frop is in a most thriving condition, has her house well furnished, has a brass bedstead, and swears that she will have red satin curtains put on it and that it shall be for Davy. This in gratitude for the many favors that she has received at Davy's hands, and particularly for her last run of custom. I have bored you with a most outrageously long letter. Give my love to all, and if you meet with Taylor[17] or any other officers of your regiment with whom I had the

[17] Capt. Nelson Taylor of the New York Volunteers and a dentist, settled at Stockton as a trader, member of first California legislature.

pleasure to serve give my warmest regards to them. Tell Bonny I wrote him a letter and sent it up by a little Frenchman named Buett. I hope I shall have the pleasure of meeting you in San José or Monterey, about the 10th of April. The weather has been very bad—rain and cold—, the mountains back of the mission are covered with snow—nearly to the foot of them—, the grass is bad, and the horses are still poor. Everybody is going to the mines, and of course I must do the same. I hope to meet you, if not to hear from you.

Your friend,
J. S. Griffin

One hundred copies printed for
Glen Dawson by Wm. M. Cheney

EL QUACHENO

HOW I WANT TO HELP MAKE THE CONSTITUTION OF CALIFORNIA—STIRRING HISTORICAL INCIDENTS

BY
STEPHEN CLARK FOSTER, DELEGATE TO THE CONSTITUTIONAL CONVENTION OF 1849

★

DAWSON'S BOOK SHOP, LOS ANGELES
1949

Introduction

Stephen Clark Foster was twenty-eight years old when, in 1849, he was elected a delegate to the California Constitutional Convention. He had already graduated from Yale University, taught school in Virginia and Alabama, attended the Louisiana Medical School in New Orleans, practiced medicine in Missouri, traded in New Mexico and Sonora, served as interpreter for the Mormon Battalion and as Alcalde of Los Angeles.

In the 'fifties he served as State Senator, member of the first Los Angeles Board of Health and of the first Board of Education. He was also the first Superintendent of Schools and inaugurated the public school system of Los Angeles.

As Mayor in 1854 he persuaded would-be Vigilantes not to hang David Brown, promising to lead them if the courts failed to act. When Brown won an appeal Foster kept his word, resigned as Mayor and led in the lynching. In 1856 he was elected Mayor again and resigned to take charge of the estate of his brother-in-law, Isaac Williams.

Foster married in 1848 Merced Lugo, daughter of Don Antonio María Lugo. Foster died in 1898 in his seventy-eighth year. His later life was not so notable as his earlier, but he kept up an interest in the history and records of this area.

A brief biography of Foster by H. D. Barrows is in the Annual Publication of the Historical Society of Southern California *for 1898. In earlier issues of this publication are several articles written by Foster, the most interesting of which*

INTRODUCTION

is in the 1887 issue entitled, "My First Procession in Los Angeles."

When the second Constitutional Convention was about to be held, our author was fifty-eight years old and wrote this account of his trip to Monterey in 1849. It is printed here from the Los Angeles Evening Express of March 8 and 9, 1878.

We have reproduced the subtitle as it appeared originally: "How I want to help make the Constitution of California —Stirring Historical Incidents." It seems probable that "want" is a typographical error for "went," a word more in accord with the theme.

GLEN DAWSON

El Quacheno

In 1842 the cattle owners of the district of Los Angeles began to complain of Don A. M. Lugo, that he owned more stock than his ranchos San Antonio and El Chino could support, and that they were encroaching on their lands. As the old Don already had granted to him all the land the law allowed, he procured a grant of eight leagues in the San Bernardino valley to be made to his sons, and moved on it a portion of his immense herds.

Hunting Grizzly Bears

The adjoining mountains then swarmed with grizzly bears, and they at once commenced their depredations on the cattle. To guard against them the vaqueros were sent out every evening to drive the stock away from the timber on the creeks and the foot of the mountains into the open plain, and some of them kept watch all night. During the night there was often heard the bellow of some unlucky bullock followed by the rush of his frightened companions. By day-break, all hands were in the saddle, and bruin gorged with his feast was overtaken before he could reach shelter, by some four or five vaqueros, and would soon be stretched out with a riata around his neck and each foot, when one of the riders making fast his riata to the horn of his saddle, and trusting to the horse to hold it

EL QUACHENO 3

taut, would dismount and with his knife dispatch the helpless bear. Three or four were sometimes the result of one morning's sport, and several hundred were killed before they were driven back into the mountains and no longer molested the cattle. This business required skill and coolness on the part of both rider and horse, as the failure of any one would lead to fatal accidents.

The Horse "El Quacheno"

Among the most dexterous in this dangerous sport was one of old Lugo's sons, and his favorite horse was a stout bay horse, of the brand of Ygnacio Sepúlveda,* nicknamed

*Ygnacio Sepúlveda was twenty-eight years old at the time of his death. He was one of five children of José Dolores Sepúlveda. Records in the Palos Verdes Library show that Ygnacio sold his interest in the Rancho Palos Verdes in 1840 to his brother-

"El Quacho," who was killed Jan. 8th, 1847, charging the American square at the "Paso de Bártolo," on the San Gabriel river. Besides the brand, the horse was marked with the scars of wounds inflicted by a grizzly's claws, caused by some awkwardness of one of the vaqueros, but he held his ground unflinching until the monster was secured and dispatched.

Riley's Proclamation

June 3d, 1849, Gov. B. Riley, in accordance with instructions from Washington, issued his proclamation to the people of California, to elect delegates to a convention, to meet

in-law Nathaniel Miguel Pryor, who came to California with Pattie in 1828.
  Benjamin Hayes in the *Centennial History* (1876) spells the nickname as "El Cuacho."

EL QUACHENO

at Monterey, Sept. 1, 1849, to form a State Constitution.*

The war with Mexico had ended with the acquisition of California and New Mexico, but Congress, instead of giving them at once a Territorial Government, entered into a fierce fight on the eternal slavery question, and the Cabinet took steps to force Congress to do something to secure a government for the newly acquired Territories. How, after a delay of two sessions, the whole matter was settled by the famous "Omnibus Bill," the last work of Henry Clay, is a matter of history.

The writer, who had acted as Alcalde of Los Angeles from January,

---

*This *Proclamation* was printed in broadside form and in 1942 reprinted by the Grabhorn Press for Thomas W. Norris.

1848, to May, 1849, had just been relieved by the election of an Ayuntamiento by the people, when the proclamation was received, and at the same time came a private letter from H. W. Halleck, Captain of Engineers, U. S. A., and Secretary of State, urging the paramount necessity of Southern California being fully represented in the Convention, as the parallel of latitude, 36° 30', the Missouri Compromise line of 1820, south of which slavery might be established, ran just below Monterey, and requesting me to use my influence to have the people hold the election, and saying that the United States propeller Edith would be sent down to bring up the delegates from San Luis Obispo to San Diego.

Election as Los Angeles Delegate

I acted as he requested, and saw that due notice was given to the different precincts, but so little interest was felt that the only election held was in this city, and only forty-eight votes were polled, and there was but one ticket in the field. The discovery of gold had deranged everything in California. Vaqueros and others, who had always worked for their $15 per month, were off to the mines. I knew that every thing was at fabulous prices at the north, and although I knew that one could travel from one end of California to the other, and stop at a place among the Spanish speaking population as long as he wished, I knew no one in Monterey, and as we had no idea where the money was to come from to pay our expenses, I was at first dubious about going, hardly considering that the honor to be acquired by helping the administration out of its difficulties would be a fair consideration for the money to be paid out of my own pocket. Not one of us dreamed that our Constitution would stand, but supposed that it would force Congress to give us a Territorial Government, to save the country from anarchy. The permanent population of California did not then exceed 25,000, nearly all ignorant of our laws and language. There were between 100,000 and 200,000 more, but nine out of every ten had come to get what gold they could and then go home.

I then had a consultation with my old father-in-law on the subject.

Antonio María Lugo

He said: "So the Mexicans have sold California to the Americans for $15,000,000 and thrown us natives into the bargain. I don't understand how they could sell what they never had, for since the time of the King, we have sent back every Governor they ever sent here. With the last they sent 300 soldiers to keep us in order, but we sent him with his ragamuffins back too. However, you Americans have got the country and must have a government of your own, for the laws under which we have lived will not suit them. You must go, and you can stop with my sister, Doña María Antonia, the widow of old Seargent [sic] Vallejo."*

"But you must give me a letter to her."

"A letter," was the quick reply, "I can't write, and she can't read, for we had no schools in California when we were young. They tell me the Americans will establish schools where all can learn. I tell you what I'll do. I will make José loan you 'El Quacheno.' My sister knows the horse, for I rode him to Monterey three years ago, and she knows my son would lend that horse to no man in California except his old father.

Los Angeles as Capital

"I will tell you how I happened to ride to Monterey at my time of

*Ignacio Vallejo (1748-1831) married María Antonia Lugo in 1790.

EL QUACHENO

life: In 1845, when Don Pio Pico became Governor, he established the seat of government in Los Angeles, as the Mexican Government had directed in 1836; but there was no Government house, so I made a trade for a house for $5,000, for which drafts were given on the Custom House in Monterey, and, like an old fool, I went security for their payment. [The house and lot occupied the ground from Main to Los Angeles streets, and from Commercial street to the County Bank]. The owner was pushing me for the payment, so I had to go to Monterey to see if that hopeful grandson of my sister, Gov. J. B. Alvarado, then in charge of the Custom House, would pay them. I found him and Castro preparing to come down and deprive Pio Pico of the Governorship, and they had use for all the money they could get; so I had my ride of 300 leagues for nothing. Plague take them all, with their pronunciamentos and revolutions, using up my horses and eating up my cattle, while my sons, instead of taking care of their old father's stock, were off playing soldier. The Americans have put a stop to all this, and we will now have peace and quiet in the land as in the good old days of the King. When you get to Monterey you go to my sister, and tell her for me, by the memory of our last meeting, to treat you as I have ever treated her sons and grandsons when they visited me."

The next step I took, was to go to D. Luis Vignes, old "Aliso," as the

EL QUACHENO

people called him, one of our few moneyed men, and borrow $100. "El Quacheno" was good for my transportation and my board and lodging in Monterey, and I was now in a position to act as an independent delegate from the District of Los Angeles.

Journey to Monterey

We had no news of the promised steamer, the Edith (she was lost off Point Concepción), so on August 20, 1849, Stearns, Domínguez, Carrillo and Foster, natives respectively of Massachusetts, California and Maine, started from this place together on horseback, for Monterey. Hugo Reid,* a native of Scotland,

*Hugo Reid. For his biography and writings on the Indians of Los Angeles County see *A Scotch Paisano* by Susanna Bryant Dakin.

was already in Monterey, and completed the full delegation. The common mode of making long journeys here then, was to take four or five horses to each rider. The loose horses were driven along, and when ever any horse showed signs of fatigue a fresh horse was caught, the saddle shifted, and the tired horse turned into the band, and the rate of traveling was 60 or 70 miles a day.

The scarcity of servants, caused by the gold fever, was the cause that the two Californians and myself started each with one horse. Don Abel Stearns,* as "El Rico" of the delegation, took along a vaquero with six spare horses, but, since, if he rode California fashion he would

*The biography of Stearns is found in *The Cattle on a Thousand Hills* by Robert Glass Cleland.

have to go alone, he concluded to jog along with the rest. There were no hotels from San Diego to Monterey then, and each night we lodged at some private house, free gratis. No greater insult could have been offered to a ranchero than to offer pay for one's accommodations.

Story of Diego Olivera

On the road from Santa Barbara to San Ynez there accompanied us an old soldier, named Olivera. He pointed out to us a live oak beneath which they found the body of D. José Dolores Sepúlveda, the great-grandfather of the Misses Lanfranco of this city, who was killed in 1822,*

---

*José Dolores Sepulveda received permission to keep cattle on a portion of the Rancho San Pedro in 1821 and in 1822 began a series of disputes between the Sepúlveda and Domínguez families. Sepúlveda was killed in 1824, not 1822 as Foster relates.

when the Indians of the Missions La Purísima and San Ynez revolted. He was coming from Monterey to Los Angeles, and ignorant of danger, arrived at San Ynez the morning of the outbreak. He was pursued by some Indian vaqueros, and he had no arm except a short sword, a useless weapon against the riata in the hands of men who could throw it fifty feet with the accuracy of a rifle, and his only hope of safety was to reach Santa Barbara, distant some fifty miles. He succeeded in crossing the Santa Ynez mountain, and had rode some seven leagues when the foremost vaquero overtook him and lassooed him, but before the riata could be tightened he cut it with his sword. A second vaquero overtook him, and this time dragged him from his horse, but he again cut the riata and remounted his steed, but the third time his pursuers dragged him off, and then sharp knives did the rest, and when the soldiers from Santa Barbara, of whom Olivera was one, went out to rescue the little garrison, besieged in the guard house of San Ynez, they found but his naked disfigured corpse.

Story of Indian Uprising

The sight of the old Mission of San Ynez recalled to my mind an incident that occured there at the time of the outbreak. When the Indians rose there were two Spanish priests in the Mission. One of them fell into the hands of the Indians, and was put to death under circumstances of the most atrocious cruelty. The other, a powerful man, succeeded in breaking away and escaped to the guard house, where, as in all the Missions, a guard of four soldiers, commanded by a corporal, were always kept as a sort of police force. The Indians were destitute of firearms, but their overwhelming numbers and the showers of arrows they directed against the portholes had demoralized the garrison when the priest took command. It must have been a singular scene, the burly friar, with shaven crown and sandalled feet, clad in the gray gown, girt with the cord of St. Francis, wielding carnal weapons, now encouraging the little garrison, now shouting defiance to the swarming assailants.

"Ho, Father," cried a young Indian acolyte, "is that the way to say Mass?"

"Yes, I am saying Mass, my son; here (holding up his cartridge box) is the chalice; here (holding up his carbine) is the crucifix, and here goes my benediction to you, you ——," using one of the foulest epithets the Spanish language could supply, as he leveled his carbine and laid the scoffer low.

There was a large force collected from the different towns, the Indian converts were followed into the Tulare valley and captured, the ringleaders shot and the others brought back to their missions, and things in California were again quiet, when my informant had occasion to go to Monterey, and on his way, arrived at the Mission of San Luis Obispo where he found the hero of San Ynez. "Welcome, countryman," was his greeting. "The same to you, father," was the reply, "but father, they tell me you are in trouble." "Yes, my son, the President of the Missions has suspended me from the exercise of clerical functions, for one year, for the unclerical language I used in that affair at San Luis [San Ynez]. The old fool, he knew I was a soldier before I became a priest, and when those accursed Indians drove me back to my old trade, how could I help using my old language?" Then taking out a couple of decanters from a cupboard, he continued, "Here, countryman, help yourself, here is wine, here is aguardiente. The old fool thinks he is punishing me, I have no Mass to say for a year, and I have nothing to do but to eat, drink and sleep."*

San Miguel Mission Tragedy

We stopped over night at the ranch of Santa Margarita, and from there to the Ojitos, some fifty miles, there was not a single resident. On our way that day we stopped at the San Miguel Mission, the scene of the massacre of the Reed family, eleven in number, in December, 1847, the first, as it was the most atrocious of all the crimes that "auri sacra fames," the accursed thirst for gold, brought upon California. We entered the once hospitable hall and

*The priest referred to was Father Francisco Xavier Uría. There is no documentary evidence for this story and it must be considered at least partly apocryphal.

looked at the dark red stains on the floor, where the assassins had piled up their victims, with the intention of firing the building, and on the wall was another dark stain, where one of the fiends had caught up poor Reed's baby-girl by the feet and dashed out its brains against the wall. We visited the churchyard and stood by the long grave where were buried the eleven victims, the jovial hospitable English sailor, his pretty California wife, with her infant and unborn child, the old motherly midwife, Olivara, with her two grown-up daughters, and all the servants. Not one escaped to tell the tale, but it was afterwards told by the murderers, who were arrested, tried and shot in Santa Barbara.*

*Three of the assassins, Joseph Lynch, Peter

Carrillo-Domínguez Dispute

The second night after, we stopped at the San Antonio Mission, and from there we rode to the Soledad. We had got along peaceably together so far, but that day occurred the only difficulty among us that happened on the trip. The two Californians got into an animated discussion as to whether the world was round or flat. C. maintained that it was round, that all the books and scientific men so maintained and proved. D. insisted that it was flat, that he had traveled from San Diego to San Francisco, and he saw it was flat, and the sailors that came from Boston and China found the ocean always flat, and he would

Remer, and Peter Quinn were tried on December 28, 1848, and executed the same day.

believe the evidence of his own eyes in preference to all the books and scientists in the world. They agreed to leave the decision of the question to me. I said I had come all the way from down East, in Maine, to California by land, some 4000 miles by the roundabout way I came, and, as far as I could tell by the eye, it was flat, and perhaps D. was right, but I could not decide between them. The dispute was kept up until D., annoyed at the sarcastic language C. used, refused to say anything more, but spurred his horse and rode ahead of us in sullen silence. I told C. that would never do, that we were delegates from the oldest and most substantial section of California, and that our business was to see that the interests of our section were protected, and it would never do for us to quarrel among ourselves, that we should have all those Yankees from San Francisco and the mining districts to contend against, and that the matter in dispute between them had nothing to do with making a Constitution. "You are right," he said, "and I will make it up," and spurred his horse to overtake his countryman. How they settled it I never knew, but from that time on we had no further difficulty.

Story of the Trained Cattle

Our last day's ride was from the Soledad Mission to Monterey, down the west bank of the Salinas river. About half-way Carrillo pointed out a large oak tree where, about

1846, was found the dead body of his uncle, D. José Ygnacio Lugo, the grandfather of the Wolfskills of this city, who are his only descendants. He was over eighty years of age, and all his life had been eccentric, and as old age came on this eccentricity became more marked, until it bordered on insanity. He owned a few cattle and horses, which he tended himself, permitting no assistance from others, and which he kept under complete control. He had been in the habit of traveling from Los Angeles to Monterey and back again, as the whim took him. He always drove his cattle with him, and whenever he unsaddled to pass the night, they were trained to come up and remain quiet all night near him, and not leave until he gave the signal in the morning. He started for Monterey on his last trip, and a vaquero, about sunset, returning from his rounds, found him lying beneath the oak, apparently asleep. He was a handsome old man, with long, snow-white locks. His cattle were lying down near him, quietly chewing the cud, while the mares and their colts stood by, and standing over the old man was his riding horse, mutely gazing on his master. He had evidently stopped to rest at noon. The vaquero spoke to him, but there was no answer. He dismounted and touched him. The Angel of Death had been there, and, apparently without a struggle or a groan, the spirit of the old soldier had gone to meet his God.

We arrived at Monterey near

sunset, after a warm, dusty day's ride. Stearns stopped with Don David Spence, an old resident like himself. Carrillo and Domínguez rode on to the house of Doña Angustias de Ximena, a niece of the former. Carrillo pointed out to me the house of the Señora Vallejo. I asked him to go with me and introduce me to his aunt, but he shrugged his huge shoulders and said: "She gave me a good scolding the last time I met her, and I don't care to face her now."

Señora Vallejo

I rode on to the house, where I found my hostess seated on the porch. I recognized her at once from her resemblance to her brother. She was over 75 years of age, and must have been a handsome woman in her prime. She politely rose to return my salutation. I gave her her brother's message, while she fixed on me her keen, black eyes, from beneath the heavy eyebrows. Two of her daughters had long been married to Americans, who had come to California in early times, and she liked the old residents well enough, but could not bear the newcomers. When the bear flag was raised in Sonoma by the newly-arrived American emigrants in 1846, before news of the declaration of war had reached California, they had imprisoned two of her sons, and made free use of their cattle and horses. When I finished, she asked me to dismount and gave me a warm welcome, for her brother's sake.

Memories of Foster's Mother

There were tears in the eyes of the aged woman, caused by the memories recalled by my message, and there were tears in the writer's eyes, as he remembered the warm embrace of the New England mother, when she parted from her first-born, long years before, far off on the rock-bound coast of Maine. I did not know until months afterwards, that that mother was in her grave, and that the last news she ever had of her wayward son was a catalogue issued in 1845, of the alumni of Yale College of the class of 1840, where in the column of remarks opposite my name, was the entry, "Last heard from in northern Mexico. Reported to have been killed by Indians."

I will here insert the circumstances of the "last meeting" mentioned in the message I bore.

Meeting of the Lugos

In March, 1846, Doña María Antonia was seated in the porch of her house, which commanded a full view of the town and the southern road, accompanied by one of her granddaughters. Three horsemen were seen slowly turning the point where one coming from the south can first be seen. The old lady shaded her eyes and gazed long and exclaimed, "Yonder comes my brother." "Oh, grandmother, yonder come three horsemen, but no one can tell who they are at that distance." She replied, "But, girl, my old eyes are better than yours. That tall man in the middle is my brother, whom I have not seen for twenty years. I know him by his seat in the saddle. No man in California rides like him. Hurry off, girl, call your mother and aunts, your brothers, sisters and cousins, and let us go forth to welcome him." The horsemen drew near, and a little group of some twenty women and children stood waiting with grandmother at their head, her eyes fixed on the tall horseman, an old, white-haired man, who stopped his horse and then flung himself from the saddle and, mutually exclaiming "Brother!" "Sister!" they were locked in a warm embrace.

We met at the time appointed in Colton Hall and organized.*

*A reprint of the *Constitution* (San Francisco,

Writing the Constitution

We finished our work in the early days of October, for Gov. Riley's proclamation calling upon the people to vote on the Constitution, is dated Oct. 12th, 1849. Whether we did our work well or ill is not for the writer to say, but, under that Constitution California, from a state of anarchy in 1849, has become a prosperous and well-organized State in 1878.

In regard to our compensation, it was fixed by ourselves, and paid out of a fund arising from duties col-

1849) with an Introduction by Robert Glass Cleland has been issued by the Friends of the Huntington Library. See also J. Ross Browne's *Report of the Debates in the Convention of California on the Formation of the State Constitution in September and October, 1849* (Washington, 1850).

lected on foreign goods, in virtue of a tariff established during the war for Mexican ports occupied by the U. S. forces, as Congress, in its first session after the acquisition of California, failed to extend the revenue laws over California.

Convention of 1878

Another Convention is now to be called, and when the Los Angeles delegation go up to attend it they can have their choice of the steamer or the palace car, and, if compensation is allowed, they have the treasury of a rich and powerful State, while the writer thirty years ago had to go dependent on old Lugo's bear horse as his means of transportation and letter of recommendation, and the old Frenchman for funds to defray his necessary expenses.*

*The reader may make his own comparisons with the situation in the centennial year of 1949.

ONE HUNDRED COPIES PRINTED FOR
GLEN DAWSON BY WILLIAM M. CHENEY

☆ ☆ ☆

THE LUGO CASE

A Personal Experience

Written by

JOSEPH LANCASTER BRENT
Brigadier-General C. S. A.

NEW ORLEANS
SEARCY & PFAFF, LTD.
1926

Copyright, 1926
By MRS. JOSEPH L. BRENT

All Rights Reserved

THE LUGO CASE

When I reached Los Angeles, California, in the early fifties, it was a city of about twenty-five hundred inhabitants, including the population in the gardens and vineyards clustering along the river bottoms. There were barely seventy-five Americans permanently settled in the city, but at times the American population was increased temporarily by persons seeking a mild climate for health, by the arrival of the cattle buyers from the North, and by a large number of gamblers, who found much profit from the almost universal gambling habits of the native Californians.

The Americans were in such small numbers comparatively that there was a feeling of uneasiness and anxiety, arising from the ability of the native Californians, if they chose, to accomplish temporarily a revolution against the American Government. It was said that the matter was frequently discussed among the Californian population, who, accustomed all their lives to pronunciamentos and revolutions, regarded an effort to overturn the Government as an exciting political campaign, rather than as a treasonable effort involving the gravest consequences. I have often heard in the night cries of "Viva Mejico" as some enthusiastic Mexicans or Californians, inflamed with liquor, dashed their horses at full speed through the streets, but I have every reason to feel certain that none of the native Californians ever seriously thought of revolution, though some of the Mexicans, especially the men of Sonora, may have talked of it, when filled with aguardiente. But the mere mooting of the matter inflamed the always active race-feeling of the Americans, so that whenever an occasion of real or supposed danger arose, most of the Americans considered they were in the presence of an enemy. So strong was this feeling that some wags availed themselves of it to work upon the apprehensions of the mayor of the city, who was an American named Hodges, and made him believe one night that hostilities had really broken out and that the revolution was in full blast. Men were ordered to ride rapidly in, and report to the mayor that the Californians were seen in numbers now in this quarter and then in another.

The mayor, full of credulity and fight, rushed around calling upon all the Americans to arm themselves and report to him for service, until at last all the Americans in town took part in the joke. The mayor sent out pickets to cover the centre of the town, and then the pickets began firing and retreating on the centre, reporting the advance or retreat of the enemy. A chicken was killed, and some of the men were daubed with blood and exhibited to the mayor, as being shot by the enemy, and others were brought in on barrows, as if gravely wounded. The mayor was wrought up to an inconceivable excitement, the burlesque continued all night and people left their beds to enjoy the fun. But about daybreak some friends of the mayor informed him that it was a joke; and when he realized it, he swore a solemn oath that he would shoot the first man who ever spoke to him about it; and all next day I saw him holding himself apart from the people, refusing to speak to or greet anyone, but having a big six shooter very conspicuously displayed: and no man dared to refer to the colossal joke. But underneath all this existed the strongest race prejudice amongst most of the Americans against the Californians, which gave color and cause to the matters I am about to relate.

I had originally settled in San Francisco, and had the most promising beginning, when, for the first and only time in my life I was attacked with serious sickness. I got well and then relapsed, and so it continued for many times.

At last my doctor, a competent man, told me that in my feeble state, the climate of San Francisco in the summer was too harsh for me; and that my best chance was to seek a milder climate, which could be found in Los Angeles. I had no remedy but to follow his advice and I went down to that city, intending to return as soon as I recovered my health. But I became fascinated with the life, the beautiful climate and valley and the pleasant friends I made. When wearied and enfeebled I reached the beautiful Pueblo, and rode from out the dry and parched plains into the lanes and corriestas of the old San Pedro entrance to the city, the sun had just gone down, the west was all ruddy, and the earth green and scented with odors of that blooming oasis. The beauty and charm of the sky and earth entered into my heart and filled it with a love for the place that still holds now, after the lapse of near half a century.

I was in my twenty-third year when I opened my law office in Los Angeles. I was a perfect stranger in the town, and the tongue of nine-tenths of people was Spanish, which I could not speak. But in a very short time, owing to necessity and constant practice, aided by my acquaintance with French and especially Latin, I began to talk with Spanish clients, and was, among other things, able to discuss the question of fees with precision. At first business was very slack and clients few; but in a few months my acquaintance extended and I was doing fairly well.

Business was very dull for some time after my arrival, and my finances ran uncomfortably low, but my youth and restored health enabled me to enjoy the strange and novel surroundings of the new world and the new life, with an intensity belonging only to that happy period of existence.

Murders were very common, but not among the resident or settled population. In fact even in the carnival of murder which subsequently broke out, it was a rare thing for a respectable citizen to be a victim. But amongst the Indians, the emigrants from Sonora and Chile, murders were fearfully common.

At that time there were large numbers of Indians in Los Angeles, and I have frequently seen crowds of them in the stores and streets: and upon Saturday evenings they assembled from the whole valley and for a long time were accustomed, in the suburbs of the town, to play a game called "Pion".

They were divided into two sides and were seated opposite to each other in front of large fires, and the game consisted in one side passing from one to another a little stick, and the other side guessing where the stick was. The accompaniment of the game was a deep guttural song, sung with the shaking of the body to keep rhythm, and it was during these shakings and movements that the little stick was deftly passed. It was something on the principle of the children's game of hiding the ring. These games produced enormous excitement and extravagant betting, and the bystanders took sides, including the women, who were desperate gamblers. The games were protracted through the night and the players, stimulated by heavy drinking, indulged in frequent fights and murders.

I remember one played between the San Luis Rey tribe and the Cahuillas from San Bernardino, which was widely advertised and numerously attended, and resulted in a tremendous battle. The game was played above the Plaza, well back of the Catholic Church and near the foot of the high hills curving back from it, which was entirely destitute of houses. I was awakened during the night by the fierce noises of the fight, and going to my door heard and distinguished the awful shrieks and war whoops of the combatants. My room was just opposite the residence of Don Abel Stearns, which shows that nearly the whole Pueblo heard the din of the battle. Next morning dead Indians were found in every direction. Alex. Gibson, our one eyed coroner, summoned a jury, of which I was one, to view the dead. We found thirteen dead in the vicinity of the fight. These all had their heads mashed beyond recognition, which is the sign manual of Indian murder: but these Indians did not scalp. Dead and wounded Indians were discovered everywhere, and it was a moderate estimate that fifty lost their lives. Shortly after this these games were prohibited by the city ordinances.

Law business was for some time principally monopolized by two Missouri lawyers, men of a rough exterior but of great ability. One of these, Mr. Jonathan R. Scott, was one of the most remarkable men I ever met. He was a very large man, and gave you the impression of a wood chopper. His mental gifts were very great, his process of reasoning clear and his ability as a trial lawyer unrivalled. With all of this he was rough in his manners and affected even a greater roughness. He rarely wore a coat even in court, and always smoked a pipe. I have frequently seen him stop while addressing the court or a jury, to refill his pipe with tobacco, while court, jury and crowded audience would watch with interest the uncertain spluttering of a doubtful match and the feeble glow of the tobacco, which grew into an ember as he lighted it after repeated whiffs.

He was born a New Yorker, and was connected by blood with the Van Rennselaer family, as he told me; his middle name was Rennselaer, the Van having been dropped as making his name too long. He was, however, a thorough and accomplished lawyer, having evidently in his earlier years been a close student, and under his garb of roughness of manner, originally affected, I think, but which became afterwards natural, he possessed the power of moulding judges and juries equal to any man I ever knew. He had lived in the frontier counties of Missouri, and had there acquired that roughness of appearance and disregard of conventionalities which characterized him. He had brought from Missouri one special characteristic, and that was a constant readiness to head a lynching party, which was inconceivable in one trained as he was to law. I have mentioned him because his belief that a community had a right to enforce lynch law, had a bearing upon the matters I am about to narrate.

About 1852, a year or two after my arrival in Los Angeles, I was surprised to receive at my offices a visit from four Californians, some of whom I knew by sight, three of whom were members of the Lugo family, which was one of the wealthiest and most influential in the country. It was interesting to see the superb and rich appearance of these opulent rancheros, as the owners of estates stocked with cattle were called. With saddles heavily plated with silver, rich jackets and trousers trimmed with silver bullets or buttons, mangas or riding cloaks fringed with heavy gold bullion, fine horses, as pretty as Arabians: and swords attached to the saddles, and not to the person, they made a strange group as they rode up and stopped at my office door.

They had come to employ me as counsel to defend two young lads, sons of one of my visitors, who had been arrested upon the charge of murder.

I was much pleased that such substantial clients had come to retain me in a case of such

THE LUGO CASE. 11

gravity and to confide its management entirely into my hands; as they stated, answering a suggestion made by me, they desired to employ no associate counsel.

Thus was the beginning of my connection with an extraordinary case, which in itself and the numerous incidents attending its progress, was full of episodes and adventures threatening at one time a race war and envolving and costing many human lives. It is utterly impossible for me to give more than a portion of the incidents of this affair, as they could readily be swollen to fill a three volume history.

The murder and the circumstances leading up to it were as dramatic as were the results of the efforts of the authorities to punish those believed to be its perpetrators.

When the Mormons settled themselves in Salt Lake Valley, some few years before the incidents I speak of, they made friends of the neighboring Indian tribe, which resulted in many ways beneficially to both parties. The Mormans had great need for horses and the Indians for arms, and the Utah tribe of Indians made considerable profit in supplying the horses and became rich and well armed upon the fruits of their trade. But as the home market for horses became exhausted, while the Morman demands were still unsupplied, the Utah tribe determined to send a foray into Southern California, which was several hundred miles distant and abounded in fine horses, far superior to the Indian ponies which they had already sold.

Accordingly a band of thirty or forty Utahs descended the Eastern slopes of the Rocky Mountains, and, crossing the Mojave River and desert, penetrated the Coast Range of Mountains through the Cajon Pass, scattering themselves over that section of Los Angeles County which, extending from the Pass up and near to the San Gabriel River, abounded in great herds of cattle and bands of fine horses, which were allowed to roam at large over the unfenced country. In two nights the Indians were able to gather three or four hundred fine horses and mares and drive them through the Cajon Pass.

The Californians, not suspecting at first the present of the Indians, commenced to search for their horses, and when it was known how many had disappeared, and it was found that all the trails led to the Cajon Pass, they soon realized that they were suffering from an Indian raid. Most of the principal stock-holders of the raided section took part in the search, and were present when the conclusion was reached that the Indians were the robbers, and they immediately determined to equip a party of forty or fifty men and send them in pursuit of the Indians.

Two of the Lugo family were owners of a ranch, or estate, called San Bernardino containing about 50,000 acres of land and contiguous to the Cajon Pass of the Coast Range, through which the Indians had passed. The rancheros determined that the expedition should assemble that very night at San Bernardino and should start in pursuit at daybreak upon the following day. These men were in control of very large estates, having many employees or cowboys; and there was no difficulty in their assembling that night near fifty men at the Lugos', who marched at daybreak in pursuit of the Indians.

The expedition was composed principally of the employes of the ranch owners, but eight or ten rancheros joined the expedition. They were very poorly armed, only a few having pistols. In the expedition were the Lugo brothers who owned the ranch of San Bernardino, and who had lost a considerable number of horses, and with them were Francisco and Menito, two sons of Jose Maria Lugo, one of the brothers. These sons were mere boys, one barely eighteen years old, who was named Francisco, and was generally called Chico, and the other about sixteen years old, called Menito, and these boys were the parties accused of murder and who became my clients.

The expedition rapidly marched through the Cajon Pass, thus crossing the Coast Range and following the broad trail of the Indians into the Mojave Desert. They suffered much for water, and upon reaching some springs their advance guard was ambuscaded by the Indians, one or two men killed and the rest driven back upon the main body. The Indians were reported well armed and numerous.

Demoralized by this ambuscade and the want of proper arms, their horses worn out by their rapid march, and men and horses alike suffering for water, the leaders concluded to abandon the expedition, and they accordingly returned home, worn out and defeated. As they passed through the Cajon Pass on the first day, in pursuit of the Indians, the expedition overtook two men driving a wagon. One was an Irishman and the other a civilized Creek Indian, called Bob, both of whom were well known in Los Angeles. When the expedition returned, it met the same two men driving their wagon, passed them and went into camp about ten miles from the point where the wagon was passed. Next morning early the expedition reached the home of the Lugos and was disbanded.

A few days after, news was brought to Los Angeles that the Irishman and the Indian had been found murdered in the pass. The coroner, the same Dr. Hodges who was the mayor spoken of above, visited the pass, which was over sixty miles from Los Angeles, and held an inquest over the bodies and buried them.

No evidence was adduced before him showing the guilty parties, but he summoned before the jury the principal Californians who belonged to the expedition, all of whom testified to the fact that they had seen the men going and returning from their vain pursuit, and that they had no knowledge whatsoever as to the parties who killed them. The coroner's jury found a verdict of "killed by unknown parties;" but the murder was a good deal talked about amongst the Americans in Los Angeles, where the men were well known. They had been employed by a company to carry out supplies to a mining camp, which was engaged in an effort to develop a gold mine at a place called Amargosa on the confines of the Mojave Desert; some Los Angeles men were interested in the mine; and thus the matter of the murder was not forgotten.

I must now go back and take up another series of incidents that seem to have relation to this matter. About a year previously an immigrant train, seeking California, struggled with difficulty across the desert, and entered the Los Angeles Valley through the same Cajon Pass. Suffering from hunger and with animals almost broken down, they reached the San Bernardino ranch of the Lugos, and being kindly received, rested there some time until the people and animals were resuscitated.

Amongst these immigrants were an Englishman and his wife, who were in great poverty and destitute of resources. They were evidently people of poverty and labor but the wife was exceedingly pretty and of cheerful and bright disposition. Her appearance and her wants attracted the favorable attention of Mrs. Lugo, the mother of the boys Chico and Menito, and she had the woman frequently at her house, giving her help and light work, and manifesting great kindness to her in every way.

The English woman made friends of all the Lugo family; but it was soon seen that the husband had no tenderness at all for his wife and was rude and even cruel to her. He was kindly remonstrated with by the females of the Lugo family, but shortly afterwards some quarrel took place between the husband and wife and he beat his wife brutally in the presence of the females of the Lugo family. When the two boys, Chico and Menito, returned they were told of this act. They were then seventeen and fifteen years old respectively, but stout for their age; and they had become, with the rest of the family, most kindly disposed towards the English woman. When they heard of the brutal conduct of the husband, exhibited in the presence of their mother, seized with anger, they rushed out and attacked the husband, whipping him severely with switches and light sticks. He made little resistance and took his punishment quietly.

Next day the man disappeared from the ranch, taking his wife with him, and afterwards turned up in Los Angeles. The sheriff at this time was hunting for a jailer, and the husband applied for the place and was appointed. When he was settled, he undertook to get even with the Lugos, the remembrance of whose kindness was entirely erased by the smart of the whipping. He employed Messrs. Scott and Hayes as his attorneys, and brough suit against the father of the two boys for $50,000 damages for the assault and battery committed by them upon him.

Some time after the verdict of the coroner's jury was rendered a Sonorena named Iquera, apparently a worthless fellow, was arrested for some petty crime and committed to the jail. It seems that this Iquera had been a member of the expedition which pursued the Indians; and after he had been in jail for some time the jailer notified the district attorney that Iquera had an important statement to make. Being brought before the attorney he made oath that after the expedition of the Californians against the Indians had returned through the pass, passed the murdered men and gone into camp ten or twelve miles from the men, during that night Chico and Menito Lugo proposed to him and a man named Elisalde that in the morning they should return and kill the two men; and that accordingly before daylight they left their camp, reached and killed the men by sunrise and returned to camp before it marched away. Mr. Scott, who was the attorney for the jailer, was also a justice of the peace and he received the affidavit and issued warrants of arrest, under which the two Lugo boys and the man Elisalde were arrested and placed in jail.

The father of the Lugo boys and his brother, Jose Del Carmel Lugo—who was widely esteemed and had been an Alcade under the Mexican regime—had both accompanied the unfortunate expedition against the Indians, and declared to me that they knew not what new testimony was discovered, but that it was an impossibility that the two boys had taken part in it, because they were always under their sight.

Next day the examination of the prisoners began before Mr. Scott, and the State was represented by Mr. Hayes, who was county attorney, and was also the partner of Mr. Scott; and both were attorneys of the jailer in the suit against the Lugos.

The news of the arrest of the Lugo boys, upon the testimony of a party confessing to be an accomplice in the murder, produced a great effect and excitement among the Americans, and they immediately announced their belief in the guilt of the prisoners. A very long and tedious examination was had.

The only evidence adduced by the State was the confession of Iquera, who declared himself an accomplice in the murder, and stated, also, that the Lugos determined to kill the men because one was an Indian and they believed both must have been confederates of the Indians who stole the horses. He was an ignorant man who could not read or write; he drank and gambled, and was generally out of work, was without family or relatives in the country, and belonged to the large class of people from Sonora who were regarded by Americans and Californians as desperate and criminal men. He adhered pertinaciously to his story, asserting that he took part in the killing simply because he was requested, and that nothing was promised or given him for his assistance. Immediately after the expedition, he abandoned his employment and drifted into Los Angeles City, and led a loafing life, devoted to petty crimes, for some of which he had been arrested and imprisoned, though he was never brought to trial.

The story itself was singular and improbable in this, that the witness confessed himself to have participated in a murder of people whom he did not know, without any motive whatsoever except to comply with a mere request from two boys with whom he was not especially intimate, who offered him nothing for his assistance. This was regarding the story by itself; but he was absolutely without any corroboration whatsoever.

Fifteen or twenty members of the expedition were examined, who testified, unequivocally, that the accused remained with them all the time, that they never left camp upon the morning of the murder, but were seen by them at all hours when, according to Iquera's confession, they must have been absent.

His story implied that they rode at least twenty miles, going and returning from the place of the murder, which, considering that their horses were not very fresh, and that a certain time must have been consumed in the murder itself, would imply an absence of not less than two hours and a half, while their return into camp must have been in the morning, when it would have been impossible for four men to ride into camp without attracting attention.

The witnesses who denied the possibility of the absence from and the return to the camp of the four men as testified to by Iquera, were as respectable men as could be found among the Californians, many of them not connected in any way by blood or otherwise with the accused; and I argued that to allow the uncorroborated testimony of one man, a confessed accomplice, to overbalance that of twenty men, was unreasonable. However, Mr. Scott, the justice, held them prisoners for trial and committed them to jail without benefit of bail.

The sentiment of the American population overwhelmingly approved this action; and while there were no threats of lynching, yet the opinion and belief of the Americans, generally, was that the boys were guilty. I always thought that race feeling rather than a fair consideration of the circumstances, led to that belief.

Under the judicial system then prevailing, a case of murder could only be tried before the district court, which held its terms only twice, perhaps three times a year; but indictments were found by the grand juries impanelled by the county courts. Very soon after the committal of the prisoners the grand jury found a bill of indictment for murder against them. Some months after this the circuit court met at Los Angeles, the prisoners were arranged and the indictment and proceedings being grossly irregular and defective, they were, on my motion, set aside by the circuit court. I then moved that the prisoners be bailed, but after hearing testimony the circuit judge refused the application and recommitted them to jail.

This resulted in a long imprisonment of the prisoners in the custody of the jailer who hated them with the venom of a man who had undergone a whipping at their hands because he beat his wife with cruelty. His bearing towards them was harsh and cruel, the food he served absolutely unsuitable, and he would not allow their friends to feed them. He refused to allow the boys to see anyone except myself; and availing himself of the plea that the walls of the jail were not very strong, he kept the prisoners heavily ironed day and night. And now about this time was developed another series of events which produced grave complications and led to very tragical events.

A party of Americans came down from the North and went into camp on the Arroyo Seco about two miles outside of Los Angeles. At first there were only a few men, but accessions arrived until they amounted to over twenty-five or thirty men.

It was given out that these men were forming an expedition to go into Sonora, the adjoining Mexican State, and work rich mines of which they had knowledge; but it was soon whispered around that the expedition was to be a freebooter enterprise to plunder the Mexican frontier and to intercept Mexicans returning with gold from the Californian placers. The citizens spoke of them habitually as bandits, when none of them were around. They mixed freely with the people, were orderly and troubled no one, so that they were upon good terms with the community.

They were commanded by a man named Irving, who, from his red face and beard was called "Red Irving." He was a native frontiersman who had grown up in Texas along the Rio Grande and had been conspicuous on that bloody frontier. He had been engaged in many a feud, and foray into Mexico, had great experience as an Indian fighter, and his reputation commended him as a proper leader for any perilous enterprise.

He, as well as others of his band, mingled freely with the people and I came to know him casually, as well as several others of his band. When the grand jury assembled again, after the quashing of the indictments, the county attorney submitted new indictments against the Lugos and Elisalde, but the grand jury refused to find them, and so, when the district court assembled for the second term, there were no indictments at all against the prisoners; and according to the settled practice and principles of law, the prisoners were entitled to be let out on bail. As far as I know there was no existing excitement against the Lugos up to that date and the people had almost ceased to discuss their case.

One morning I went into the district court and moved that the prisoners be admitted to bail, as the grand jury had ignored the bills against them. The district judge and the district attorney came from the adjoining county of San Diego, and after the district attorney had examined the papers, he stated to the court that the prisoners were entitled to bail and the judge so ordered, and fixed the bond at $10,000 each; and the law required the sureties should each be worth double the amount of the bond. I asked the court to defer the matter until 2 P. M., when I would have the bondsmen ready.

There were several people in the court when the judge agreed to bail the prisoners, and the news soon spread over the city. I immediately sent messages for the bondsmen who lived in the country, notifying them to be in court at 2 P. M. Entirely unconscious of any excitement concerning the prisoners, I returned to my office; and in about an hour after my return two men entered my office.

One of them was a mechanic and machinist, who had been doing business and residing in the city ever since I had been there, and whom I knew very well. With him came a man named Evans, who was the officer next in command of Red Irving's band. The machinist said to me with confusion that he hoped I would "take no offense" at him as he thought he had a "good opportunity to make money just as others were doing." I asked him what he meant; and he began to stammer, and beads of perspiration gathered upon his face.

Evans spoke up bluntly and said, "The matter is about the Lugos. Our boys have been given the job of taking them out of jail; and now we hear the judge is going to turn them loose, and we don't intend to stand it."

"Why do you come to me," I asked, "with this nonsense?"

"You are the lawyer of the boys, and we think it fair to let you know that they can never be taken out the jail alive, until we are settled with. We want you to tell their father that if he don't pay us the $10,000 we were promised, to capture the jail and liberate his sons, when we started for Mexico, the boys must stay in jail, or lose their lives if they come out."

I at once sprang up and ordered the men too get out of my office immediately, which they did, Evans saying as he went out, "They think it is cheaper to buy the judge and district attorney than us, but those boys will never get out alive except with our consent, and they had better know it."

I was tingling with anger and excitement as they left; and my principal feeling was indignation that my clients had entered into lawless negotiations with these bad and desperate men, while I felt confident that the boys would be acquitted by the operation of the law, as I in good faith believed them to be innocent.

But I was also eager to punish the men for daring to make a demand for $10,000, before the prisoners could obtain the release on bail, to which they were entitled, and turning to the Criminal Statutes I began preparing an affidavit for their arrest for attempted blackmail. But then the reflection struck me, could I expect the men to submit to arrest, and, if backed by their bandit companions, they resisted, was it practicable for the sheriff to enforce their arrest?

The sheriff was a weak good natured man, without resolution enough to arrest any men that resisted or were even reputed as dangerous. Whenever it became necessary to arrest any of the desperate characters who broke out into violence, he went around among the American residents, and asked their assistance, which was most generally given. I suppose that in more than half a dozen cases I had been called upon by him, and with others had gone with him to effect the arrest of some desperado; and in no single instance had any of them undertaken to resist when the citizens' posse sided with the sheriff. But in this Lugo case I knew the feelings of the Americans were strongly prejudicial against my clients, and that their sympathy would be with some lawless banditti in their hostile efforts, from whatever cause, against the Lugos. This was so clear and apparent to me that I gave up the idea of arrest as absolutely impracticable.

A little before two o'clock the father of the boys, and half a dozen men to act as sureties, rode up to my office. In great anger I greeted the father, and told him I withdrew from the defence of the boys because he had entered into unlawful negotiations with Red Irving and his men for the capture of the jail and the release of his sons; and that he must get other counsel.

He seemed utterly confounded and declared, with a solemn oath, that he had never had any negotiations whatsoever, and knew of none, with the bandits; and that I was totally misinformed. He then asked his brothers who were with him if they knew anything about the matter, and they denied all knowledge.

While we were speaking I heard a great clatter of horsemen in the street and, upon looking out, I saw twelve or fourteen of Irving's men racing by at full speed. A block away from us a road left the main street, and, ascending a sharp slope, approached the public jail, which, standing by itself upon a high hill, overlooked the town.

When these racing horsemen reached the road leading to the jail, they turned into it, rode up the slope, and, in the presence of the whole city, dismounted and stood at guard over the jail. It was evident that this bold action was intended to carry out the threat of Evans, their leader, made to me, that the prisoners should not be released by process of law unless they paid them a toll of $10,000.

The reckless boldness of the seizure of the public jail, in open day and in sight of the whole city, was a proof the men relied upon the sympathy of the American population, which belief was justified by the fact. The street leading to the Court House was filled with people attracted by the hour of the meeting of the court and the knowledge or anticipation that something was about to occur; and expressions of approval of the action of the bandits were frequently uttered.

As soon as the seizure of the jail was completed before our eyes, I said to my clients,

"Now you see the result of your imprudent transaction with the bandits." They renewed their positive denial and asked me what was the meaning of what they saw. I told them that these men claimed they had been promised by the Lugos $10,000 to capture the jail and to liberate the boys; and that they now declared they would kill the boys if they were brought out of jail to give bond, unless the $10,000 was paid them.

At this point I heard the call of the sheriff that the court was open. The seizure of the jail was effected only a few moments in advance of the meeting of the court and this explains the hot speed with which these desperadoes rode in order to arrive before the opening of the court. I told my men to wait for me until I return from court.

The crowd evidently was expecting me, as the next figure in the drama that had just opened; and when I entered the court room the crowd rushed in. Many Americans were present, and among them were Evans and some of his men; but fortunately, as I think, Red Irving was not there, and I understood that he had gone on an expedition, and that a messenger had been sent for him, but he could not get back until next day.

I stated to the court that I was not ready that evening to furnish the bond for the Lugos, and asked that the matter be postponed until the next morning. The court thereupon adjourned, and, as the crowd passed out to the street, I heard loud laughter of derision. It was fully appreciated that I dared not bring the boys to court for fear of their being killed by Evans and his men; and it was evident to me that the sentiments of the Americans of the city encouraged and supported the lawless action by which the jail had been seized and the prisoners made subject to their lawless captors.

The position that confronted me was grave and full of responsibility. I believed the prisoners were innocent, and I was satisfied that their parents had not entered into any negotiation with the men who now held them prisoners.

None of my friends, and at that time I had many amongst the Americans, gave me any encouragement or support. Those I conversed with signified their belief in the guilt of the accused, and their hope that they would be hung by anybody that would undertake it. No one seemed to feel any indignation that a desperate band of strangers had seized the jail and overturned the reign of law to enforce a lawless claim for $10,000, and I perfectly satisfied myself that no reliance could be placed upon a single American in the struggle between the authorities and Irving's men, and without their assistance nothing could be done.

We had no military organization whatsoever, though the United States had a cavalry force at San Diego, more than a hundred miles away, and utterly unavailable to save the lives of the prisoners, the question of whose death was to be determined in twenty-four hours or less. The payment of the $10,000 ransom could not be advised by me for many reasons. It was immoral, or, if not immoral, considering the vis major that demanded it, it was impolitic, because its payment would be regarded as a confession of guilt, and the sentiments of the American citizens had to be reckoned with, who might punish with death those whose life had been bought from the bandits.

I was animated with the desire to save the lives of these innocent boys, as I believed them to be. Their parents had, in the fullest faith, entrusted their lives into my hands, so far as the courts were concerned; and I knew that even outside of the courts they had no other reliance but me. The father was a quiet man, submissive to law and totally wanting in any aggressive qualities. In the long incarceration of the boys, the family wrongfully had been denied, against my best efforts, the right to visit them, through the hostile co-operation of the jailer and the local judicial authorities. The mother frequently visited me to learn about them and send them messages, and rarely did she see me without shedding tears over the cruel fate of her children. In her sufferings she exalted her belief in my ability to restore her children to her, declaring that her only hope was in me, and manifesting her friendship in every way that a tender mother can find, to show her reliance upon one whom she thought able to save her children. If I failed to exhaust every resource to save her children, my conscience would condemn me.

It was easy for me to confine myself to my strictly legal duties as a lawyer, and next day to bring the prisoners into court to be bailed, and to let the authorities protect them as best they could; but that was simply to sentence them to death. I was utterly unwilling to do that. I was determined, as far as it was within my power, to devote myself and all my resources to the struggle for the lives of my clients, a struggle which, as far as I could see, must be determined under conditions envolving, in the maintenance of the law, the probabilities, nay, the certainty, of a bloody combat with this desperate band of Irving, having, strange to say, at its back the moral, if not physical, support of many of the American citizens.

No one then regarded the native Californian population as a factor, in determining any question in the community, which was to be solved by physical force. The Californians lived in the country, separated by their large estates of rarely less than five thousand acres, and more often of thirty and forty thousand acres. Their business was stock raising, which required but few hands comparatively, and their houses were widely scattered. It was difficult to assemble one hundred men of the race: and impracticable to assemble two hundred except with great delay. They were little accustomed to firearms, though most of them had pistols, but it was a rarity if one possessed a gun or rifle.

Seeking in every direction for the means to save the lives of the Lugo boys, I could think of no other than to call upon this ill-armed and peaceful population to take up arms, and oppose themselves to the twenty-five well armed, desperate and experienced men led by the redoubtable Red Irving.

There was one consideration, however, that much increased my anxieties. If the native Californians appeared in arms ready to attack Red Irving and his men, who were Americans, there would be a development of the race feeling and sympathies; and I well knew how strong that was and how, when blows were struck men would take position according to their race. Especially would this be liable to occur when the issue at arms was raised over the Lugos, believed by the American population to be guilty men. In addition, the appearance of the Californians in arms would be an unusual and unexpected event, and might be looked upon by the Americans as hostile to the newly established American domination for reasons hereinbefore set out.

If hostilities broke out, they might not be determined by one combat; and if the Lugo boys should be killed by the bandits they would be pursued by the Californians, and if any members of the bandits were killed, the survivors, reinforced by sympathizers, would seek revenge and the war might become flagrant throughout the country.

This view struck me with great force; and I believed then, and believe now, that the above consequences were inevitable if we had carried out our plans.

I had my own feelings on the subject and I looked with bitter repulsion upon any course which, if the American settlers and the Californians were to be opposed in arms, made me apparently stand separated from my own race.

What was the escape from this probable clash of arms? I could see none, unless from selfish motives I abandoned my clients and withheld the only advice which afforded any prospect of saving their lives.

I therefore determined that there was no possible hope of saving the prisoners, except by rapidly organizing the Californians and bringing them to the city in sufficient numbers to fight or overcome the lawless band of men. These conclusions, which jeopardized my own life, were only reached after anxious debate with myself, for I had absolutely no one to take counsel with.

I rejoined the party of Lugos and their friends who were awaiting me in my office.

I explained to them fully the situation; telling them that nothing could be expected from the civil authorities and that the jail and the prisoners were in possession of lawless men, who held them for ransom. They were very indignant, denying that they, in any way, had treated with the band for the liberation of the boys.

They asked what they could do to save the boys, and I told them that if they could assemble seventy-five resolute men of their race, and bring them into town as soon as possible, the boys might be saved. The men must be armed as well as possible, and must be ready to fight, if necessary, to retake the jail, under authority of law.

They eagerly accepted the idea, and said if the matter were to be determined by fighting, they were willing to so settle it, and they could get plenty of men.

Amongst the party was a Mexican named Vincenti Elisalde, who was the brother of the Elisalde who was charged with assisting the Lugo boys in the murder and was in jail with them. This Vincenti was a bold and energetic man and immediately took the lead in discussing plans.

I told them to get twenty or thirty men in town as rapidly as it was possible; that the banditti in possession of the jail, tired of remaining on watch, might determine to kill the boys during the night, and that they should be watched by a sufficient force to attack them, if necessary. It was also explained that the men must come in secretly and hide themselves in the upper part of the city, in which there were many walled yards where they could not be seen; that they must not show themselves until in the morning, when I would send for them to attack, if necessary, and drive away the banditti guard around the jail, seize the prisoners and bring them into court, and guard them until released. They were further told that the men would act under the authority of the court and sheriff.

It was then about three o'clock and the five or six men parted, each pledged to send out messengers to summon their hands to gather together. All that evening and late into the night, swift couriers carried over a great area of territory a summons that found ready response. About dusk some of the nearest men began to come in; and Vincenti Elisalde reported that he would soon have thirty men in town.

Shortly after dark a heavy fog came up from the sea, as was often the case, and it was difficult to see a horseman across the street. After dark the fog became very heavy, and Elisalde soon announced that he had placed in the ravines around the jail thirty men to watch the banditti on guard, with orders to attack them at once if they discovered any suspicious movement against the prisoners.

Up to this point I had acted entirely alone without the advice of a single friend or associate; and the steps taken demanded the utmost secrecy, because if it were known that armed Californians were being brought into town, there would be immediate union between large numbers of the Americans and the band of Irving, which would probably result in the immediate hanging of the prisoners.

As I walked through the foggy streets and recognized the camp fires at the jail, which Irving's men had lighted as they kept their lawless watch, and reflected that outside of, and around, them were lying other men, ready, if an occasion arose, in a moment to engage them in a bloody struggle, and when I considered that, under my advice other men were arming and coming into the city to take part in what seemed a contest inevitably provoking bloodshed, in which perhaps the whole community might be involved, it is not wonderful that, while not relaxing in my resolution to preserve the lives of my clients, I felt a wish and desire to have someone of greater experience to join me in counsel, and in control of the events that seemed moving on to a bloody climax.

Under these feelings I selected a lawyer named Ogier, a South Carolinian, who had been an officer in the Mexican War, and afterwards became United States District Judge, who seemed to me a man of resolution, and employed him as associate counsel. I offered him a fee of one thousand dollars, to be paid by me out of my fees, and which he readily accepted. When I disclosed to him the situation and asked him for suggestions, he had none to give, except to persevere in the course which I had taken, the perils and hazards of which he recognized in almost a greater degree than I.

We sat up late in consultation, only interrupted by reports that were brought to me, from time to time, as to progress made in the call for men, and as to the continued quiet at the jail. Neither of us slept much that night, and I was called early in the morning about pressing matters. At daylight our guard was withdrawn from around the men who were holding the jail, and we had altogether, a little after sunrise, over sixty men in all carefully concealed in the upper part of the city, and other men kept dropping in until we had a total of about seventy.

The district court had finished all its business except the bailing of the Lugos; and the district attorney, a very capable, intelligent gentleman, had agreed that he would get the court to meet when I notified him I was ready. Ogier, my associate, and myself were earnestly discussing the hour when the court had best meet and when our Californians should appear upon the scene. Neither of us had a ray of hope of avoiding a desperate fight in our efforts to save the lives of the prisoners.

We were conversing about eight in the morning in the street in front of my office, when I suddenly heard the tramp of horses, and, looking up, saw wheeling into the main street, from a side street, a column of United States dragoons, which as it stretched out displayed about fifty men. If the men had descended from Heaven, my surprise and my pleasure could not have been greater. There marched law and order, and the physical power to support them; here had appeared a relief from banditti rule, and the peril of bloodshed.

This troop of cavalry was commanded by Major Fitzgerald, and had been stationed at San Diego: and a few days previous had marched from there northward for one of their periodical changes made in the ordinary routine of service.

As soon as possible we interviewed Major Fitzgerald, who said his troops would camp all day in Los Angeles, and resume their march next day. When the actual situation was disclosed to him, he was in great doubt what he could do.

He was shown the guard of Irving's men still camped at the jail. Major Fitzgerald knew and esteemed our district judge and Mr. Sutherland, the district attorney, both of whom lived in San Diego; and he had interviews with them. He said it was not competent for a United States officer to interfere with his troops in the domestic affairs of a state except on order from the President; but that it had been held that the soldiers were amenable, with the consent of their officers, to be called like other citizens by the sheriff to act as members of his posse; and that under the extraordinary circumstances, he would allow the sheriff to summon his men individually as members of his posse. He himself, and his officers, could not be summoned, and his men must act under the non-commissioned officers; but if there should be resistance and a fight he would take command. He was ready to go to his camp with the sheriff and allow him to summons privates and non-commissioned officers, to act as a posse, and he would direct the first serjeant to take charge of the men and report to, and obey the sheriff.

This resolution of the major filled us with rejoicing, as it was self-evident that with the presence of the soldiers, we could recapture the jail and the prisoners, if we kept from them all knowledge of our contemplated action.

But difficulty now was met from a most unexpected quarter. The sheriff refused to summons the soldiers as a posse. He was a good man, but timid, and he feared that if the prisoners were brought before the court under the protection of the troops, they would be shot down in the court room, and, with them, many others, including the judge, lawyers, etc.

"These men," he said, "are desperadoes and they will never allow the prisoners to escape alive."

This was the answer he gave my associate, who came to me entirely disheartened.

Fortunately the sheriff and myself were very excellent friends. He relied upon me in all troubles and followed my advice, and when I showed him how wrong his position was, and urged his action, he agreed to act as we desired.

It was agreed that the sheriff, Major Fitzgerald and my associate should visit the camp and summons the men, but that they should go separately so as not to attract attention; and the strictest secrecy was urged, as we all agreed that, if the fact that the soldiers would intervene were known long enough in advance for the leaders of the mob to consult, the prisoners would be hung in the jail before we could reach them.

The soldiers were all individually summoned to serve upon the sheriff's posse, and the sergeant was directed to be at the court house a little before 2 P. M., for it was arranged that the court should be called as soon as the prisoners were safely brought out of the jail.

It was with difficulty that the Californians whom we had brought in could be prevented from showing themselves in such numbers as

THE LUGO CASE. 41

to attract attention, but they were cautioned to hold themselves ready at two o'clock to act if called on.

THE COURT HOUSE SCENE.

While the apprehensions of a bloody struggle between the Californians on the one side, and Irving's band and their allies among the American citizens, on the other side, were allayed, owing to the presence of the United States cavalry, the anxieties of all cognizant of the circumstances were very great.

Sheriff Burrell described the danger when he stated that this desperate band would not allow the prisoners to escape alive, and would probably butcher them and others either in the court room or when leaving it. There was not one of us who did not consider this probable; but there was no other choice than to take these chances, and we faced them as best we could.

The whole town was in turmoil all the morning and business was almost suspended. No one had the least idea that the soldiers were to take part in the scenes, but the whole community was on tip-toe expecting some denouement, such as the hanging or shooting of the Lugos.

At ten o'clock, when it was supposed the court would convene, crowds were on hand; and all of Irving's twenty-five men but himself were present, except a few who still were in possession of the jail. Those present were conspicuous in the vicinity of the court by their flannel shirts; and their openly displayed six shooters and knives made them easily recognizable. I was pleased to see that none carried rifles, as this omission gave some proof that they had heard nothing of the assembling of the Californians.

It was evident that I was closely watched, principally, I think, because of a general belief that I was not ready to allow my clients to be sacrificed without a struggle, and of curiosity as to what method I would pursue.

So impressed were the district judge, attorney and clerk with what would be the personal peril to them in the court room that they took precautions to protect themselves. Four discharged soldiers, who were well known as good men, were employed by these officers, armed and placed in the clerk's room, which opened just behind the judge's seat, with instructions in case of firing to cover the exit of the judge and officials into the clerk's office, and then to defend the room against all comers.

I knew nothing of these arrangements, until after the matter ended. My plan was to send the soldiers with the sheriff up to the jail where Irving's guard was, who could make no resistance, and to take the prisoners, and, surrounding them and the sheriff, to bring them to the court-room.

It was impracticable for the cavalry to enter the room; and there were objections made to dismounting some of the men and bringing them inside, which was regrettable. The result of which was that the prisoners would be in the court room only in the charge of the sheriff and a deputy, and with them would be the several bondsmen and their father, while the room would be filled with their enemies.

The court-room was an oblong room, entered from the street at its back, with no partition whatever between the bar and the public. There were two windows opening on the street and a man standing on the pavement could look in. If a row were started, the shots directed at the prisoners would reach their relatives and friends who had come forward to serve as their bondsmen, as well as the officers of the court and the lawyers, who were all grouped near together at the end of the narrow room. This whole position was carefully considered before the meeting and its hazards and perils foreseen.

It seemed that the only security we could have inside the court room must come from ourselves, except the moral influence of the court which was an important element, as its character and standing were high. I had the Californians on hand, but their appearance on the scene might be regarded as a challenge, which would be taken up.

These were the instructions I gave: A selected body of Californians, at 2 P. M. should approach the court-house but not so as to be seen. These men were intended for two purposes.

1st—To receive, protect and carry off the boys, in case they were bailed without accident.

2nd—To be ready to respond at a moment's notice, when called to come to our relief, and to force an entrance into the court room.

I judged that I would be able by personal observation in the court-room to determine when an attack would be made. My associate and myself, under advice, were armed with pistols.

It would be almost impossible for the boys to be shot without my observing preparations for it; and I felt confident that I would be able to discover preliminary symptoms in time to anticipate the shooting.

It was arranged, therefore, that Vincenti Elisalde, whose readiness and alertness I have already spoken of, should see this group of selected Californians in position and then should come to the court-room,—dismounting outside and holding his bridle in his hand ready to mount instantly,—and station himself at the window in front of the trial table near which I would be, ready at an agreed signal from me, to mount and bring down his men prepared to force their way into the room, unless halted by me.

The agreed signal was that I should take from my pocket a key, and shake it at him; and in two or three minutes at the furthest, it was estimated, that the men would be at the door.

A few moments before 2 P. M. the troops drew up in front of the court-house, and the sheriff went on foot with them. The crowd that hung around all the morning had no suspicion, even then, of the meaning of their appearance; and eager questions were asked as to where the soldiers were going, and some supposed they were about to continue their northward march. But when passing down the street they suddenly wheeled to the right and were seen winding up the ascent to the jail, the whole truth flashed on the crowd.

"They are going for the Lugos, and the sheriff is leading them," was exclaimed, and then bitter and violent execrations broke forth. As court had not yet been opened, Irving's men were scattered, ten or twelve at the jail, more throughout the town, and only a few present. Irving himself was absent, though I understood he was momentarily expected.

No resistance was made at the jail, and there was only delay enough to take off the irons from the three prisoners, and then the cavalry formed a hollow square and inside of it marched the sheriff and the three prisoners.

Men were running rapidly to and fro, gathering together Irving's men, but before that was effected the sheriff arrived and with the prisoners entered the court room. The judge came in from the clerk's room and in a loud voice proclaimed the opening of the court. Not a word was spoken by the crowd, but scarcely any of the citizens entered the court-room, into which, a few at a time, came Irving's surprised men.

The proceedings immediately begun, and consisted only of the court examining the sureties as to their competency. Each surety was to be worth double the amount of bond and they were all to be worth $120,000. The district attorney was very particular in making each bondsman enumerate his property, and it seemed to me the exciting crisis was unduly prolonged.

There were collected in the court-room about twenty spectators, nearly all belonging to the band. Evans, their first lieutenant, was there, and he and a few of his men talked earnestly in whispers, but events had moved so rapidly and unexpectedly that it seemed evident to me they had not time to form any plan, though their faces expressed passion.

The sun beat with great heat upon the soldiers, who had remained drawn up and in front of the court-room, and the sergeant not understanding the importance of their remaining as close as possible, moved his troop to the opposite side of the street, where there was shade. I was startled very much at this, but the want of any concerted plan amongst the angry audience seemed apparent to me; and I made no move to get the soldiers back.

But suddenly there was a movement, the crowd of citizens who blocked the doorway without entering, was rapidly divided, and in stalked the redoubtable Red Irving. Tall and spare, with steely blue eyes and red beard, dusty, heated, and evidently harried, he gazed for a moment around the room and then eagerly advanced and talked with his leaders, who gathered around him. His coat was off and outside of his shirt was belted his six shooter and hunting knife.

During all the proceedings I kept walking to and fro on the side of the trial table, which was nothing unusual for me to do, but which gave me the opportunity, without attracting attention, of observing every movement in the room. I immediately approached the sheriff, and in a whisper told him to immediately order the cavalry to cross the street and draw up on our front so as to bring them nearer to the court.

When Irving entered and was recognized, there was a murmur, and for a moment not a word was spoken, expectation waiting upon what action he might take. I saw from the conference going on that he was giving no orders, only asking questions. The whole crisis had arisen in his absence, and he was ignorant of the details, and especially the presence of the cavalry was unknown to him until his arrival.

Presently the tramping of horses and rattling of sabers showed me the long line of blue coats extending along the outer side of the court-room. Irving left his companions and walked to the front and carefully ran his eye over the arrangements.

The prisoners were seated on a bench along the wall, and in front and by the side of them sat their father, uncles and two or three other friends. No shots could reach the boys without traversing the bodies of their father and other friends.

Suddenly he wheeled around, and went back amongst his men, and half a dozen gathered around him. For the first time noting their angry and excited faces, I felt impressed that some action was about to be taken.

All during the proceedings I could see, touching the window, the swarthy countenance of my friend Elisalde. I can see him now, as he was then, his bright black eyes never leaving me, his bushy black beard and dusky face. Over his shoulders was his dark riding coat, bound with a broad band of gold lace, in one hand were seen the reins of his horse, whose head I could just see beyond him;—bold, resolute, obedient, a very electric button, ready upon a touch to rouse into action forces charged with perils to life.

THE LUGO CASE.

Moved by this second conference of Red Irving and his men, I withdrew the signal key from my pocket but carefully concealed it, hesitating to launch my messenger upon his ominous mission until developments made it necessary.

In a few moments Irving again appeared in the front. No whispering or movement of his men indicated preparations for attack. He stood out conspicuously, his angry eyes now resting upon me and then seeking the prisoners. I had frequently met him and we had always exchanged greetings, though when his eyes rested upon me there was no shade of salutation in them. The mental processes that governed him and his men were clearly perceptible.

The rapidity of events, following the appearance of the soldiers, the absence of Irving, his actual ignorance of the situation by which he was surrounded, his inability to estimate all the defensive resources arrayed against him, and therefore the absence of all prepared plans, left him and his men absolutely impotent; and he represented standing there, baffled wit in the presence of law resting on force.

I returned the signal key to my pocket, conscious that the crisis had passed. In a few moments more the bonds were approved, and the sheriff, as soon as the court wrote its approval, started to the door with the prisoners surrounded by their friends. Again the cavalry formed a hollow square around the discharged prisoners, who were conducted into another street, where fifty Californians with led horses awaited them and escorted them safely away.

* * * * * * *

At that period the "Bella Union" was the principal hotel in Los Angeles, and almost every American took his meals there. I went that night late to my supper. There had been, I understood, great and bitter excitement after the discharge of the prisoners. A great deal of liquor was drunk and many ugly threats had been made. When I sat down to take my supper, there were only a few men in the room. I had nearly finished my meal when looking up I saw Red Irving approaching me.

He was evidently under the influence of liquor and he drew near me slowly, keeping his eye fixed upon me. I felt a certain apprehension that he might insult or outrage me. I was totally unarmed, but I was eating with a steel fork of some sharpness and strength and I felt that I was not absolutely without some kind of defense.

When he reached close to me he stood for a moment gazing upon me with the pertinacity of a drunken man, and then raising his hand—fortunately only as a gesture—he exclaimed:

"Young man! I don't blame *you!* You did your duty. But for Fitzgerald and his soldiers I have the greatest contempt!" and then followed a string of oaths and scurrilous abuse incapable of repetition. He said he could whip the soldiers and that he had sent word to Major Fitzgerald he would fight him in the morning, with his men at his back, on foot or on horseback. He wanted to know what business Fitzgerald and his soldiers had to interfere "in our private quarrels" as he stated it.

He then directed his attention to the Lugos, whom he villified as murderers; always by way of defining his position, declaring that he did not blame me: and even adding that I was a gentleman, as evidence of his personal sentiments.

But he wound up his invectives by declaring that he would get even with the Lugos for their rascalities and then said: "I solemnly swear that during June I will have their hair or be in hell". I have described this incident for the purpose of stating the awful oath, which in view of subsequent events, bore a mysterious significance, which has left it impressed on my memory.

HOW RED IRVING SOUGHT TO FULFILL HIS OATH AND ITS RESULTS

Things quieted down after this, but the Lugos were advised to keep away from the city and its vicinity until Irving and his men left. Some weeks after it was reported that Irving announced that his party was ready to go into Mexico and begin mining. It was well known that they were well armed with rifles and had bought large supplies of provisions. They were said to have twenty-five men and several servants. They left their camp in the Arroyo Seco and their first march carried them into the San Jose settlement where they slept. In the morning they openly went about seizing horses.

Many of the rancheros came into Los Angeles complaining of horses being taken. This produced some excitement, but no action followed, as it was supposed that the next day the band would have continued their march towards the Colorado desert, which it was known they intended to cross.

That evening the band marched to the vicinity of the Chino Rancho, where is now the great Chino Beet Root Factory. They continued seizing horses, openly driving up many and selecting the best horses; in addition they killed several beeves belonging to the people; and announced their intention to remain there until they dried the meat in the sun, making what is called "Taso" or sun-dried meat, which would keep unspoiled, and which was the usual supply of meat for parties setting out upon expeditions.

Very many rancheros came into the city complaining of the seizures of their horses, and amongst them were many influential ones,—Don Julian Workman of the Puente, Senor Palomares of San Jose and Julian Williams of the Chino. They made a great clamor, demanding that the county should be raised and the sheriff should proceed and arrest them.

The city was aroused and great indignation was felt at the boldness of this lawless band. Lawyers were employed, and writs of arrest and writs of replevin were issued.

It was well understood that it was a very grave matter to capture this bold and well armed band; and Russell, the sheriff, used every effort to collect a strong force. He succeeded in getting together over fifty men, amongst whom were some of the gamblers, very resolute men. A full day was lost in getting the posse, but they sallied forth pretty well armed and very resolute in purpose; as many of them had suffered from the depredations of the band and others feared they might also be robbed.

On the second night they reached the Chino Rancho, and learned that the band had left there that morning at daylight and that it had divided itself into two parts; one, composed of its wagons and loose horses, servants, and a small guard, had followed the main road to the Colorado, crossing; and the other, composed of eighteen men, headed by Irving, had marched off on the road to the left leading to the San Bernardino Rancho, with the open declaration that they were going to kill the Lugos.

This movement against the Lugos did not take them by surprise. The first day that the band broke up their camp at the Arroyo Seco, an American who lived principally among the Californians and was called by them Martinsito, came to see me. He was the best friend of and sympathizer with the Lugos that I knew, and he had frequently sought to serve them.

He came to tell me that he had positive information that the band had started for Mexico, and that Irving had told some of his friends that before they left the country a party of his men would visit San Bernardino and settle with the Lugos. Remembering Irving's oath, I felt satisfied that this was true, and I felt it was very important that this information should be sent to the Lugos without delay.

I asked my informant if he would go as the messenger. The distance to San Bernardino was about sixty miles, and he said it was a long ride and he might fall in with some of Irving's men. He then remarked it would be dangerous to write, as the letter might be lost or captured by Irving who would be on the lookout. But finally he agreed to go, saying while he would carry no note that I must give him some token which, when shown by him to the

Lugos, would be recognized as coming from me and accredit him.

The custom of sending personal tokens, instead of letters, was a very common one. I knew an old Californian who was accustomed to send in his hat to a money-lender as authority for a loan to the bearer, and frequent and considerable transactions were carried on without confusion upon the faith of the hat. So when Martinsito demanded that I furnish him a token I was not at a loss.

During the progress of the affair, the mother of the boys had seen me frequently, and upon one occasion had given me a gold ring which she said she had long worn, which was hammered out by some rude Mexican workman and had a cross upon it. I knew this would be immediately recognized and I gave it to the man, with the message that I advised the Lugo boys, with their father and uncles, not to sleep in their houses at nights and to keep good and careful watch all day, until they were satisfied that Irving and his men had left the country. Martinsito carried his message and returned with great rapidity, seeing me the day that the sheriff's posse marched, and telling me that the Lugos would carefully follow my advice, and that there was no danger of their being caught.

When the sheriff's posse learned this, it was determined by the sheriff that next morning, early, they would march to San Bernardino, as it was evident there would be a tragedy there. Some of the posse that day returned to Los Angeles, instead of following the sheriff, so that the news spread that Irving had gone in pursuit of the Lugos; but I felt confident that he would not catch them.

It is now necessary to make a digression in order to clearly understand the new elements that entered into this affair.

The original settlements in California resulted from the efforts of the missionary fathers to Christianize the Indians. They promoted their religious work by the social changes they carefully and laboriously wrought amongst the Indians, who were assembled at the missionary stations, and who were taught to sow and reap grain, to cultivate crops and to weave clothes and live in houses. It is impossible here to say more than to refer to their labors which resulted in greater happiness and development than the Indians had ever elsewhere received at the hands of the European races.

Professional reasons imposed upon me the search of the missionary fathers' old archives in manuscript, especially of the mission of San Gabriel, and I speak as one who is not without considerable information. Only those Indians that voluntarily came to the missions were accepted and no violence was used to compel any tribe to join themselves to the mission.

There was a small tribe of Indians called Coaillas, settled upon what was afterwards known as San Bernardino County, who never joined the missions; and the remnants of the tribe still occupied upon the Lugos' rancho their original rancherias or huts. They were always recognized by the Spaniards as "Indios Gentiles". They were few in number at that time, and in no way had they made any improvement in civilization, except they had learned to work for wages for the Lugos and their neighbors, and to get drunk.

I had occasion frequently to see these and other Indians who came into Los Angeles. The men were very ugly and apparently stupid, wearing but few clothes and devoted to drink; but under all the changes of government they had preserved a separate tribal existence. They were only a few, possibly not over forty men, speaking their native language and a very little Spanish. Their chief while I was there was a man called Juan Antonio, a taciturn man, saying little, and seemingly having a capacity to talk but little.

The first time I ever saw Juan Antonio was when he was cited to appear before our county court. It seems that two of his young Indians got drunk, and one killed the other. By the law of the tribe the fact of killing was to be punished by death without any inquiring into the circumstances. So upon the day after the killing, Juan Antonio and his men went with the killer to the place where the dead man was to be buried. They gave the killer a spade and made him dig a grave and when they considered it deep enough they placed in it the dead man, then knocked the killer on the head and tumbled him into the same grave. Some busybody heard of this incident and rushed into court and made affidavit against Juan Antonio for murder and prayed his arrest. Instead of executing the warrant literally, the sheriff sent Juan Antonio word to come to court on a certain day as the authorities wished to see him.

I was in court accidentally when the old fellow came in with three or four others of his tribe. One of the judges was a Californian and he explained to Juan Antonio that the court had heard about his killing an Indian, and wished to know about it.

The old fellow with great frankness described the whole process, including the knocking on the head and burying the two in the same grave. And when the county attorney asked what right he had to kill the man, he simply said "he had killed the other man".

Another lawyer and myself immediately volunteered as friends of the court and suggested that it was not competent to inquire into the matter occuring amongst a savage tribe according to its law; and though this view was opposed by the county attorney, the court accepted it, and discharged the whole matter.

The old fellow knew nothing of what was going on, and when he was told he could go, he went away without the slightest idea that there had been a question raised as to his power to administer justice.

The few remnants of this tribe, with their chief, lived upon what were the Lugo lands, and were their cowboys and laborers when called upon. Their only weapons were bows and arrows, if we can call weapons that which were only used for securing food; and I think there never was a record of their having made war on the whites.

When Irving and his men arrived at San Bernardino they immediately surrounded the two residences of the Lugos, which were about a mile apart, and found no men in them. Though the ladies of the family were there, they began to be abusive, breaking up a few things and especially in the last house they became very disorderly, searching the house, wantonly destroying some of the clothes, and indulging in terrible threats against the men. They unfortunately found wine and some of them became quite excited, mounted their horses, and charged about the grounds, firing their pistols. While these things were going on, four or five of the Indian servants, attracted by the noise, came and stood outside, looking upon the actions of the men.

At last Irving called his men to mount, declaring he would return again and wreak his vengeance.

Some of the men rode their horses at a gallop, suddenly jerking them up and firing their pistols; and at last one exclaimed: "Let's try our pistols upon the Indians," and a fusillade was opened upon the surprised Indians; the result of which was a ball in the arm of an old man. The Indians immediately disappeared and rushed off to their rancherias and informed Juan Antonio and the others of what had transpired.

Juan Antonio told his men to take their bows and arrows and they all went back to the house. The lawless men had not left and were still hallooing and charging around. When the Indians returned, as soon as they were seen, they were fired on, though Irving tried to restrain his men, and at last he got them started.

Instead of returning down the valley and following the road through the open country, they determined to shorten the road by riding up to the head of the valley and then crossing a range of foot hills, thus emerging well upon their road to the Colorado desert. None of them knew the country but they believed that it was easily practicable for them to cross this range of foot hills, which, though high, were nothing like a mountain range.

As they started off, some of them rode and fired in the bushes where they thought the Indians were concealed. The Indians, incensed by the wounding of the old Indian and the unprovoked firing upon them, still continued at a distance to follow; and when the men recognized the Indians, they began to whoop and halloo as if it were a great joke. They were all armed with six shooters and many, probably all, carried extra cylinders which could be readily fitted in their pistols. They had left in their wagons their rifles, believing they would have no use for them.

That these miserable California Indians, with their bows and arrows should follow them, excited only their laughter, and every now and then some would gallop to the rear and fire in the bushes. But the Indians on foot continued to follow at a distance, while the country remained open.

But as the men advanced, the open places became fewer, and the density of the chaparral increased. Before them loomed the steep range of mountains, crowned by the San Bernardino mountain, the loftiest of the Coast Range, and at right angles shot out from this mountain the range of foot hills that interposed between them and their desert road. Evidently they were seeking for some pass to cross the foot hills, and at last they came to a canyon or glen that seemed to penetrate the hills and give promise of a pass. As they turned towards the canyon the density of the chaparral and its height continued to increase, until the hill-sides were covered with it.

As they entered into this dense chaparral the time came for which the Indians had been waiting. Though often fired at they had not replied by a single arrow. Now entering into the chaparral and running through it like rabbits they came up beside the horsemen, and concealed by the brush growth, opened at short range with their bows and arrows.

A man was shot and fell off his horse, whereupon his companions charged back, but there was nothing to be seen but chaparral. Another fell and one was wounded and rode rapidly away. The horsemen attained the mouth of the glen and entered it. It was a dry canyon and covered very densely upon its sides with growth, but the centre, where in rainy seasons the water ran, was a little more open. The Indians availing themselves of the dense growth, swarmed up along the whole line of horsemen, who, without seeing an enemy, received their arrows, shot from almost under their horses' feet. Panic now seized the riders, and they rode up the canyon at full speed, leaving their fallen companions; but at last a halt was ordered and it was determined to charge.

Here evidently was the last rally, for eight or ten men fell here close together. Red Irving with his arm extended up to fire his pistol, was shot by an arrow entering under his armpit and extending through and beyond the body.

Thus perished this formidable band of hardy and lawless frontiermen by the hands of Indians utterly unpracticed in war and generally looked on as one of the low types of life, and considered incapable of protecting themselves and using only the same bows and arrows with which their fathers were armed when Columbus discovered America. But the conditions under which they fought gave the Indians resistless advantages, as was evidenced by the fact that they were but little more numerous than the whites, and that they reported that not one of them was even wounded, except the old man who was wantonly shot for play, and whose wound was the principal moving cause of the death of Red Irving and his men.

It was supposed for a long time that every man with Irving had perished, but one of them by pushing rapidly ahead before the Indians caught up with the head of the column, and not returning when he heard the firing, escaped with his life. The road he advanced on became impassable and he abandoned his horse and struggled along on foot, reaching the men in charge of the wagons and extra horses of the band. Upon communicating the fate of his comrades, the men divided up the baggage and property left, and each separated, seeking roads which did not lead them back to

Los Angeles. The man who escaped was Evans, whose name I have mentioned above.

The sheriff's posse, whom we left in full march to the Lugo rancho, heard before arriving a rumor of the destruction of Irving's band by the Indians, but could scarcely believe it. The posse was composed of about one half Californians and one half Americans, and amongst them ten or fifteen gamblers and frontiersmen from Los Angeles. They rode rapidly forward and were piloted to the bloody canyon where the tragedy had been consummated.

The Coailla Indians had inherited from their forefathers a barbarous custom which prevailed extensively in the valley. This inherited habit taught them not to believe that an enemy was dead unless his head was crushed by stones.

When the sheriff's posse followed up the line of dead men until they reached the spot where the last stand was made, and where the bodies were almost piled one on the other, it was discovered that the hideous Indian custom had been followed in the case of each body of the killed. When the posse drew up at this last scene, they began talking about it. The Californians, inflamed with anger at the lawless band, which had robbed them of their horses, which had attempted to kill the Lugos —with whom many were united by blood— and which has perished in a lawless raid in pursuit of what was simply murder, expressed their gratification at this result while the Americans, moved by the brutal spectacle of the butchery and annihilation of seventeen of their countrymen, resented the gloating over the dead of their race by the Spaniards.

Words were bandied to and fro, and excitement grew high; threats and menaces flew from man to man. Then the two races of the posse separated, one on each side of the canon, with only the mutilated and the dead between, confronting each other with bitter words and threats. Pistols were freely drawn upon each side, and it looked for a moment as if the baleful influence of the lawless men who had just perished was still potent for bloodshed. However, before a shot was fired, one or two men of prominence and influence rode between the angry and separated lines, and quieted the outburst of what would have been a bloodier fray than that before them. Turning away, the posse rode back sullenly and dispersed.

THE END OF THE LUGO CASE

If there were a disposition to extend this already unreasonably long narrative, ample material exists for it in other episodes that occurred; but the narrative will be henceforward curtailed within narrow limits.

Shortly after these events the grand jury of Los Angeles found an indictment for murder against the Lugos, this reversing the action of the preceding grand jury, as was their right. The county attorney notified me of that fact and of his intention to apply to the county court for an order of court, based on their bond given in the district court, requiring the Lugos to present themselves before the county court and abide its order.

Though Irving and his band had disappeared, I feared that the appearance of the Lugos in court would be attended by great danger to them, which danger was aggravated by a certain unreasonable resentment felt by a great many that Irving and his men had perished through their efforts to kill the Lugos.

There was in addition an energetic and hostile influence against the boys, proceeding from most of the county local authorities and shared by many of the American residents, who thought they were appropriate subjects for lynch law.

When the motion was made in court for the order to appear, I filed objections to it for very substantial reasons. The bond was taken by the district court and by its conditions and under our practice I claimed that the county court had no jurisdiction at all over the bond. The court overruled my objections, and passed an order for the accused to appear before the county court at a fixed day.

I told the court that my opinion was clear that they had no jurisdiction to pass the order, and I would advise my clients not to obey it. Upon the day fixed by the court, the accused were called at the court house door and made default. Whereupon the court ordered the forfeiture of the bonds and the issuance of warrants of arrest. I repeated in the court my belief that the forfeiture of the bonds and the warrants of arrest were null, for want of jurisdiction, and that I would advise my clients to disregard them.

Then began a series of efforts by the sheriff to arrest the accused. Posses were raised and raids by day and by night made in every direction in which it was supposed the accused could be found.

When the next district court met the indictment was returned to it. There were many substantial defects in the indictment and proceedings, which nullified them, and the district court was compelled on motion to set aside the indictment. Then as there was no indictment the district court refused to order the accused to appear, holding their bond was still in force. Notwithstanding this, the county authorities, persisted in their efforts to arrest the accused.

Very many dangerous and exciting episodes occurred in this illegal attempt of the local authorities to arrest the accused; and I always believed that behind these efforts was a strong and resolute organization to hang the Lugos if they were ever brought to town.

The county attorney could never get a grand jury to find another indictment against the Lugos. The evidence of a dozen or more responsible men in direct contradiction of the informer, was too convincing to allow the finding of another indictment.

Things drifted along this way for more than a year, greatly to the discomfort of the accused, and the greater discomfort of the sheriff. The lapse of time blunted many of the prejudices against my clients. Other American settlers came into the county, who outnumbered the older and more prejudiced residents, and who had no feelings at all in respect to the Lugos.

I then believed that the time had come when the affair might be settled, and with some misgiving I determined to make surrender to the sheriff.

One evening about three o'clock the accused came by previous arrangement into town with competent bondsmen and went to the private house of the county judge and waited the arrival of the sheriff. I had prepared all the proceedings for a writ of habeas corpus; and new bonds had been carefully made out, ready for immediate execution. At three o'clock I went to the office of the sheriff and notified him if he would come immediately with me I would give him an opportunity to arrest the

Lugos. He was much surprised at this and asked if he should take a posse with him. He was told there was no necessity for it. He called his principal deputy and both armed themselves, the deputy carrying with him a double barreled shot gun. As we passed the office of the county attorney, I advised that he be notified to come with the sheriff.

We all went to the house of the county judge, where were the Lugo boys and their friends. The boys were immediately arrested by the sheriff, who wished to carry his prisoners at once to jail; but I had explained the whole matter to the county judge, and as soon as the arrest was made, I presented to him papers asking for a writ of habeas corpus which was immediately granted. As there was no indictment pending, the judge immediately allowed bail to the prisoners. This was assented to by me, as they were already under subsisting and valid bonds, but it was thought better to allow the arrest to be made and to give new bonds for the sake of peace. In a very few moments the new bonds were executed and approved and the prisoners discharged.

No further indictment was found against the accused; and this ended the Lugo case; without ever having been brought to trial; and all excitement in relation to it disappeared.

THE END

PEOPLE VERSUS LUGO

*Story of a famous Los Angeles murder case
and its amazing aftermath*

BY W. W. ROBINSON

1962

Dawson's Book Shop
Los Angeles

Copyright 1962

W. W. ROBINSON
Los Angeles, California

Library of Congress Catalog Number: 62-10883

CONTENTS

		PAGE
I.	Death in Cajon Pass	1
II.	Jailed for Murder	5
III.	The Indian Raid	9
IV.	J. Lancaster Brent to the Rescue	13
V.	Conspiracy	17
VI.	Red Irving and His Gang	21
VII.	*Californios* Versus Bandits	25
VIII.	In the Courtroom	29
IX.	Red Irving Pays a Visit to San Bernardino Valley	33
X.	The Lugo Case Ends	37
	Sources on the Lugo Case—with Comment	43

PEOPLE VERSUS LUGO

DEATH IN CAJON PASS

O N JANUARY 27, 1851, an Irishman named Patrick Mc-Swiggen and a Creek Indian named Sam were murdered in desolate Cajon Pass, connecting twenty-mile link between the grim Mojave Desert and the lush San Bernardino Valley.

This launched the "Lugo Case," famous in Southern California crime annals, a proceeding that created an unparalleled state of tension in Los Angeles and unloosed a chain of amazing incidents.

In a setting of green hills and distant mountains, Los Angeles in 1851 was still a Mexican-California pueblo in looks and feelings. Its homes and its shops were one-story adobe buildings, centered about a bare and dusty plaza. Nine-tenths of its three thousand people were Spanish-speaking—either *Californios* or Sonoran newcomers. The other tenth were mostly recently arrived Americans. For two years at least it had accustomed itself to a brawling street life, to the presence of innumerable gambling houses ("monte banks"), and to a routine of fights, stabbings, and killings. The scum of northern mining communities was finding it a convenient rallying place, and embittered Sonoran miners

2 : PEOPLE VS. LUGO

from the Mother Lode made it a center for criminal activities. Indians, too, were present in great number and on Saturday nights were rough. Close to the period of the McSwiggen-Sam murder, a party of San Luis Rey Indians had played "peon" with Cahuilla Indians from San Bernardino Valley and had ended their game with a great battle fought on the hill back of the Plaza Church. The next morning dead Indians strewed the scene of the fight. A member of the coroner's jury, summoned to view the men with mashed-in heads, counted 13 in the immediate area and made a moderate estimate that Indians killed totalled fifty. Los Angeles in 1851 was well used to sudden death.

At the time of the Cajon Pass murder a company of American soldiers was encamped at Cucamonga, a few miles southwest of the mouth of the pass. They were members of Company A, 2nd Infantry, United States Army, which at that time had headquarters on Isaac Williams' near-by Chino Rancho. Two days after the murder a detachment of these soldiers was riding toward Cajon Pass. Presently they met "four Spaniards"—that is, *Californios,* and on getting near the mouth of the pass they came upon six stray, yet harnessed, mules and then saw a wagon on the left of the trail. Without investigation, they went further and camped for the night. The next morning, January 30, Captain Walker and 12 men came to the camp and told the group that two men had been murdered. Four of the soldiers—James Dempsey, John A. Jackson, William I. Henry, and W. G. Gee—immediately went back to the wagon. There they found two dead men, one on the right and one on the left of the road or trail.

The white man's clothes had been drawn up over his head and his pockets were turned inside out. Further examination of the corpse showed the head and face much bruised, as from being dragged over the rocks. There was a bullet wound and clotted blood on the head, and the face was black. The livid mark on one leg could have been caused by a rope. A few yards away was a hat with a small bullet hole and, upon the tail of the wagon, there were spots of blood. The body of the Indian, on the other side of the trail, also gave evidence of having been dragged.

The soldiers quickly buried the dead as best they could, covering them with stones and bushes. On each side of the trail they put up a wooden cross with this inscription: "Murder committed here, Jan. 27th, 1851."

News of the double murder soon reached Los Angeles, and presently the identity of the dead men. They were teamsters employed by a gold mining company, operating in the Amargosa Desert on the road to Salt Lake, in which Benjamin D. (Benito) Wilson and other prominent Angelenos were interested. Coroner A. P. Hodges in due time visited the scene of the killing, held an inquest, and re-buried the bodies which by that time had been partly eaten or torn by coyotes.

This murder excited Los Angeles, since the victims were known, but the town boiled over when two members of the richest and most influential family in Southern California—the Lugo family—were arrested, jailed, and charged with the murder!

JAILED FOR MURDER

Almost a month had passed after the Cajon Pass killing before Coroner Hodges, from the Chino Rancho, summoned Justice of the Peace Louis Rubidoux of near-by Jurupa to meet him the next day (February 26) in the Pass. At this meeting testimony was heard and the coroner's jury made its finding.

"A white man came to his death by criminal and violent means," the jury reported, "from a gunshot wound through the head ... by the hands of some person or persons of a party or parties who went after a band of outlaw Indians and part of whom were met by the witnesses before the jury on January 28, 1851, on their return, and said party met being Francisco Lugo, Jun., Francisco Lugo, Sen., Francisco Argüello, Luis Castro, Guadalupe Rendon, Manuel (a Frenchman), Ysidro Higuera, and others not known." Any sheriff, constable, marshal or policeman was "therefore commanded forthwith to arrest the above named persons, and take them before the nearest or most accessible magistrate in this County." (At this time the San Bernardino County

6 : PEOPLE VS. LUGO

area was within Los Angeles County.) A similar verdict covered the death of the Indian.

The two Lugos included in those named were the young sons of José María Lugo, one of the owners of the huge Rancho San Bernardino. Francisco Lugo, Senior, was at least 18 years old and was usually called "Chico." Francisco Lugo, Junior, was at least 16 years old and was known as "Menito."[1] Both were "stout for their age." Their grandfather (father of José María) was the famous, wealthy, and respected Antonio María Lugo, landowner and stockraiser. Don Antonio was a distinguished figure on the streets of Los Angeles and a frequent visitor to San Bernardino Valley. He rode erect in the saddle. With a sword, Spanish style, attached to his saddle, he symbolized the California ranchero. In 1839, in the name of one of his sons, José del Carmen Lugo, a permit had been obtained to colonize the San Bernardino and Yucaipa valleys. The colony plan collapsed, but three sons and a nephew of Don Antonio moved into this fabulous and frontier region. They received a grant from Governor Alvarado in 1842. The nephew, Diego Sepúlveda, brought horses and cattle from Rancho Palos Verdes into Yucaipa Valley and built an adobe home that still stands. The three sons made their home on the floor of the San Bernardino Valley area: Vicente Lugo on a hill overlooking Politana and the site of present day Colton; José del Carmen

---

[1] Joseph Lancaster Brent, who handled the defense in the Lugo Case, gives the ages of the young men as 18 and 16 in his *The Lugo Case*, written a half century or more after the events. Possibly, as their defender, he liked to think of them as younger men than they were, though other contemporaries referred to them as "boys." The varying and conflicting ages given in the Padron of 1836, the Padron of 1844, and Census of 1850 are puzzling. They lead one to believe that the census takers estimated ages or were often given incorrect information. The young Lugos were listed as 8 and 6 in 1836, as 14 and 12 in 1844, and as 23 and 16 in 1850. Not too much reliance need be given the stated figures when one notes that the mother of the boys, María Antonio Rendon, perhaps exercising a feminine privilege, was described as 40 in the Padron of 1844 and as 39 in the Census of 1850.

Lugo in the old Asistencia de San Bernardino, a landmark from Mission San Gabriel days; and José María Lugo on the site of San Bernardino's present Courthouse.

Through the 1840s and until Mormon colonists from Utah bought them out in 1851-1852, the Lugos led the pastoral, feudal, self-sufficient way of life typical of that of most California ranchos. This life revolved about the raising of longhorned cattle. It included horsemanship of a superb order, rodeos presided over by the judge of the plains, lavish hospitality, celebration of religious holidays, bull and bear fights (with bears obtained from the Highland area), and horse races. Always threatening this simple, medieval living were the raids from desert Indians, especially from the far away Utes who were constantly tempted by the fine horses of the valley rancheros.

Such was the rugged background of Chico and Menito Lugo—now accused of murder—a background highlighted by resistance to Indian raids.

By the end of March Sheriff George Burrill (through Deputy W. B. Osburn) had taken into custody Chico and Menito Lugo and a third man named Mariano Elisalde. The sheriff acted under two commitments signed by Justice of the Peace Jonathan R. Scott, charging the three arrested men with the murder specifically of Patrick McSwiggen and Sam, a Creek Indian. All three defendants were members of the party which had been seen in Cajon Pass returning from the pursuit of raiding Indians.

Preceding the arrest there had been several weeks of testimony and of cross examination of witnesses before Justice Scott. All of the statements and answers are preserved in a fat bundle of hand-written, yellowing, hard-to-read sheets in the criminal files of the Court of Sessions sequestered in hard-to-find cabinets in the Hall of Records, Los Angeles.

8 : PEOPLE VS. LUGO

In the cramped and dirty quarters of their new adobe home, the Los Angeles *calabozo* or jail, located on a hill overlooking the Courthouse and the town, the Lugo boys and their friend Mariano had a world of time to recall the details of the recent Indian raid on Rancho San Bernardino and its aftermath.

III THE INDIAN RAID

HORSE STEALING RAIDS on San Bernardino Valley during rancho days were master-minded by a Ute chief named Walkara. The whites usually called him Chief Walker. He was a superb horseman and commanded a band of two hundred well-armed, well-mounted Utes, Paiutes, and Snakes. From headquarters in Utah, south of the Great Salt Lake, the raiders swept down through the Cajon Pass, usually at the full of the moon, to drive off herds of horses from Southern California ranchos. These they sold in the Salt Lake Valley or to New Mexican traders. When Walkara began his raids in the 1830s he was simply an Indian wearing a loin cloth, a shell necklace, and a blanket. With success, he adopted, for his forays, a "full suit of the richest broadcloth generally brown and cut in European fashion, with a shining beaver hat and fine cambric shirt." To these he added "his own gaudy Indian trimmings." So garbed, he rode at the head of a troop with "richly caparisoned horses."[2]

So great was the Indian menace in the San Bernardino

[2] Quoted by Paul Bailey from contemporary sources in his *Walkara—Hawk of the Mountains* (Westernlore Press, 1954), page 16.

10 : PEOPLE VS. LUGO

Valley during the 1840s and until Walkara's death in 1855, that a group of New Mexican colonists was established at Politana, to be succeeded by a band of friendly Cahuilla Indians and also, finally, by a body of American soldiers—for attempted protection of this frontier region.

The murder of Patrick McSwiggen and Sam the Creek Indian was in the wake of a typical Walkara raid. Thirty or forty mounted Utes rode down into the valley and drove several hundred fine horses, mostly belonging to José María Lugo, stampeding up Cajon Pass. Lugo organized a pursuit party of about twenty men, neighbors, vaqueros, and possibly Cahuillas. Lugo's two sons, Chico and Menito, were in the party.

On the way through the pass they met McSwiggen and Sam—Los Angeles-bound—who were encamped near their wagon. They asked them some questions about the horse-thieves. They continued, following a trail that was still fresh. The second day they camped in the Mojave Desert at a cienega near the present site of Victorville. The next day their advance guard overtook—or were ambushed by—the raiders, who were well armed. Lugo's men not only failed to recover their stock but they lost one man killed. Demoralized, they returned to the valley, and during this return—it was charged—certain members of one group came upon the Irishman and his Indian companion and shot them to death.

Fragmentary information about this raid, together with a bewildering mass of data about specific activities and movements, were revealed in testimony and statements made before Justice Jonathan R. Scott in the preliminary hearings on the double murder. In the yellowing documents—171 handwritten pages—where testimony is preserved are also many odd or picturesque bits of data. For example, weapons mentioned included not only rifles and pistols but swords and lances. Ygnacio Alvarado, a member of the pursuit party, testified Sam "was not a Yutah," for "Yutahs generally have no eyebrows or eyelashes"—an interesting comment, perhaps, on Ute customs. Another participant testified that Chico was riding a silver roan horse when leaving camp and a cinnamon-colored one against the Utes. A brother-in-law of the Lugo boys, Francisco Argüello, told of his conversation with the Irishman and that the latter and Sam were short of food.

For nearly a month after the meeting of the coroner's jury Justice Scott listened to the courtroom talk of a procession of men—rancheros, vaqueros, and American soldiers—who had chased the raiders or who had been in the vicinity of Cajon Pass at the time of the murder. The Lugo boys and Mariano Elisalde were in court under the coroner's warrant. The courtroom was in the Bella Union Hotel, on Main Street, where since June of 1850 the county had rented three rooms having wooden floors—for its courthouse and clerk's office—and one room with an earthen floor for a jury room.

"Do you know the names of any of those you met?" Private Dempsey was asked.

"No, but would know their persons," he replied.

"Do you recognize any of that party among the prisoners now present?"

"No."

In similar manner all four soldiers testified. All failed to identify the prisoners as being members of the party of Californians or "Spaniards" they met in Cajon Pass. The members of the expedition, likewise, with one exception, failed to implicate the accused.

The climactic testimony was that of Ysidro Higuera, a Sonoran, who had been a member of Lugo's pursuit party. In a deposition made on March 10, 1851, he claimed to have

12 : PEOPLE VS. LUGO

witnessed the killing, described it in detail, and named the Lugo boys and Elisalde as the killers—with Chico as the leader. Higuera admitted, too, that he himself participated, along with another man whose name he did not know.

On the strength of Higuera's testimony the Lugo boys and Elisalde were committed to the sheriff and jailed. Higuera—already in jail on another charge—became the star witness for the prosecution.

IV. J. LANCASTER BRENT TO THE RESCUE

Shortly after Chico and Menito were jailed, a group of four mounted *Californios* drew up at the Main Street office of Joseph Lancaster Brent. Brent was an able young lawyer, a native of Maryland, who had arrived in Los Angeles in time to go before the District Court in October of 1850 and be admitted to practice. His office was a room in an adobe building across the street from the residence of merchant-landowner Don Abel Stearns.

In the rising cloud of dust Brent recognized three of his callers as members of the Lugo family. They were dressed in the resplendent manner of wealthy rancheros: jackets and trousers decorated with silver buttons, riding cloaks fringed with gold. Their horses—"as pretty as Arabians," Brent later recalled—were equally resplendent, the saddles silver-plated and with swords attached. They had come to hire Brent to defend the two sons of one of the visitors against a charge of murder. Brent accepted the case, after being assured by José María Lugo and his brother José del Carmen Lugo that the two boys could not have committed the crime since they were always within their sight during the Cajon Pass episode. Chico and Menito became Brent's clients.

The young attorney found himself in the middle of a tense and explosive situation. Already Los Angeles had made up its mind. The Americans were instantly convinced that the boys were guilty. The *Californios* were pro-Lugo and certain of their innocence. Back of these conflicting views were the prejudices of the English-speaking group, the minority group, against the Spanish-speaking majority—and vice versa. The Americans feared the native Californians and had feared them since the close of the Mexican War. At any moment an uprising or revolt by the Californians could wipe them out. The *Californios* were jealous of the newcomers. Race feelings were strong and rampant.

Brent studied closely the testimony of Ysidro Higuera and was able to cross-examine him before Justice Scott had finished the preliminary hearing.

Higuera's story—still obtainable from the bulging bundle of 110-year-old papers in the criminal files of the Hall of Records—was that on the night before the killing the men who had gone in pursuit of the Indians were assembled at the mouth of the Cajon. "Many were there, perhaps 20. The defendants were there, the Alvarado party was there also." In the morning, he said, the Alvarados went to San Jose—meaning the San Jose (or Pomona) Valley. José María Lugo took some of the party and went to his rancho. "The defendants remained at camp."

Then Chico sent him (Higuera) after José María Lugo's party "to get a lance." When he returned, according to the Higuera version, the defendants were talking to a white man and an Indian who were with a wagon. The white man was on a mule, the other in the wagon. Chico asked the Indian to let him see his rifle. The Indian could not speak Spanish and made a sign of refusal. Chico talked about swapping. The Indian "made a sign he did not understand." Then Chico took a pistol out of his holster case. "He fired the pistol at him, and the other two fired; the Indian fell dead in the wagon; the white man then dismounted and ran behind the wagon to keep them from killing him." Then they took the white man out into the road and "Lugo *major* shot the white man with his other pistol; Lugo shot first, then the others," including a man whose name Higuera did not know who had two pistols. Elisalde had a rifle.

Continuing, Higuera said the mules ran with the wagon but they caught them and cut the harness. Higuera loosed the mule tied behind the wagon. This rope Chico tied to the feet of the Indian and ordered Higuera to tie a rope around the white man's feet and drag him out of the road, which he did—"as Lugo *major* was the captain of the company." He dragged him some distance off the right of the road. "Lugo *menor* fastened a rope to the Indian's legs, hauled him out of the wagon and hauled him some distance to the left of the road . . . Lugo *major* told witness to say nothing about matter; the murder was committed between 8 and 9 of morning; Lugo *major* brought away the Indian rifle."

Higuera ended by saying he "heard no reason for killing the two men." On cross-examination he stuck well to his story, and freely admitted his own participation as well as that of the two Lugo boys, Elisalde, and the man whose name he did not know.

Justice Scott ordered a search made of the Lugo house for the rifle of the Indian, which Higuera said had been taken by Chico. A constable searched but he reported he could find nothing.

In spite of the argument of the defense that it was unreasonable to permit the testimony of one man—an admitted accomplice in the murder—to counterbalance the testimony of a procession of twenty responsible men, Justice Scott ordered the defendants held for trial and committed to jail.

At the conclusion of the testimony and of the examination of witnesses, the attorney for the defendants (J. Lancaster Brent) and the county attorney (Benjamin J. Hayes) stipulated, on March 31, "That all the depositions of witnesses taken in the examination of Francisco Senior shall be considered in evidence and subject to be read and referred to as evidence in this case."

Hayes, the prosecutor in the Lugo Case, with Scott as a partner had begun the practice of law the year before. They were the first American lawyers to open a law office in Los Angeles. Both were Missourians. When Brent came to town he found they had a practical monopoly on local law practice. At Los Angeles County's first election, held April 1, 1850, Hayes had been elected county attorney and Agustin Olvera county judge. Both Louis Rubidoux and Jonathan R. Scott were elected justices of the peace to serve—with Judge Olvera—as the Court of Sessions which began to function on June 24, 1850, and which had limited criminal jurisdiction.

Meanwhile the attorney for Chico and Menito was exploring some interesting and illuminating data that concerned not only the star witness for the prosecution but the Los Angeles jailer who was keeping the Lugo boys in irons day and night.

V CONSPIRACY

TEN DAYS BEFORE Ysidro Higuera made his damaging statements implicating the Lugo boys, a horse belonging to an Angeleno named Francisco Botiller was stolen. Along with the horse, the thief took a bridle, a pair of *botas*, a pair of spurs, and other of Botiller's personal belongings.

Higuera was arrested as the thief and was jailed in the *calabozo* on the hill a week or so before the Lugo boys joined him as fellow prisoners.

Higuera's jailer, it turned out, was a bitter enemy of José María Lugo and Lugo's two sons. He had reason to hate them because of the rough treatment they gave him one July day the year before. The jailer was George W. Robinson, a Kentuckian, who, with his attractive wife, had originally come to California, and through the Cajon Pass, with an immigrant train. They had arrived at Rancho San Bernardino in a destitute condition. While they and their animals were recuperating, Mrs. Robinson became well acquainted with the wife of José María Lugo, was often at her home, helped her in her housework, and made friends with the household.

She was treated badly, even cruelly, by her husband, to the outrage of all the Lugos.

The job of jailer happened to be vacant. George W. Robinson went into Los Angeles and was given this job by the sheriff. He returned to the ranch, presently, to get his wife. He came into the house, spoke harshly to her, and took hold of her. Mrs. Robinson screamed. Louis Rubidoux, who was present, ordered the man out, while José María Lugo, also present, struck him in the mouth. Chico Lugo and his brother-in-law Argüello, in the room, too, pointed swords at Robinson. Drawing a pistol, the latter went to his wagon, followed by Rubidoux—Justice Rubidoux—who told him to give up his arms. Instead, he ran, but was overtaken by the Lugo men. They fought. Robinson was badly beaten, tied up, but was later released at the intervention of Rubidoux. The Lugos were charged with assault with deadly weapons, and Robinson sued for damages in the amount of $30,000—all of which is revealed in detail in the still extant court files of early days, along with the case involving horse-stealing charges against Ysidro Higuera. The jury in the assault case found the two Lugos, father and son, guilty and recommended a fine of $2.50 each. The suit for damages was the first action—Case No. 1—brought in the District Court of the 1st Judicial District. It drifted on for years and then, apparently, was switched to another county because Robinson's attorney (Hayes) had become District Court judge. Jailer Robinson's heart was filled with a terrible bitterness toward the Lugo family.

After Higuera had been in jail a few days the jailer told County Attorney Hayes that Higuera had a statement of importance to make. This turned out to be his story of the Cajon Pass murder. This statement, in the form of a deposition, was placed in the hands of Justice Scott, who also happened to be Higuera's attorney.

J. Lancaster Brent came to the natural conclusion that the jailer had coaxed a false confession out of Higuera, whom he later described as a "worthless fellow," a Sonoran who belonged to a class of illiterates both "desperate and criminal." Actually Higuera could have made up his story—so logical in some of its details—out of the testimony given by the American soldiers who first found the bodies of McSwiggen and Sam the Creek Indian.

Chico and Menito had gone to jail in March of 1851, with the hearty approval of the Americans in Los Angeles who had a simple explanation of the whole affair. They believed that the two Cajon Pass victims had misdirected the pursuing party by telling them the horsethieves were armed only with bows and arrows. So, on the return from the disastrous ambush, the Lugos had taken quick revenge. In April their attorney was trying to get them out of jail on bail. During that month a party of men rode into town from the north who gave a strange twist to the Lugo Case and who brought a condition of almost unendurable tension to the people of Los Angeles.

VI RED IRVING AND HIS GANG

Under the command of Captain John Irving—called "Red Irving" because of the color of his face and beard—a party of about 25 mounted men arrived in Los Angeles from the north in April of 1851.

Irving, a former Texan ranger, said they were on their way to Sonora to fight Indians. One of his band, however, stated they were going to Mexico "to rob some of the specie conductors," that is, the silver trains whose route was between the mines and Mazatlan.

These newcomers, many of them reputed to be notorious "Sidney Ducks" from Australia via San Francisco, camped a short distance out of town in the Arroyo Seco. Townsmen looked upon them as bandits and called them just that—when they were out of earshot. During their several weeks of stay "they excited the terror of the citizens and many offences were charged upon them." The quotation is from the Los Angeles *Star* of May 31, 1851.

Hearing of the Lugo Case, Red Irving or members of his gang approached wealthy Antonio María Lugo and made him a proposition. The gang offered to break open the jail, free Don Antonio's grandsons, and take them to safety in Sonora. Red Irving's price was $50,000, according to the *Star* (of June 7, 1851); $10,000, according to Brent's recollections. Don Antonio rejected the offer saying he had an attorney named Brent who was looking after his interests.

This violent proposition coincided with Brent's attempts to get the Lugo boys and Elisalde out on bail, though the judge had refused the first application. The parents of Chico and Menito were greatly worried, for they were not permitted to see the prisoners and they knew the boys were in chains and were not getting decent or sufficient food. The father, José María Lugo, was a quiet, well thought of man, who had been honored during the Mexican administration by being named "judge of the plains." The mother, Doña María, often visited Brent to send messages through him to her boys, and on these occasions was usually in tears. Elisalde had a blackbearded brother named Vicente, and this brother was much concerned, too. The jail was a tough place to be in, especially on week-ends when it was packed with drunk Indians who would be auctioned off Monday mornings to the highest bidders for private labor.

Attorney Brent went into court with a new motion to have the prisoners admitted to bail. The court was the District Court—which corresponded to the modern Superior Court, with a broader jurisdiction over criminal matters than the Court of Sessions. (San Diego and Los Angeles counties comprised the First District, with Judge Oliver S. Witherby presiding.) After Judge Witherby had carefully examined the papers, he gave Brent a favorable decision and bail was fixed at $10,000 each. He gave the attorney until 2 p.m. to produce the necessary bondsmen.

The news spread rapidly through Los Angeles, and crowds of men began to gather in the streets, especially on Main Street where the Courthouse was located.

An hour after Brent returned to his office, a man named George Evans entered. He was a member of Red Irving's gang and second in command. As remembered by Brent, Evans came to the point immediately, saying in effect:

"We have been promised $10,000 to capture the jail and free the Lugo boys. Now we hear the judge is going to turn them loose. Just tell their father this: If he don't pay us the $10,000, those boys must stay in jail or lose their lives if they come out."

Brent ordered Evans out of his office, furious at the attempted blackmail and also at the thought that the Lugo family was apparently double-crossing him. If he could have the gang members arrested he would take the necessary steps at once. But he knew that the sheriff arrested desperate characters only when he had American help—and this time the Americans would be backing the bandits.

When José María Lugo came into Brent's office a little before 2, with men to act as sureties, Brent told him he was withdrawing from the defense, because Lugo was dealing with Irving. Lugo denied this, and his brother agreed. The attorney was wholly misinformed, they said. This satisfied Brent that the Lugo family was playing fairly with him.

As they were talking, a group of Irving's men raced by at full gallop and turned up the steep slope to the jail. They dismounted and took up guard about the adobe building. This seizure of the jail was in full sight of the town.

The street in front of the courthouse was now full of men. They were anticipating a momentary shooting or hanging, and the Americans heartily approved the bandits' hillside action.

Just then Brent heard the sheriff announcing that court was open. It was 2 p.m. Telling José María Lugo and the others to wait for him, Brent entered the courtroom, along with a crowd of Americans pushing in. Among them were George Evans and some of his companions. Irving was not present, for he was out of town—though a messenger had already gone to summon him.

Brent did the only thing he could under the circumstances. He asked for a postponement of the hearing until the next day. He was not ready to furnish the bail bonds for the Lugo boys, he said.

Upon adjournment, the crowd pressed out to the street. Loud laughter was heard. It was obvious, from the crowd's point of view, that Brent "dared not bring the boys to court for fear of being killed by Evans and his men"—quoting from Brent's own acount.

In this life-and-death situation Brent gave serious consideration to his position. He was alone. None of his friends and no Americans backed him, though he believed firmly in the boys' innocence. There was no military organization in Los Angeles. The nearest cavalry force was in San Diego. The lives of the prisoners were really in his hands!

The only chance of saving them—it suddenly came to him—was to call upon the *Californios* to get a band of their own people together at once and oppose Red Irving's gang.

CALIFORNIOS VERSUS BANDITS

When Brent got back to his office he told the half dozen men waiting for him what he thought must be done. They agreed fully to the plan of assembling 75 bold *Californios* to save the prisoners' lives.

One of those in the office was Vicente Elisalde, brother of Mariano. Vicente was a brave and energetic fellow. He took the lead and headed the group to go out and summon volunteers. It was then 3 p.m., and it was important to get twenty or thirty men into town as soon as posible. The bandits might tire of their vigil around the jail and kill the boys during the night. They should be watched. Also, secrecy should be the motto, and the *Californios* assembled should hide themselves during the night in the walled courtyards of the uper part of the city. In the morning Brent would give further instructions.

The summoning of Californians began and continued during the night. A fog had come in and during it Vicente Elisalde was able to place thirty men in the ravines about the jail to watch the bandits.

Through the swirling fog Brent could see the flickering of the camp fires about the jail. Fearing a battle was inevitable and feeling extremely alone, he got in touch with a lawyer named Ogier. He asked him to act as his associate and to share with him the burden of the decisions. Isaac Stockton Keith Ogier had practiced law in Charleston, South Carolina, and was in partnership in Los Angeles with a Peruvian named Manuel Clemente Rojo.[3] Brent promised him $1000 out of the fee that he would receive. Ogier said yes and agreed at the same time that the plan of defense outlined was the correct one.

Shortly after sunrise Brent was informed that sixty *Californios* had been summoned and were hidden in the upper part of town—with more men coming in.

There seemed no hope of avoiding a terrific battle.

About 8 a.m. Brent heard the sound of horses hooves and saw a glorious sight, the symbol of law and order, a body of blue-coated United States dragoons wheeling into Main Street. There were fifty in the troop.

Interviewing the commander, Major E. H. Fitzgerald, he found the soldiers had been in San Diego and were making a routine march to Los Angeles. They expected to be in camp in town all day. Brent pointed to the Irving men about the jail, explained the situation, and asked for help. Major Fitzgerald told him that soldiers, like other citizens, could be summoned—with his consent—by the sheriff to act as posse members.

Brent went to the sheriff and finally persuaded this reluctant man, who feared imminent bloodshed and hangings, to visit the camp of the dragoons and secretly and individually summon them. This was done and each soldier was told to

---

[3] Ogier later was named United States District Attorney and in 1854 was appointed Judge of the United States District Court for the Southern District of California. Horace Bell in his *Reminiscences of a Ranger* recounts some of the odd adventures in which Ogier participated, referring to him not by name but as the man who "claimed to be of Huguenot origin" and as "the great Federal legal light."

be at the Courthouse before 2 p.m.—when court would open. The *Californios* were given similar advice but were asked not to appear in a group.

Los Angeles was so tense all morning that no business could be done. The town did not know the role of the soldiers or of the chosen *Californios*, but it did expect the Lugo boys to be hanged or shot. As early as 10 crowds of men filled Main Street near the Courthouse. They included the members of Irving's gang (except those around the jail) and they could be picked out by their flannel shirts, their six-shooters and their knives. They carried no rifles, indicating to Brent that they knew nothing of the defense plans. The crowds also included, dispersed throughout, the Californians who had volunteered to protect the prisoners. They were under secret instructions.

Shortly before 2 the troop of soldiers came down Main Street and turned up the slope toward the jail. The crowds now understood and were furious. At the jail Irving's men offered no resistance. The only delay in releasing the three prisoners was the time involved in freeing them from their irons. The soldiers formed a hollow square and within this were Sheriff Burrill, Chico, Menito, and Mariano Elisalde. They marched to the Courthouse and the sheriff and prisoners entered before Irving's gang could get together.

The judge also entered the courtroom, coming from the clerk's room at the rear. He made a loud announcement. Court was opened!

VIII   IN THE COURTROOM

Court opened precisely at the time the prisoners entered the oblong room and took their seats on a bench along the wall. It had been planned that way.

To protect the district judge, the acting district attorney (Thomas W. Sutherland), the county attorney (Hayes), and the clerk, four former soldiers were stationed by the prosecution in the clerk's room behind the courtroom. They were armed and were prepared, if shooting started in the courtroom, to guard the exit of the officials into the clerk's room and then take part in the general defense.

As proceedings began, Brent from his position at the trial table could see everyone in the courtroom and everything that happened. He was armed with a pistol, as was his associate at the table, Ogier.

The father, the uncles, bondsmen, and two or three friends sat in front of and beside the prisoners, making a protective wall. Sheriff Burrill was near by, conspicuous as usual by the infantry sword which he wore, a habit he learned from former residence in Mexico.

Spectators in the courtroom numbered about twenty, comprised almost entirely of Red Irving's armed gang under the command of Evans.

As Brent walked up and down the side of the trial table he could look out to Main Street through the courtroom's two windows. To his comfort he saw the bushy-bearded Vicente Elisalde at his station just outside one window. Over his shoulders was his riding coat decorated with gold lace. He held the bridle of his horse, whose head could be seen. He was ready for the signal from Brent that would cause him to summon his *Californios* and then push into the courtroom.

Brent could see Vicente and Vicente could see Brent—and the agreed upon signal was a key which the attorney had in his pocket, to be waved at the right moment.

What disturbed Brent, however, was that the troops outside had moved across the street, tying their horses to the balcony rail of Eulogio Celis' home, to escape the rays of the hot sun which beat down upon the east side.

Just then there was a movement of the crowd at the door. It divided and, as described by Brent, in strode Red Irving— "tall and spare, with steely blue eyes and red beard, dusty, heated and evidently harried." He was coatless. In his belt were a six-shooter and a knife. He began whispering with his men and questioning them.

Brent stepped over to the sheriff and quietly asked him to go out and bring the United States troops back to the Courthouse side of the street.

Court proceedings seemed interminable. Though they consisted merely of passing upon and approving the bail-bonds, the prosecuting attorney was exacting in his examination of the sureties. There were six sureties for the three prisoners and each was required to establish to the satisfaction of the court that he was worth $20,000, or double the amount of the bond.

Irving seemed angry, excited, and puzzled. He had gone to the door and seen the line-up of cavalry outside. Suddenly he turned back and gathered six of his men about him. Brent believed the moment of action had arrived. Brent took the key out of his pocket, fingered it, but kept it hidden. He hesitated.

Then Irving came to the front again, casting angry glances at the prisoners and at their attorneys. Baffled, he and his gang gave no evidence that they planned an attack.

Brent returned the key to his pocket.

The court approved the bonds.[4]

Then the sheriff took his prisoners—surrounded by friends—to the door. Again the dragoons formed a hollow square around the three men who were now free on bail and took them through the lynch-law-loving mob into another street. There fifty *Californios* awaited them with horses and all rode off to safety.

That night Brent ate a late supper in the dining room of the Bella Union Hotel—adjoining the part that was rented by the county as a courthouse. When he had almost finished he saw Red Irving—drunk—approaching him. Brent had only the fork with which he was eating to protect himself.

But Irving was polite. He placed no blame on the young attorney, who had done only his duty. Brent was a gentleman! For Major Fitzgerald, however, he had utter contempt, and said he had offered to fight him and his soldiers the next morning. As for the Lugos, he saved for them his finest profanity. They were murderers—and he would get even with them or see himself in hell!

[4] Only the bond releasing Elisalde remains today in the files of the case.

IX RED IRVING PAYS A VISIT TO SAN BERNARDINO VALLEY

LATE IN MAY of the same year of 1851—a month after the climactic courtroom scene—Red Irving and his band broke camp in the Arroyo Seco and left Los Angeles. They were apparently heading for the Colorado River.

The Lugo boys had not been seen in or around Los Angeles since they had been spirited away by their California friends, following their release from jail on bail. Presumably they were keeping close to their home in the San Bernardino Valley.

Irving's gang, well supplied and well armed, proceeded east. They crossed Rancho La Puente and helped themselves to horses belonging to its owner, William Workman. They continued to Rancho San José, which was the property of Ricardo Vejar and Ygnacio Palomares. There they stopped over night, killing cattle they needed and rounding up more horses. The band went on to Isaac William's Chino Rancho, where more horses were added to their stolen string. There they divided forces, part—with wagons and extra horses—taking the road to the Colorado. The remainder of the gang—12 men headed by Red Irving himself—continued to the rancho of Louis Rubidoux, the Jurupa, on the Santa Ana River.

From Rubidoux they obtained provisions for supper and camped for the night. They were well behaved, though Rubidoux noticed that they had six-shooters belted around their waists. They left between 7 and 8 in the morning—Tuesday, May 27—heading in the direction of Agua Mansa, a farming comunity on the Santa Ana, on the road to Politana and the San Bernardino Valley. Don Louis later stated that his impression of the gang was "that they were bad men and that they were in pursuit of the young Lugos."

Meanwhile complaints from the rancheros had been pouring into Los Angeles. The sheriff organized a posse of fifty men to proceed to the Chino Rancho. Brent despatched a messenger to Rancho San Bernardino to warn the Lugos. For identification this messenger carried, not a letter, but a gold ring embellished with a cross that Doña María Lugo had given Brent. The messenger got through, delivered the oral message (not to sleep in their houses at night and to keep watch by day), and returned by the time the posse started from Los Angeles.

With the avowed intention of killing the Lugo boys, Red Irving and his men proceeded to the ranch home of José María Lugo. (The Los Angeles *Star* of June 7, 1851 gives details.) Two members of the household saw the outlaws approaching. One of them, Alexander Martino, ran and hid in a ditch. The other, Victoriano Bega, climbed a cottonwood tree from which he could watch in safety. A third man at the house, Jesus Castro, received the outlaws who entered by the back gate. Each drank a glass of milk and began to ask questions.

"Where are the two boys?" Castro said they were in town. "Where is their father?" Castro told them the father was at the rodeo in Agua Caliente—referring to the Lugo's branding area near by.

Then the band ransacked the house. They opened trunks, and helped themselves to two thousand dollars worth of clothing, rings, and other objects, including two silver-plated saddles and bridles.

As the outlaws were leaving, one of the Lugo vaqueros, Ricardo Uribe, came in from the Agua Caliente rodeo. He had been sent by José María Lugo who had been informed of the presence of Irving and his men. He had caught up with Juan Antonio, the bold Cahuilla leader, and twenty of his mounted group—these being the Indians hired by the Lugos to work for them and protect their interests, largely from raiding horsethieves. They were on their way from Politana to José María Lugo's house, having been told by another Lugo vaquero to guard the place while Lugo himself was hiding the horses in a thicket. Uribe and the Cahuillas came in together. On reaching the house, Uribe saw the line of Americans, Irving's band. He asked questions and was answered with curses and a volley of bullets. Juan Antonio learned what had happened and found that an old Indian servant of Lugo had been wounded.

As the outlaws took the road toward Yucaipa, they were pursued by the Indians who were armed with bows, arrows, and lances. Irving's men varied their rapid retreating with occasional charges, during which they fired at the Cahuillas when they were close to them. This procedure was the strategy of Irving, according to George Evans' later statement, a strategy that proved fatal. "Irving, as if doomed, turned into the mountains along the path which led into the fatal trap."

Juan Antonio's strategy was superior. His harassing tactics caused Irving and his men to follow "the road into a ravine, the steep banks of which prevented his egress, and here it was that the whole party was slain"—except Evans who dashed into a clump of bushes where he lay till near dark. Many more Cahuillas had joined the original band for the kill. "The Indians first shot them down with arrows," Evans reported, "and then beat in their skulls with stones." Irving, mounted on a superb horse, fought bravely, but in vain. When his body was examined later, there were five arrow wounds in the region of the heart. The day after the battle the sheriff's posse entered the Cañada of Santa María which was about eight miles from José María Lugo's house, and came upon the scene of the massacre. The bodies of the eleven men were entirely naked, stripped of clothes, and "mangled in a manner shocking to behold." One Indian had been killed, it was learned, and two or three Indians wounded. Some of the American posse-members were extremely angry with José María Lugo for having "incited the Indians against the evildoers"— and at the whole idea of Indians acting as enforcement officers.

Evans, the sole survivor of the massacre, concealed by darkness, went back to José María Lugo's house. There he found a mule, saddled, which he took and "fled toward Temescal, subsequently joining the company of Sonoran miners near the Colorado, telling them that Irving would be on shortly." He is believed to have caught up with his friends at San Felipe. In November he was back in Los Angeles, staying long enough to tell his story of the affair to the editor of the *Star*. It appeared in the November 20 issue, with Evans' frank statement that the purpose of the visit to Rancho San Bernardino was to kill the Lugo boys and to steal Lugo horses.

X THE LUGO CASE ENDS

WITH THE LUGO BOYS safe at home and Red Irving and his gang routed, the Lugo Case itself appeared headed for the doldrums.

Nevertheless, between May 27, 1851, when the outlaw band was wiped out on Rancho San Bernardino, and October 11, 1852, when the Lugo Case was finally dismissed, there were incidents which threatened the defendants' freedom and even the life of one of the attorneys involved.

On August 21, 1851, the defense attorneys, in a brilliant stroke, went into the District Court and had the proceedings in the Court of Sessions judged invalid. The basis for their move was that no indictment had ever been brought—as required by law—by a Grand Jury of the County of Los Angeles.

The prosecution then moved that the papers in the case be submitted to the next Grand Jury, which would meet in October following. This was agreeable to the defense.

On October 14 the Grand Jury met, with Albert Packard as foreman. It made its findings, overruled Brent's objections, and issued indictments against the defendants, one for each murder. They were signed by Lewis Granger, who had been named county attorney upon Hayes' resignation in September. Chico was charged with the actual killing, the others being accessories. The court ordered the arrest of the defendants.

For the next two months, it is apparent, the sheriff, armed with a warrant, could not find the Lugo boys or Mariano Elisalde—to arrest them. They were following Brent's advice to keep out of sight. There were still Americans in Los Angeles who would not object to seeing these defendants lynched.

During this in-between period a seeming attempt was made to assassinate Benjamin Hayes who had been so active in the prosecution of the Lugo boys. One night in November, after a day of hard legal study, Hayes heard the sound of a horse approaching his office. He stepped to the door and opened it. The street was filled with moonlight. He saw, about four feet away, a Californian in the saddle. Instantly there was a pistol shot. The ball passed through Hayes' hat, grazing his cheek, and continued through the door.

Many Angelenos, including Brent's partner, Jonathan R. Scott, thought the Lugos were implicated. There was excitement and considerable horseback riding on the part of the sheriff. Later it was learned that Salomon Pico, a nephew of the illustrious Pío Pico and Andrés Pico, actually fired the shot. There was no prosecution but Hayes came to the conclusion that the plan had been to kill another man, Justice of the Peace J. S. Mallard, who had been using his office during his four days' absence in San Francisco and against whom Pico and his associates had at least one grudge.

When Brent thought it advisable for his clients to appear in public, they submitted to the sheriff and were released almost immediately on bail in the amount of $10,000 each.

José del Carmen Lugo and Felipe Lugo were sureties for Chico, and José Sepúlveda and Jose María Lugo for Menito. These bailbonds, dated December 19, 1851, are still in the files of the case.

Brent's account indicates that the District Court set aside the indictments because of defects in the proceedings. Be that as it may—and Brent wrote his story nearly half a century after the events—the Lugo Case definitely entered its final phase. The Lugo boys, however, kept themselves hidden, for the sheriff would have re-arrested them.

Nearly ten months passed, and the county attorney could find no new evidence to counter that originally furnished by responsible men. Moreover, Americans were pouring into Los Angeles, and these newcomers had no feelings about the Lugos and no prejudices.

In October of 1852 Brent surrendered the boys and Elisalde to Sheriff James R. Barton and, accompanied by friends, all went to the Plaza home of Judge Olvera, who presided over the Court of Sessions. The records do not disclose all that happened there, but in the Brent version the defendants were freed on new bonds which were all ready for the signing.

In any event the case was immediately dismissed. This is shown by the minutes of the Court of Sessions which are preserved in bound volumes now in the custody of the Los County Law Library. Three orders of dismissal were issued. Each followed this language: "Ordered that the prosecution in the above Case be dismissed and that the bond given by Defendant be exonerated."[5] The notation on the binder that holds the paper of the case says simply: "Dismissed—lack of evidence."

[5] Vol. 2, pgs. 24, 25, Minutes of the Court of Sessions for Criminal Business, County of Los Angeles, State of California.

So ended the case of the People of the State of California vs Francisco Lugo, et al, with no further effort made to find out who killed Patrick McSwiggen, the Irishman, and Sam, the Creek Indian, in lonely Cajon Pass.

J. Lancaster Brent was paid his well-earned fee, rumored to be $20,000.

The defendants, the defense attorneys, the prosecutors, the judges, the sheriffs, and all the minor participants in the curious and celebrated Lugo Case have long since passed into history. Some left records of distinguished achievement. Others succumbed to obscurity. Still others are known, only to genealogists, as ancestors of present-day Southern Californians.

SOURCES

SOURCES ON THE LUGO CASE
WITH COMMENT

I. *Court files in the offices of the County Clerk of Los Angeles County*

(a) Of basic importance are the criminal files of the Court of Sessions. The court cases were given no numbers until the year 1854, but are kept in bundles in steel cabinets lodged in the old Hall of Records. Here are the proceedings, apparently incomplete, of the Lugo Case (The People of the State of California vs Francisco Lugo, et al), together with the related case involving horse-stealing charges against star-witness Ysidro Higuera, as well as the one concerning the dispute between George W. Robinson and José María Lugo—both cases brought by the People of the State of California.

(b) Minutes of the Court of Sessions, now in bound volumes in the Los Angeles County Law Library, where William B. Stern has been named custodian and deputy county clerk. (See Volume 2, Pages 24, 25)

(c) District Court Case No. 1 (Robinson vs Lugo)

II. *Newspaper files*

(a) Los Angeles *Star*, issue of May 31, 1851, telling of the wiping out of Red Irving's band of outlaws.

(b) Los Angeles *Star*, issue of June 7, 1851, telling of the coroner's inquest over the bodies of the outlaws and containing interesting testimony about events leading up to it.

(c) Los Angeles *Star*, issue of November 20, 1851, giving surviving outlaw George Evans' interview with the editor.

[Note: These issues of the *Star* are apparently unavailable, but pertinent clippings, covering matters noted, are in Volume 38 of Benjamin Hayes' *Scraps* on file in the Bancroft Library, Berkeley, California.]

III. *Accounts by Participants in the Lugo Case*

(a) *The Lugo Case—A Personal Experience*, by Joseph Lancaster Brent (attorney for the defense in the Lugo Case), published in 1926 by Searcy & Pfaff, Ltd., New Orleans. Brent's reminiscences, vividly written, present the Los Angeles backround in a fascinating way. They are in general agreement with facts disclosed in the court files themselves and supplement them. Of particular interest is Brent's telling of events leading up to the climactic courtroom scene and his description of the scene itself.

(b) *Pioneer Notes—From the Diaries of Judge Benjamin Hayes*, privately published in 1929 in Los Angeles. County Attorney Hayes, the chief prosecutor in the Lugo Case, gives the Los Angeles background of the 1850s, bits about the Lugos and the Lugo Case, and goes into detail about the apparent attempt to assassinate him.

(c) *Life of a Rancher*, by José del Carmen Lugo (uncle of the two Lugo boys who were defendants and one of their chief backers), as dictated to Thomas Savage in 1877 for use by Hubert Howe Bancroft in the preparation of his *History of California*. In translation, this was published in the September, 1950, *Quarterly* of the Historical Society of Southern California. José del Carmen Lugo presents a valuable, detailed, and grim account of life on Rancho San Bernardino, including much about the Lugo family and his story of the visit of **Red Irving** and the outlaws.

IV. *Miscellaneous Historical Material*

(a) *An Historical Sketch of Los Angeles County,* by Col. J. J. Warner, Judge Benjamin Hayes, and Dr. J. P. Widney, published in 1876 by Louis Lewin & Co., Los Angeles, and republished in 1936 by O. W. Smith, Los Angeles. See pages 77 and 80.

(b) *History of Los Angeles County,* by J. Albert Wilson, published in 1880 by Thompson & West, Oakland, California, republished in 1959 by Howell-North, Berkeley, California. See pages 79 to 81.

(c) *Reminiscences of a Ranger,* by Major Horace Bell, published in 1881 in Los Angeles, republished in 1927 by Wallace Hebberd in Santa Barbara. See pages 195, 196, 197.

(d) *History of San Diego and San Bernardino Counties,* published in 1883 by Wallace W. Elliott and Company, San Francisco. See pages 77 to 79—a confused account found in the San Diego section although it relates to San Bernardino County.

(e) *Heritage of the Valley,* by George William Beattie and Helen Pruitt Beattie, published in 1939 by San Pasqual Press, Pasadena, California. This is the most important book on the general history of San Bernardino Valley.

(f) *Walkara—Hawk of the Mountains,* by Paul Bailey, published in 1954 by Westernlore Press, Los Angeles. This contains background material on Indian raids and raiders, with the life story of the man who led them.

(g) *The Cahuilla Indians,* by Harry C. James, published in 1960 by Westernlore Press, Los Angeles. Presents the story of Juan Antonio and his leadership of the Indians who routed the Irving gang.

(h) *Lawyers of Los Angeles,* by W. W. Robinson, published in 1959 by the Los Angeles Bar Association. See Chapters 3 and 13 for the organization of the courts and the practice of law in Los Angeles in the 1850s.

(i) *California County Boundaries,* by Owen C. Coy, published in 1923 by California Historical Survey Commission, Berkeley, California. See chapter on Los Angeles County.

(j) *Courthouses of Los Angeles County,* by Granville Arthur Waldron, published in the December, 1959, issue of the *Quarterly* of the Historical Society of Southern California. This establishes, from original records, the location of the buildings used as courtrooms or courthouses in Los Angeles County.

(k) *Andrew Sublette—Rocky Moutain Prince,* by Doyce Blackman Nunis, Jr., published in 1960 by Dawson's Book Shop, Los Angeles. See Chapter VII for information on the mining companies operating in the Mojave Desert for whom the (Lugo Case) murdered men worked.

(l) *The Indians of Southern California in 1852,* containing the B. D. Wilson Report with its comment on the Cahuillas and the killing of the Irving gang, edited by John Walton Caughey, published in 1952 by Huntington Library, San Marino, California.

(m) *The Story of San Bernardino County,* by W. W. Robinson, published in 1958 by Pioneer Title Insurance Compnay, San Bernardino, California. This gives the rancho background of the defendants in the Lugo Case.

(n) The Los Angeles *Padron* or Census of 1836, with editorial comment by J. Gregg Layne, and the Los Angeles *Padron* or Census of 1844, edited by Marie E. Northrup—both published by the Historical Society of Southern California in the *Quarterly* for September-December, 1936, and for December, 1960; together with the *Census of the City and County of Los Angeles for the year 1850,* edited by Maurice H. and Marco R. Newmark, published in 1929 by The Times-Mirror Press, Los Angeles.

(o) *Juan Antonio—Cahuilla Indian Chief, A Friend of the Whites,* by Gerald A. Smith, Raymond Sexton, and Elsie J. Koch, published in 1960 by San Bernardino County Museum Association. This tells the interesting story of Juan Antonio, his death from smallpox in San Timoteo Canyon, and the discovery, in 1956, of the burial site and his remains.

MERCHANTS and DONS

San Diego's Attempt at Modernization
1850-1860

By Mario T. Garcia

Mario T. Garcia has been a lecturer of Chicano Studies and History at San Diego State University from 1970 to 1974. He has also taught at the Third College at the University of California, San Diego. He received his B.A. and M.A. from the University of Texas, El Paso and will shortly complete his Ph.D. in History at UCSD. His doctoral thesis is entitled "Modernization and Labor in the Southwest: a Case Study of the Mexican Population of El Paso, Texas, 1880-1920." Professor Garcia's publications include "Jose Vasconcelos and La Raza," *El Grito* (1969) and "A Chicano Perspective on San Diego History," *Journal of San Diego History* (1972).

In January, 1975, Professor Garcia will begin an appointment as Acting Assistant Professor of Chicano Studies and History at the University of California, Santa Barbara.

I.
Introduction

The conquest of the Southwest by the United States during the Mexican War (1846-1848) represented more than just a transfer of territory. It stands as the replacement of a colonial—almost feudal—society by an aggressive capitalistic one. In 1846 Mexico was independent, but her political, social, and economic structure remained the same as during the period of Spanish colonialism. The United States, on the other hand, already stood as a leader in the commercial and industrial revolution characteristic of Western capitalism in the nineteenth century. In this article the effects of this transformation on San Diego's economy during the first full decade of Anglo-American control, the 1850s, are considered in seven areas of economic activity: (1) commercial life, principally the role of merchants; (2) the status of agriculture; (3) the impact of mining; (4) whaling and fishing enterprises; (5) the economic decline of the Californios; (6) the attempt to create an "inland empire" by establishing trade relations with Mormon settlements in Utah; and (7) the energetic but abortive attempt to make San Diego the western terminus of the transcontinental railroad.

II.

Before examining San Diego's economic history from 1850 to 1860, the background of the economy under both Spain and Mexico must be considered. At the close of Spanish rule in 1821 San Diego consisted of a small military "presidio;" a mission, which owned a vast amount of land, yet existed in an impoverished state due to enforced support of the military establishment; and a small number of settlers; totaling about 450 inhabitants.[1]

Agriculture predominated as the principal means of livelihood following the initial settlement in 1769. Members of the first expedition brought seed from Mexico, but their attempt at agriculture failed. According to historian William E. Smythe, a flood destroyed the grain which had been planted on low ground, and the early colonists harvested only a small quantity of maize and beans during the first years. By 1790, the mission friars developed a crude method of irrigation and had a limited success in agriculture, as they and the other settlers harvested 1,500 bushels of grain that year. The Spanish soldiers also were involved in agriculture during these early years. They grew peas, olives and pomegranates, and developed the first "truck gardens" in San Diego. This small production continued up to the period of Mexican independence, and by 1821 small patches of cultivated lands, called rancherias, could be found not only along the base of Presidio Hill, but out across Mission Valley. Two vineyards also had been established in the valley. Unfortunately, a severe flood that year washed away or damaged most of these rancherias. However, when he visited San Diego in 1836, Richard Henry Dana reported purchasing a variety of vegetables including onions, peas, beans, watermelons, and other fruits. Nevertheless, agriculture during both the Spanish and Mexican periods never became of great importance, although enough grain was grown some years to provide a surplus for export. Apparently the Spaniards did not consider this export trade significant and did not expand it.[2]

The chief economic resource in San Diego during the Spanish-Mexican period was livestock. Cattle flourished in the dry, warm climate of the area, and abundant pasturage existed. No data survive to give an idea as to the production of cattle, but soon after the independence of Mexico this activity was greatly accelerated by the start of the "hide and tallow" trade with New England. Beginning in 1822 "Yankee" ships put into San Diego and in exchange for manufactured products received large quantities of hides and tallow. Conceivably, the Mexicans might have increased their profits had they included horses in this trade, but according to historian Max Miller even though large numbers of range horses could be found, the rancheros slaughtered them to save the pasturage for cattle, and no "horse-trading" developed.[3]

The landing place for the American vessels was at La Playa just inside the bay on the shore of Point Loma, where certain Boston firms erected four hide-curing and store houses. La Playa became a center of activity as hide ships went from port to port and returned with hides to be stored until the voyage back to New England. On their return trip, the "Yankee" traders sold tallow to candlemakers in the South American ports of Lima and Callao.[4]

By the time of the Mexican War, cheaper hides could be secured in other areas and this profitable trade for the Californios ended, although without dire effects as their attention then turned to the meat-hungry gold miners of California. The "hide and tallow" trade left its influence in San Diego. It helped to establish an extensive cattle industry in Southern California, and led to the rise of the wealthy, land-owning Mexican families, who constituted the ruling class of San Diego up to the time of the United States conquest.

The Spanish colonial government until 1813 provided land grants to the presidio, the mission, and the pueblo. Private individuals could obtain grants only on certain conditions, which stipulated: (1) a maximum of three leagues for each individual which could not over-lap or conflict in any way with those of the pueblo; and (2) a minimum of two thousand head of livestock required for each rancho. In 1813 the Spanish government passed a decree which increased the permissible amount of private land ownership in order to improve agricultural conditions in California and to reward veterans and retired soldiers in the area. Smythe points out that by the first decade of independence at least five land grants had been made to private individuals in San Diego: the Peñasquitos Rancho, which contained nearly 9,000 acres, and belonged to the veterans Ruiz and Alvarado; the Rancho del Rey (250 cattle and 25 horses); the San Antonio Abad rancho (300 cattle, 80 horses, 25 mules, and some grain); El Rosario or Barracas rancho (25 head of livestock and some grain), and the San Isidro Stock Range (no data available).[5]

In 1832 government and mission lands not in use could be obtained by settlers. This liberalization of the land policy reached its peak in 1833-34 when the mission lands were secularized, and the period of large private landholdings evolved as the Californios divided the mission estates among themselves.

Even after the mission lands passed into private hands, the mission itself continued to be an important trade center, becoming the principal customer of the "Yankee" ships. In exchange for cash and hides, the mission acquired cargoes of sugar, tea, coffee, and clothing, which were sold to the rancheros. The mission friars thus became the first established merchants of San Diego, an activity that by 1850 would pass into Anglo-American control.

A final economic activity of some importance during this period was fishing. Off the kelp beds of Point Loma and what is now La Jolla large numbers of sea otters could be found. Valued for their furs, they were hunted by the "mission Indians," who turned over the furs to the friars. In their role as merchants, the priests exchanged the pelts for New England manufactured goods. This trade ended in the 1850s when the supply of sea otters was depleted. The hunt for the sea elephant (seals) took its place for a short while until the "Yankee" whalers exterminated them.

III.

As the first decade of United States rule in San Diego opened, the geographic characteristics of the town did not undergo any fundamental change except for the enterprising attempt by William H. Davis to establish New Town. However the economic characteristics of the town did change. The major aspect of this change was the growth of Anglo-American commerce. The "Yankees" quickly built general stores, hotels, and related businesses. This significant modification in the economy, no longer dominated by the hide and tallow trade, is reflected in the 1850 census. The population stood at 650, not including Indians. Of this number, the great majority consisted of Mexicans (the exact figures are impossible to ascertain given the limited ethnic data of the census of 1850).[6]

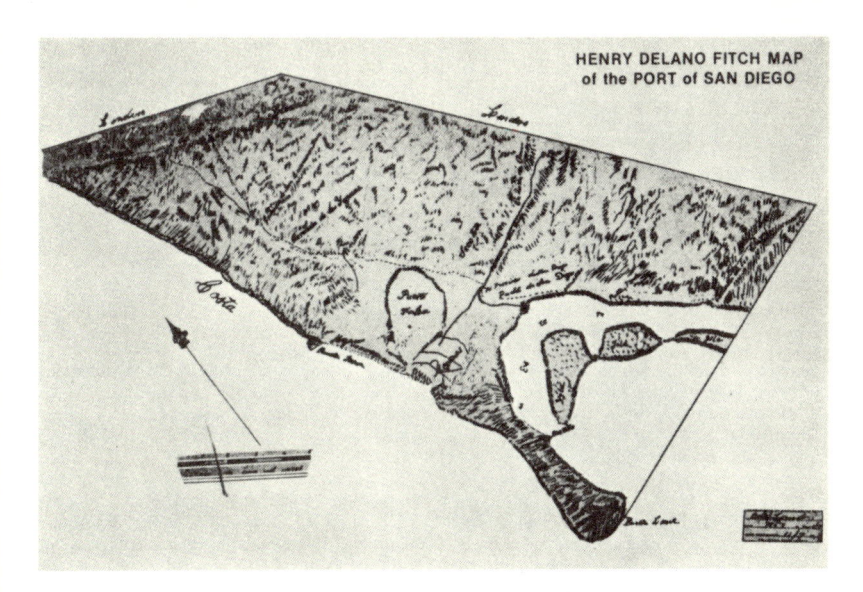

HENRY DELANO FITCH MAP of the PORT of SAN DIEGO

Compared to the Anglo population the economic resources of the colonized Mexicans, specifically the "gente de razón" or upper class, were much greater. The Taxpayers Roll of 1850 clearly reveals this. José Antonio Aguirre's property, for example, was assessed at $23,955. Other "ricos" were Juan Bandini ($23,301); José Antonio Estudillo ($21,686); José María Estudillo ($30,385); Juan Marrón ($24,349); María Pedrorena ($26,505); Rosario Aguirre ($14,457); Santiago E. Argüello ($13,742); and Juan María Osuna ($10,443). The Anglo colonizers came nowhere close to the Californios in wealth. William H. Davis came closest at $23,000. Other examples of Anglo property holders were: Cave J. Couts ($14,740); George F. Hooper ($8,900); Louis Rose ($2,580); Ames & Pendleton ($3,150), and Julian Ames ($1,692). The total valuation of Spanish-surname property (county figures only are available) was $413,471.25, while that of the English-surname was $142,428.25. The per capita valuation reveals the disparity even more between the two ethnic groups: Spanish-surname, $8,269.42; English-surname $2,848.56.[7]

A breakdown of the census of 1850, which must be done for the county, since this census did not separate the township in the survey, reveals these additional facts. First of all, the number of so-called graziers or rancheros was reported as six, all of them Mexicans. However, the high valuation found in the tax rolls suggests the figure is too low. The number of "farmers" (some of these, without doubt, rancheros also) is listed at 21: 10 Mexicans, 10 Anglos, and one Indian. There were 14 "traders" in San Diego in 1850: 12 Anglos and 2 Mexicans. The number of listed merchants is 18, with the great majority being Anglos (13) as opposed to Mexicans (5). Of those who can be classified as professionals or artisans (the census lists these occupations: lawyers, dentists, physicians, millers, bookkeepers, cabinet makers, carpenters, blacksmiths, saddler, agent, butchers, tanners, and engineers) there are 36, all of them Anglos. This figure combined with those of traders and merchants reveals the increase in commercial activity in San Diego, primarily among the Anglo population. Finally, 126 people worked as laborers: 56 Mexicans, 54 Anglos, and 16 Indians. Lacking additional data for this study, one can only presume that most of this labor concentrated in military-related work, on the ranchos of the Californios, in the building of New Town, or in the construction of business houses in Old Town and La Playa. A report of 1851, for example, reveals that the army employed civilians as laborers and teamsters at the supply depot in New San Diego.[8]

IV.

One of the significant developments in the economic life of San Diego was the rise of commerce during the 1850s. Perhaps the most ambitious business project undertaken came at the start of the decade when a group of investors headed by William H. Davis began the development of New Town. Davis, a San Francisco merchant and investor, had married into a prominent Californio family in San Diego, the Estudillos. It was the head of the family, José Antonio, who in 1849 aroused Davis' interest in establishing a business enterprise in San Diego. Estudillo concluded that in order for the town to prosper it had to become a seaport. This, however, entailed the re-location of San Diego, or the establishment of a new settlement, closer to the bay. Andrew B. Gray, chief surveyor for the U.S. Boundary Commission, enlarged on Estudillo's suggestion a year later. Gray explained to Davis the economic advantages of the location of a town at the foot of what is now Market Street. Davis concurred and both he and Gray agreed to call the undertaking New Town.[9]

In his autobiography, *Seventy-Five Years in California, 1831-1906*, Davis commented very little about this enterprise. This is not strange, for New Town did not prove to be one of the brightest stages in the life of this California capitalist. Davis did write in 1850 he expected that if and when San Diego became a port of entry, the town, and no doubt he too would prosper. San Diego, Davis foresaw, would be the chief supplier for the northern Mexican state of Sonora and for Baja California, as well as possessing a lucrative commercial tie with San Francisco.[10]

A look at a map of San Diego reveals that the physical site represents a good one, for it "juts" out into the middle of the bay.[11] Here, Davis and Gray in partnership with prominent rancheros, José Antonio Aguirre and Miguel de Pedrorena, and Anglo merchant, William C. Ferrell, obtained from the municipality of San Diego a tract of 160 acres for which they paid $2,304. Davis, according to historian Andrew F. Rolle, purchased from his partner Pedrorena an additional thirty-two quarter blocks of land

San Diego, 1850, after the sketch of Lt. Powell

(102 lots) at the New Town site for $13,000 or $14,000.[12]

At the same time Davis and his associates began their project, the other two populated areas of San Diego, Old Town and La Playa, had visions of expansion and profit. The settlers at both places agreed with Estudillo that the future of the town rested upon its development as a seaport, and consequently a rivalry began between Old Town and La Playa for leadership in this development. County Assessment Rolls, the earliest dated 1854, show that many property owners in Old Town also purchased lots in La Playa. No doubt the aim was to be in a position to profit from either development.[13]

One object in this rivalry, which came to include New Town, involved the construction of a U.S. Army depot that would supply southern California and western Arizona. Before Old Towners or La Playans could persuade the army that their locations would be the best for the depot, Davis persuaded the quartermaster at San Diego, Second Lieutenant Thomas D. Johns, to build an army camp at New Town. In return for his cooperation, Johns received shares in Davis' enterprise. Johns later resigned his army position to assist Davis in the construction of a wharf. He also obtained a contract, apparently in conjunction with Davis, from the army to supply the troops with coal. When his coal concern failed in 1851 due, undoubtedly, to the collapse of New Town, Johns sold most of his coal and left for San Francisco.[14]

In addition to the army depot, Davis and his partners gave land to the federal government on which the army built a corral and what became known as the "San Diego Barracks," which served as the supply depot. Davis, moreover, constructed a wharf and a warehouse at the new site, besides financing the erection of other buildings. The wharf itself was a major undertaking. Its uniqueness lay in its immense cost, especially for the small size of San Diego. Almost twenty years

57

later Davis stated that he paid $60,000 to build it, which made it equal in cost to wharves constructed on the Great Lakes.[15] Davis did not anticipate it would be that expensive however, since Charles H. Hill, who agreed to construct the wharf, told him the expense would be $13,000.[16] The possible explanation for the higher cost might involve the fact that Davis had to pay for transporting lumber and other construction materials from San Francisco. He also agreed with Hill to pay a fee of $50 for "each day's delay for want of materials." No records are available to indicate the cost of labor. Thomas D. Johns mentions the use of Indian labor at New Town which conceivably might have been used for the wharf.[17] If this was the case, labor costs would not have been too high, although the actual wage scale for Indian labor is unknown. White labor was more expensive. In 1853 Lieutenant George H. Derby of the topographical engineers in San Diego reported that he had to pay civilian workers $60 per month, which, according to Derby, represented higher wages than in the Atlantic states.[18]

The actual construction of the wharf began in September, 1850, and ended in August of the next year. Rolle describes the pier as being "eleven hundred feet long and twelve feet longitudinally and a bulkhead or T at the end thereof one hundred feet long by fifty feet wide." When completed, this lengthy and expensive wharf stood as a monument to Davis' ambitious project at New Town. Unfortunately, his wharf proved to be as weak as his project.[19]

Besides the army depot and the wharf, other establishments soon located themselves at New Town. J. Judson Ames' *San Diego Herald* was situated over George F. Hooper's wholesale and retail store. Other businesses included: Ames and Pendleton, lumber and merchandise; Slack and Morse, general merchandise; the Boston House Hotel; and the Pantoja House owned by Davis. Davis also attempted to have the federal government establish a post office and a customs house at New Town. To persuade officials in Washington to do this, Gray returned to the East, only to meet disappointment as the post office and customs house were established at Old Town and La Playa.[20] The reasons for this decision remain unclear, however, it may be that the property holders at both places proved to be more convincing to federal officials than Davis and Gray. In 1852 even after little remained of New Town, Davis still unsuccessfully attempted to convince both the postal and treasury departments to move these facilities to New Town.[21] Despite these setbacks, Gray continued to encourage Davis. "You will have the satisfaction of knowing and feeling," he wrote Davis from the East, "that you have been the founder of a lovely . . . . flourishing and beautiful town. Ten years—and they will soon pass away and you will still be young—and will be surrounded by a delightful society—and heavy business population."[22]

Regrettably for Davis and his associates, Gray's vision did not materialize, and by 1851 business in New Town lay in a state of deterioration. Perhaps the best example of this condition is Davis' wharf. Even though it was the only wharf, few ships utilized it after its completion. Ames and Pendleton reported in 1852 that it provided no income, and "no sailing vessels ever enter." If this was not bad enough, in 1853 Davis, who had returned to San Francisco, received word that the steamer Los Angeles had crashed into the wharf. The extent of the damage proved great as the ship tore away thirty feet of the structure, which constituted the "most valuable part of it, it being the only berth where vessels of deep draft could lay." Pendleton believed the cost of repairs would amount to at least $750, but the damage was never repaired. Apparently it had been so poorly constructed that "the wharf's piles were . . . so brittle that they were 'snapping like pipe stems.'" Indeed by 1855, ships had to anchor a short distance from the wharf and transport their goods there by the use of winches. Eventually the only revenue Davis received were wharfage fees from the government and the few private ships that used his facilities. For this, Davis later claimed, he received $150 per month between 1851 and 1861. One other source of income from the wharf was the fees charged the "cartmen" who transported goods from the wharf to Old Town. Despite the fact that the government and the merchants used the wharf to some extent during the decade, it remained a "financial millstone" for Davis. His attempts to sell it, moreover, proved fruitless. Finally, in 1862 the U.S. Army destroyed the wharf, using the timbers for firewood. Davis' complaint about this action did not receive attention from the U.S. Congress until 1885, and then his only compensation was $6,000.[23]

MIGUEL De PEDRORENA

The failure of the wharf had its impact on the merchants at New Town, and an examination of the correspondence sent by Davis' agents to him in San Francisco reveals dull business conditions. Few people moved to New Town, and by 1852 most of the inhabitants were either soldiers or connected with the boundary survey. That same year the frames of some of the houses were torn down and shipped to San Francisco. Some of the merchants drifted back to Old Town, while others packed up and left for Baja California. As for Davis, he sold most of his New Town real estate during the next few years. What remained of New Town later formed the nucleus of a second, but more permanent enterprise headed by A. E. Horton. Thus, in a short period, Davis' ambitious project collapsed and New Town became "Davis' Folly."[24]

This failure, according to Rolle, can be ascribed to several difficulties. The most pressing was the lack of water. Another item in short supply was wood, which had to be transported from San Francisco. Foodstuffs, also, were in short supply due to the lack of good soil in the area. John Russell Bartlett, the U.S. Boundary Commissioner, recognized these problems and commented in 1852:

> A large and fine wharf was built here [New Town] at great expense; but there is no business here to bring vessels here, except an occasional one with government stores. There is no water nearer than the San Diego River, three miles distant . . . wood has to be brought some eight or ten miles [apparently this wood was not considered adequate for the wharf]; nor is there any arable land within four miles. Without wood, water, or arable land this place can never rise to importance.[25]

The rivalry between New Town, Old Town, and La Playa played a part in the New Town failure as "Old Towners" and "La Playans" effectively discouraged settlement at Davis' site. "We meet with much opposition from the inhabitants of the old town and beach," Davis wrote in 1850, "they make every effort in the world to crush us. . . ." Finally, Rolle maintains that the repeal of the city charter in 1852 (for an unknown reason) and the serious Indian rebellion, the Garra revolt, during the same time influenced settlers not to move to New Town.[26]

Despite this failure, Rolle believes Davis and New Town merit more attention than has been given. "In some respect," he notes,

> Davis deserved more credit than he received. In recent celebrations of California's centennial years much attention was paid to her Gold Rush, to American acquisition, and to the province's evolution into statehood. Forgotten, however, were the sacrifices made by the many town builders like Davis who, too early for their own benefit, tried to create order out of confusion. By attempting to provide stopovers for dusty travelers such men anticipated the growth in population of rude shacks. In a remote corner of the United States his experiment, though patently unsuccessful, forms a part of the largely unwritten urban history of the American West.[27]

The local historian Smythe recognized that the business cycle of San Diego during the 1850s consisted of prosperity in the early years, a less prosperous period in the middle of the decade, and by 1859 a definite economic downturn. Despite this fluctuation, the establishment of new businesses represents an important addition to the predominantly ranching economy of San Diego.[28]

The expectation of economic growth led the common council of the town in one of its initial meetings in 1850 to draw up an ordinance regulating the licensing of commercial activities. Those persons, according to the ordinances, responsible for petitioning for a license included:

> . . . merchants, auctioneer, grocer, butcher, hotel or tavern keeper, or keeping a restaurant; or of

JOHN JUDSON AMES

vending, bartering, selling, exchanging, or otherwise disposing of liquors of any kind. . . ; or of keeping a Monte Bank, Fan Bank, Roulette Table, or other Table, Billiard . . . or of giving an exhibition of Theatrical or circus performances of any other public amusement; or of driving a . . . cart, waggon. . . .[29]

The license fee was computed on the amount of business trasacted by each firm. As such, five categories for taxation became established. Class one included those whose monthly sales amounted to $2,000; class two—$1,500; class three—$1,000; class four —$500; and class five, under $500. Failure to purchase a license, furthermore, would result in a fine of $50. Still another licensing ordinance stipulated that anyone selling retail from any vessel lying or being within the port of San Diego had to pay a license fee or a percentage on all goods sold. The actual number of licenses issued during the 1850s cannot be determined. Neither the minutes of the Common Council nor the county tax records contain such information. What remains significant, however, is the detailed commercial ordinances adoped in 1850 and 1851. Undoubtedly, the "city fathers" expected increased commercial activity as the decade began. It may be that the ambitious plans of Davis, plus the "gold rush fever" heightened these expectations.[30]

As a protection for residents of San Diego who desired to establish a business, the Common Council in 1850 passed an ordinance that "our city inhabitants [are] to get choice lots for themselves in preference of strangers, the latter will in future be allowed to compete with them for any lot not yet disposed of." In addition, lower prices for city lots would apply to residents. Most of these lots throughout the first part of the decade were purchased by merchants such as Louis Rose, D.B. Kurtz, G. P. Tebbetts, Joseph Rheiner, and E. W. Morse. As Secretary to the Board of Trustees of San Diego in 1853, Morse advertised that "the above real estate being situated upon one of the best harbours on the Pacific Coast and in a delightful climate, offers a rare opportunity for investment."[31]

Morse's invitation was accepted by a number of businessmen during the decade. A survey of advertisements in the *San Diego Herald* reveals the preponderance of general merchandise stores such as Hooper & Co.; Ames & Pendleton; the "Tienda Barata" of Marks & Fletcher; Harp & Noell; Hoeff & Tebbetts; Goldman & Strauss; Strauss & Kohn; G. Lyons & Co.; Katz and Co.; Louis Rose's Commercial House; the general store of Juan Bandini and Joseph Reiner of which the *Herald* commented that ladies in preparation for balls and parties could find an assortment of fancy dry goods there. "Mr. Reiner," the *Herald* noted, "is [an] acknowledged 'ladies man,' and we are sure will spare no pains to please you and will take pleasure in showing you the fine things even though you do not purchase." The Whaley House was still another general goods store; and the influential merchant E. W. Morse had his "New Store" built in 1855. Some of these companies did not last the decade, and dissolved for either financial or personal reasons. An example is Marks & Fletcher, who sold off their stock in 1852 and returned to the East.[32]

These general stores received some of their business from the U.S. Army which had troops stationed at both New Town and the mission. The army accepted sealed proposals from merchants who desired to supply the troops. A good portion of this activity declined by the middle of the decade when the army no longer used the San Diego depot to supply by overland route the forts at Yuma and Jurupa. However, W. C. Ferrell, collector of customs, reported in the middle of 1851 that the army no longer occupied the depot.[33] Instead, goods were shipped to these places via the Gulf of California and the Colorado River.[34] The Californios with their large ranches formed a second market for the San Diego merchants, and, thirdly, the merchants sold to customers from ships stopping in San Diego for supplies.

Another form of business catering to the coastwise shipping consisted of hotels and saloons, such as the Exchange Hotel and Billiard Saloon which advertised itself as "fitted up for the accommodation of the resident or travelling community." Moreover, "the Bar is abundantly supplied with the Choicest wines, liquors, segars [sic], preserved meats, fruits, etc.; and every attention paid the convenience and accommodation of guests." Similar establishments to be found in San Diego included the Pantoja House operated by Charles J. Laning; the Colorado House of Cave J. Couts which boasted "an elegant Billiard table," which, "has just been put up and the Bar stocked with the best Wines, Liquors and Cigars to be had in San Francisco;"[35] the Boston House of Slack & Morse; the Ocean House; the New Orleans Hotel at La Playa; the Playa Hotel situated near the entrance to the Bay; the American Hotel, and Bandini's Gila House which he later sold to Anglo proprietors, and of which Ames stated:

> There is not on the shores of the Pacific so pleasant and agreeable a place to spend the summer months as San Diego; and we are surprised that some enterprising Yankee does not rent that beautiful and spacious Hotel of Mr. Bandini's—the Gila House—and fit it up for the reception of company. If that house was opened and advertised in the San Francisco papers, hundreds on hundreds of invalids and persons of leisure, would flock to this delightful southern clime, who are now deterred from coming for the wont [sic] of proper accommodations.[36]

Many of these hotels, like the general stores, did not survive the entire decade, and those that did apparently did not make much profit, since the visitors and tourists to San Diego dwindled in the middle and late years. This trend can be seen by an examination of the advertisements in the *Herald* throughout the period. The years when the tourist trade would play a key role in the economy of San Diego still lay ahead.

A variety of additional firms in San Diego could be found during this decade. Charles R. Johnson, for example, sold lumber to ships which entered the harbor; Leany & Sexton operated a butcher shop and claimed that "our prices being about *one half less* than the San Francisco market will be an inducement to Panama steamers to touch in here for supplies." James H. Smith advertised himself as a "house, sign, and ornamental" painter, although he had competition from C. H. Pond & Co. Louis Rose, before opening his general store, owned a butcher house in Old Town, and supplied meat to both residents of San Diego and to the vessels that put in. Two years later, Philip Crosthwaite also went into the meat business with his establishment on the Plaza at Old Town.[37]

All of these businesses underwent financial fluctuations because of the tenuous state of the economy during the 1850s and the dependence on both ranching and the coastal trade. Despite shortcomings, the business firms of San Diego provided material comforts and even luxuries to a near-isolated and small town. "Dull times we *may* have," the *Herald* stated, "but [we] shall always be content if attended with the means of personal comfort we now enjoy, and if any are less fortunate in their feeling, we are confident in the hope that for them 'a better time is coming.'"[38]

While business in the form of general stores and other services achieved some success, manufacturing in San Diego during this period barely existed. An examination of the Manufacturing Census of 1860 discloses that only four manufacturing concerns could be found. Two of these were fisheries (no information is given to indicate exactly where in the county they were located) with an annual value of products of $18,000, and 16 employees. Another consisted of a saddlery and harness establishment with an annual value of $2,000 and only one employee. Finally, one individual constructed wagons and carts with an annual value of $1,750. In total, the annual value of manufactures in San Diego County in 1860 came to $21,750.[39]

One final addition to the commercial life of San Diego in the 1850s was the coastwise trade. A number of ships utilized the harbor of San Diego at the start of the decade. The Panama steamship line, for example, established in 1849, sent its vessels to San Diego on

WILLIAM HEATH DAVIS
c 1850

a regular basis. During 1851 the notice of arrivals in the *Herald* lists a number of steamers arriving from Panama en route to San Francisco. On their return trip to Panama and to the Atlantic coast these steamers, plus some schooners and brigs, put into San Diego. Here they acquired coal, lumber, provisions, and their passengers rested at the town hotels and acquired fresh supplies. On June 5, 1851, the *Herald* observed that four ships had arrived. San Diego historian Carl H. Heilbron notes that for the year that ended June 30, 1852, 29 foreign ships (19,016 tons) arrived in San Diego. Clearance for foreign ports during the same period went to 13 ships (5,169 tons), 12 of which flew the U.S. flag.[40]

Regular steamship service began in 1851 when the steamer *Goliah* inaugurated a schedule between San Francisco and San Diego carrying freight and passengers with stops at Monterey, Santa Barbara, and San Pedro. In 1853 another steamer, the *Southerner*, augmented this schedule. Early in the period the Pacific Mail Steamship Company began regular mail service, and even contemplated the purchase of Davis' wharf. This possibility elicited from Ames a most hopeful expectation:

> This will undoubtedly prove a fruitful source of material benefit to the town and the Company, for while the town enjoys the benefits to be derived from increase of trade, which must necessarily occur on the arrival of each steamer, the boats will have the advantage of lying alongside a good wharf, with a much greater facility of communication with Old Town, and of taking in such stores of beef and water as they may be in need of.[41]

The "good wharf," of course, proved to be otherwise, and Ames' hopes never were fulfilled as the Company decided not to purchase the structure. Moreover, by the middle and late years of the decade the coastwise trade declined due to depressed economic conditions throughout the state. Unfortunately, it is difficult to document the rise and fall of shipping activity in San Diego (number of ships and tonnage) since the customs records are limited and provide only sparse information.[42]

A facet of this decline concerns the status of the U.S. customs house in San Diego. Under Mexico the town had served from time to time as a port of entry, with the customs house at Ballast Point on Point Loma. After the United States conquest, San Francisco became the only customs district in California, with the San Diego customs collector designated as a deputy collector. This arrangement reduced San Diego from a port of entry to a port of delivery along with Monterey, while San Francisco became the sole port of entry, which meant that vessels arriving from foreign ports were required to pay duties on cargo at San Francisco, before proceeding to the ports of delivery. San Diego's status under this arrangement lasted only a short time and then reverted to a port of entry.[43]

W. C. Ferrell, who had been one of Davis' partners in New Town, served as the first collector for the district of San Diego with headquarters at Point Loma. In Ferrell's acknowledgment of his appointment, he informed the Acting Secretary of the Treasury that more employees and new facilities would be needed. Ferrell expected an active movement of cattle and sheep from Sonora into the United States through San Diego. He also reported that steamers in the area chose to ignore customs regulations. Finally, Ferrell suggested it might be best to move the customs house to New Town, but provided no justification for this suggestion.[44]

Two weeks later Ferrell reported to Washington that he occupied a small house at La Playa, which now served as the customs house. Apparently the old Mexican structure had become so dilapidated it could no longer be used. Ferrell later noted that the new customs house was "advantageously located," being five miles from Old Town and eight or nine miles from New Town by land, but only five by water. This facility did not have a storehouse, but Ferrell believed he could get along without one. He did suggest, however, that the government depot at New Town might be used for a storehouse since the army no longer needed it. Ferrell further suggested the transfer of the customs house to this abandoned site.

In 1852, John G. Brown, who acted as an agent for Davis in Washington, proposed to the Secretary of the Treasury, Thomas Corwin, that the customs house be moved from La Playa to New Town. He informed the Secretary that La Playa was isolated and that New Town possessed a "new" wharf that extended 1300 feet into the channel, cost $40,000,[45] and served any class of naval ship. In addition, Davis would build the customs house and charge no rent for one year. Corwin made no decision on this proposal, and, instead, sent it to Ferrell authorizing the collector to "use his judgment on the matter." Ferrell's connection with Davis in 1852 cannot be determined, but he did not make the selection in favor of his former associate. He notified the Secretary that it would be best to remain at La Playa and that the majority of businessmen in the area favored the decision. The site of the customs house at La Playa did not radically influence the location of business in San Diego. The majority of establishments remained in Old Town with some at La Playa.[46]

Regardless of the distribution of business, poor conditions at the customs house mirrored the over-all economic problems of San Diego. Ferrell and the other collectors during this period found it difficult to meet expenses, especially since some vessels refused to pay any duties, and there was much smuggling. One source of revenue, Mexican cattle, disappeared when livestock was declared free of duty. The full extent of these activities, however, cannot be ascertained due to a minimum of customs house records available. J. Ross Browne, a federal inspector of customs, visited San Diego in 1853 and commented on the poor conditions:

> ... the collector is left destitute of occupation and is compelled to seek business and society in various parts of the state. Now and then, however, he is supposed to take a look at his pay account, and see that the public light on the Point keeps burning on nights, notwithstanding the roof has been blown off.[47]

Browne, further, observed that the Department of the Treasury would not even allow the San Diego collector a deputy or clerk at public expense. "I look upon this," Browne wrote in his notes, "as a very severe course to impose upon any gentleman whose services are presumed to be worth three thousand dollars per annum, and would recommend that he should at least be allowed a bottle of whisky." While Browne may have exaggerated, it remains clear that San Diego failed to achieve any considerable status as a port or commercial center in the early 1850s.

V.

Agriculture during the Spanish-Mexican period had never achieved prominence in San Diego, nor did it throughout the fifties. The importance of agriculture was perceived by some, but, despite efforts to encourage more San Diegans to pursue this occupation, it (not including ranching) remained a minor activity.

The farming that did exist was restricted to family gardens. John Hay, at his ranch about a mile from town, grew oats and barley, which the editor of the *Herald* reported in 1854 were "three feet [in] height, and from appearance, promise to yield an extraordinary crop." That same year, a report called attention to the extensive arrangements made in San Diego County to cut a large quantity of oats, likely to be quite profitable. Ames related in March, 1854, that he had been shown stalks of barley from nearby Rancho de Jamacha "32 inches high and full headed." This brought from Ames the response: "Can the 'cold and barren region of the North' equal this?" Indeed, barley represented the most important crop by the end of the decade (16,850 bushels in the county in 1860), but Irish and sweet potatoes, corn, peas, beans, and hay, were also grown in limited quantities. Ames reported in 1855 that an enormous yield of sweet potatoes had been raised on the ranch of Judge Ladd, which could be worth over $2,000. "Now in view of these facts and figures," Ames castigated some of his fellow-citizens, "is it not astonishing that there are so many idlers loafing about this town, when they can find a ready market for any quantity of produce that they can raise."[48]

Wheat also was produced, and stood as the second largest crop next to barley. A yield of 1,056 bushels in 1852 was expanded to 8,695 bushels in 1860 (county figures). [49] The construction of a flour mill in the middle of the decade encouraged the increased production, but San Diego still had to import grain from San Francisco at great cost, a fact which disturbed Ames and others:

> People cry out hard times, when there are idlers enough about this town, who have no visible means of support, whose labor would ten times more than produce enough to supply the deficiency in the article of food. [50]

Although Ames noted with delight in 1853 the increased growth in wheat and other crops, a study of the 1860 Agricultural Census for the county shows that very little agricultural production took place, with the exception of beef and wool. Nevertheless, for a man like Ames the development of agriculture represented a challenge that had to be met:

> When we reflect that the town and country with a population not over two thousand, fails to supply its own wants, but sends away forty or fifty thousand dollars yearly to pay for flour alone, we begin to believe that there is a lack of something like wholesome enterprise or industry on the part of the inhabitants. Nothing is exported here but money. That goes off in quantities, to pay for supplies that we have the means of raising at home.

> We know that men among us are accustomed to derive great satisfaction from sneering at the attempt to introduce agricultural industry, and amuse themselves and their friends by predicting the failure of every instance of trial. We rather envy the ease with which these gentlemen are entertained, but believe their satisfaction would be more enduring if the country could show, by well directed enterprise, its ability to prosper by its inherent resources. [51]

Ames' appeal remained constant throughout the decade. In 1851 the *Herald* in an extensive editorial pointed out that gold mining could be only a temporary phenomenon. The newspaper discounted the idea that California would revert to a wasteland when the depletion of this mineral occurred, but advised that to avoid this possibility, advantage had to be taken of the state's climate and natural resources in order to establish a profitable agricultural society. [52]

Others shared a similar opinion. In a letter to the editor, lawyer J. W. Robinson wrote that "few things are of more importance to us than the development of the agricultural resources of this State." Robinson encouraged, though unsuccessfully, the formation of a county agricultural society to promote, in conjunction with state and county agricultural and horticultural fairs, a diversity of crops grown in San Diego. His proposal met with little enthusiasm, for like other settlers in the state, San Diegans had come to California for more "lucrative" ventures. [53]

Another writer to the *Herald* in 1853 complained that most people in San Diego remained unaware of the value of vineyards. Others were more aware. In 1857 the biggest winery in Los Angeles produced 60,000 gallons of wine. San Diego, on the other hand, in 1860 produced only 70 gallons. [54]

In 1853 "Cincinnatus," reported in the *Herald* that among the numerous fruits that could be cultivated in Southern California, none had greater possibilities than peaches. "Every person," he insisted, "owning a farm or garden or lot of ground, ought to grow peaches, whether he consults profits or pleasure. The growth and maturity is rapid—the fruit sells high—and who can deny the luxury of a fine ripe, luscious juicy peach?—no one." [55]

To encourage agriculture, the *Herald* stressed the value of saline land between Old Town and "False Bay" (Mission Bay) and between Mission Valley and the bay, an area which had always been considered useless for agriculture. According to a state geological survey, the *Herald* reported, saline land could be profitably cultivated. Corn seemed to flourish better in this type of soil, as well as barley and wheat. As evidence, the newspaper pointed out that at his ranch located on saline land by the bay, Judge Hays had raised two crops from one sowing of barley, and "his potatoes and other vegetables are superior to any we have ever seen in the southern part of the State." [56]

Not only could such crops be grown, but for a nice profit. Ames reported in 1855 that potatoes in the area sold for from four to ten cents per pound throughout the entire season and that onions sold for eighteen cents per pound. Despite these high figures, there continued to be little interest in agriculture on the part of Anglo-Americans in San Diego, and it irritated Ames to see his town dependent on other areas for foodstuffs, the only exception being fresh beef. In this respect, it is of interest to note Ames' neglect of the contribution of the Californios, for without their production of beef, wool, butter and cheese the economy of San Diego, not to mention local palates, would have suffered even more. Apparently, Ames did not consider the Spanish-speaking inhabitants as participants in the growth of California.

Besides the need to diversify the economy and gain profits, Ames believed there existed a higher motive for the development of agriculture. "Among the variety of pursuits of men," he wrote in true Jeffersonian style,

> ... few are found to leave more lasting evidence ... than the agriculturist—that first and most useful employment of man. And certainly no man contributes so largely to the permanent wealth of the State, as the cultivators of the soil. The millions dug from our golden mountains, and teeming gulches are carried by every steamer from us, never to return. But the products of the soil remain, and make us independent, indeed. 57

Even such pious exhortations by Ames had no effect on the populace, and agriculture failed to develop in San Diego during this period. According to the Agricultural Census of 1860 San Diego County contained 4,143 acres of improved farm land and 499,863 acres of unimproved farm land. These statistics include, apparently, not only farms, but the ranches of Californios and Anglos, where land was used for cattle and sheep raising. The cash value of farms in the county in 1860 totaled $269,800, including farms and ranches. 58

These figures clearly reveal the retarded conditions of agriculture which existed in San Diego. An important factor in this retardation involved the land policy of the state government, even though as early as 1849 a state committee on agriculture urged farming as the state's most important industry. State authorities believed the mid-western pattern of small family farms could be repeated in California. To assist in this development, the state in the 1850s provided direct grants to farmers as well as tax exemptions. Governor Bigler proclaimed in 1853:

> ... the interests of both state and nation will unquestioningly [sic] be best subserved by thus donating the public domain in small tracts. It will induce emigration to the State; greatly increase the amount of taxable property; and above all, secure to us an abundance of the necessaries of life produced at home. 59

There were obstacles, however, because of the diversity of California's topography which lends itself more to large landholdings, the existence of large Spanish-Mexican grants, and the weakness of land policies adopted by the state. These policies dealt with (1) the adjudication of the Spanish-Mexican grants; (2) the transfer of federal lands to the state; and (3) the establishment of a system to administer and distribute the state lands.

The Spanish-Mexican claims, discussed later in more detail, were dealt with by the Land Law of 1851 which provided for a Land Commission to determine the validity of the grants. The commission validated some of the grants, but many others were not, and the land reverted to the state for public sale.

The transfer of federal land to the state involved a cumbersome and complicated procedure which led to much confusion over land titles. The state legislature also demonstrated a "distressing ineptitude" in its system for the disposal of state land. "No conscious planning, no weighing of policies, no careful deliberation marked this important action," historian Gerald Nash emphasizes. "Instead state policy resulted from a conglomeration of scattered, hastily enacted laws."

While the state legislature passed several laws for the sale of land, most of them led to fraud and speculation. One law enacted in 1852 called for land to be sold at $2.00 an acre for lots of 160 to 320 acres, with each purchase limited to 640 acres. By 1855, 232,000 acres had been sold. Three years later the legislature amended the law to lower the price to $1.25 an acre, and allowed purchasers to buy land on credit. They were required to put down only 20 percent of the price and given five years to pay the balance with an interest rate of 10 percent. This led to speculators "grabbing" most of the land. "Since an application for a certificate of purchase was not mandatory," Nash explains, "many simply paid the first year's interest without applying for such a certificate. Speculators were able to hold these lands after paying only ten cents an acre, while the state could not place them on the market."

Besides the problem of land speculators, a weak administrative system hampered the state in its attempts to dispose of land to actual settlers. The administration of land laws involved so much 'red tape' that small farmers had difficulty 'cutting through it' to acquire property. "The failure of the state as middleman," Nash concludes, "gave rise to the land speculator as an agent in the complex process of land distribution." Moreover, no central body existed for the distribution of lands. The result was a perplexed bevy of local bodies attempting to administer land sales. Not until 1858 did the legislature create a centralized administration which was restricted, however, by its smallness and lack of funds. The outcome of this speculation, corruption, and maladministration was that the ideal of a California society characterized by small family farms did not materialize. In fact, a small number of farmers possessed a large share of the total agricultural area. Large-scale distribution of state land did occur in succeeding decades, but the pattern of large landholdings continued.

VI

The idea held by Ames and others that San Diego needed a more diversified economy came from their belief that California's gold mining furor would eventually end, and San Diego would be forced to adjust since its economy was so dependent on cattle production for the mines. Many San Diegans, however, proved to be as susceptible to the 'mining fever' of the fifties as almost everyone else, and throughout the decade mining activities engaged various citizens of the town.

No organized mining existed during the first half of the decade, although individuals carried out their own explorations. In July, 1851, the *Herald* reported that two miners had recently arrived from Santo Tomás, 300 miles to the south in Baja California, with notice that gold in abundance could be found there. Baja California also became the scene of an unsuccessful trip made by two prominent San Diegans, Judge Robinson and Colonel Haraszthy, in search of silver. The Colonel also, in conjunction with another resident of the town, Charles R. Johnson, explored for silver in Southern California, and reported there existed a good possibility that silver mines in the area could rival those of Mexico, although this never happened.[60]

The successful exploitation of these mines required enterprising individuals. This sentiment, coupled with a touch of "Manifest Destiny," found expression in the *Herald* after its announcement of the discovery of rich deposits of gold, silver, and copper near the ranch of Juan Bandini, south of the border. "It will not be longer," Ames contended,

> ... ere some of our enterprising spirits, thirsting for novelty, and love of adventure, so truly characteristic of California, will be winding their way to the Silver diggings. The country is now, and has been ever since the resignation of Don Castro as Governor, in a state of anarchy and confusion, which we think will not terminate till they come under the protection of the Stars and Stripes, which we are credibly informed is the will and wish of a very large majority of the people of lower California. Will the people who are the source of all power, rise in their majesty and declare their wishes? Is this beautiful peninsula, rich in nature's choicest gifts for ever to be desecrated, and stained with human blood in this enlightened and progressive age?[61]

Perhaps the most excitement came in May, 1852, when the *Herald* reported the discovery of gold under the headlines:

> **Gold Mine In San Diego!!**
> **San Francisco Rivalled!!!**
> **Southern Port Triumphant!!!**[62]

This excitement resulted from the arrival of two Indians who brought with them some specimens of gold bearing quartz, "full of the 'real stuff.'" The Indians explained they had discovered the gold in one of the gulches between Old Town and the mission. "Should this report prove true," an inspired Ames pronounced, "that there does exist such a mine in our immediate vicinity, we may expect to see San Diego, with its superior natural advantages, soon rivalling our famed sister, San Francisco." Unfortunately, for Ames and San Diego, this report proved to be false.

On the other hand, coal was one mineral discovered and exploited. Reports existed as early as 1849 of possible coal deposits in the cliffs of Point Loma. Davis wrote a year later that a few explorations for coal had been made in the area, but that no extensive coal beds had been found.[63] In 1855 what came to be considered substantial coal deposits were found on Point Loma. The extraction of this deposit began after city trustees, on November 22, 1855, leased a tract of 40 acres on the ocean side of Point Loma for fifteen years to four San Diegans who formed the San Diego Coal Company: H. C. Ladd, Ephraim Green, G. W. Servine, and Seth B. Gainer. One month after its formation the Company advertised in the *Herald* that shares of its stock could be purchased for $100 per share. This discovery and exploitation of the coal deposits led Ames to exclaim that "there is no doubt as to the quality of the coal, and should the vein prove abundant it will become a great source of wealth."

Point Loma Coal Mine

Picture taken in 1953

This hope never came true, although the Company did work the mine for two years, employing several miners from San Diego and other areas. The Company purchased mining equipment from San Francisco including a steam engine and force pumps which they operated day and night. Misfortune struck the Company several times when operations had to be halted because of flooding and defects in the engine and machinery. These delays prompted from the *Herald* a criticism of the San Francisco suppliers. "We sincerely wish," Ames wrote, "that the parties in San Francisco, who palmed off the defective machinery on this Company, were sunk to the bottom of the shaft and obliged to remain there till the engine they sent down here could pump off the water and 'dry them up.'" [64]

Discoveries of other coal deposits near San Diego soon followed, and one other company, the Pacific Coal Company, was formed, but quickly failed. By 1858, the San Diego Coal Company apparently ceased operations. The total output of these coal operations cannot be determined. It probably was not very large, and by 1860 only ten miners remained in San Diego County. [65]

In 1857, copper deposits in Baja California attracted the attention of San Diegans. At the Jesús María mines about eighty miles south of San Diego, copper specimens were uncovered which contained 50 to 60 percent pure copper. At the same time, reports arrived that other copper deposits had been located. [66]

These discoveries led to the demand for miners, and many San Diegans crossed the border to work in the mines. Others viewed the discoveries as an opportunity for investment. San Diego merchant Louis Rose invested in the Buena Vista mine. T. R. Darnall wrote to his parents explaining he had entered into copper mining speculation in Lower California, "and have invested every cent that I can call my own and a little *more.*" Ephraim Morse used his resources as a merchant to engage in mining activities south of the border. In late October, 1857, he returned from the Jesús María mines to report that vigorous work characterized the mines, and that new ones had been opened. [67]

That same year news arrived that investors from San Francisco had made arrangements for a line of steamers to operate from San Diego to the mouth of the Colorado River, touching the Mexican ports of Santo Tomás, Ensenada, La Paz, San Blas, Mazatlán, and Guaymas and return, to connect with coast steamers to San Francisco. The *Herald* was moved to comment that "the mineral riches of the region south of San Diego are being constantly developed and should be a strong inducement on the part of our Government for its purchase from Mexico, independent of the growing necessity of controling [*sic*] the navigation of the Gulf of California." [68]

The idea of annexing Baja California increased in intensity following some conflicts between Anglo miners and Mexican officials in September, 1857. To protect the miners, some citizens proposed that a large group be sent to their assistance, and sent word to Los Angeles to have more men available in case they were needed. That some of these people contemplated more than just a rescue of the miners is evident in the *Herald's* boast that "if our people ever cross that boundary line, Mexico may as well say farewell to Lower California, for the rich silver and copper mines there are too valuable a prize for the Yankee, ever to relinquish their grasp upon."[69]

Excitement increased when word came that T. R. Darnall, who had gone to Santo Tomás to assist in the trial of the miners, also became a captive. "Everybody who had horses volunteered them to mount a party for the rescue of our citizens who are held in the custody of those outlaws, and the whole town was ready to march on the Frontier, as soon as arms could be procured." Things calmed down, however, and no "invasion" became necessary when the Mexicans released Darnall and the miners. Nevertheless, these "harassments" by Mexican officials gave support to the argument that the United States should take this additional Mexican territory. No better expression of "Manifest Destiny" can be seen than these words by Justin Ames:

> The signs of the times seem to intimate that ere long the stars and stripes will float over this territory, and for the sake of those interested herein God grant that it may be so. Even the people themselves [the Mexicans], although they say it is hard to be sold with their country like so many cattle or sheep, yet they admit that their condition would be infinitely better under the administration of our laws—at any rate their condition cannot be worse. But still the evil is in themselves—ignorant and lazy, they are content with existing. . . . [70]

Although Baja California never came into the physical possession of the United States, investment in the copper mines by some San Diegans continued to the end of the decade. San Diego gained not only from this investment (although total production records are not available to determine profits and/or losses), but in the sales that the town merchants made to the mining companies and to individual miners. The records and letters of E. W. Morse show that a sizable percentage of his store's sales were to mining concerns in the south during 1857-1859. On October 8, 1857, the San Ysidro Mining Company purchased goods in the amount of $251.11 That same month the Jesús María Mine bought $350.35 worth of goods, plus an additional purchase of $1,000 over the next two months. Individual miners received their pay in scrip and exchanged it for either goods or cash at Morse's store.[71]

Besides supplying miners, Morse had a direct investment in the Jesús María mines to the tune of $3,213.38, and in several letters he wrote to the managers of the mines he exhibited deep concern for their **operations**. These letters show that the operation suffered from weak management and incompetent miners, both of which reduced output and profits. In a letter probably written in 1857, Morse reprimanded the managers for being too lax with the workers, both Anglos and Mexicans:

> You are too easy with the men, you don't *boss* them but let them do as they please, while I was there they were pleased to do as little as possible.
>
> . . . let them know that they are at work for you and not as companions for you. It is not exactly necessary that you should wear kid gloves but there is a proper medium between the kid gloves system and that in vogue at the Jesús María mines in my opinion.

In another letter, Morse wrote to the management along the same lines:

> If you hadn't had such a d--d set of rascals about you it would never have happened [?] and you will remember my advise was not to have them about.
>
> I am running all the risk, what risk do you run even if it is but 3 or 6,000 it is all I am worth.[72]

Morse specifically complained to his foreman that the employees at the mines worked only five hours a day. "Damn well for you," he protested, "to do it off of me you have nothing to lose . . . after my writing to you again and again you would go directly contrary to my wishes—in not getting out metal as fast as possible—putting men on other mines, and particularly not bossing them. What have you been doing!"

With these problems, Morse, by 1858, began to remove himself from his involvement in the Jesús María mines and sold his interest to investors in San Francisco. Mining in Baja California continued into the next decade, but it never reached the "boom" proportions expected by Ames.

VII

Fishing in the form of capture of sea otters represented an important activity in San Diego during the period before the Mexican War. Historian Samuel F. Black points out that, next to the cattle industry and the trade in hides and tallow, fishing was the most important aspect of the early commerce of San Diego. By the time of Anglo invasion in 1850, however, the otter had been severely depleted, and San Diegans engaged in fishing only sporadically. However, the *Herald* attempted to convince citizens that fishing was a profitable enterprise. It reported as early as August, 1851, that good fishing existed in San Diego Bay, especially the abundance of crawfish, "not a whit inferior to the lobster and scarcely less in size." When the schooner *Emeline*, which had been in the bay for two weeks taking fish for the San Francisco market, disclosed a catch of twenty tons during one day's haul, Ames wrote: "Fishing is by no means an insignificant item in this bay, and if carried on extensively we could more than amply supply the demand for the up country market."[73]

As with agriculture, most of the residents of San Diego could not be convinced of the profitability of the fishing trade, and therefore avoided it. One firm, the San Diego Fishing Company, did organize in 1853 to haul fish from the bay and sell them in the store of George Lyons and Company, but apparently it made little profit and disbanded in a short time. By 1858 only two fisheries could be found in the county.[74]

Whaling, however, did interest people in San Diego, and by 1860 it had become a growing activity. This did not represent a new trend, for the whaling trade had been carried on long before the Mexican War when Anglo whalers came along the San Diego coast. They carried out this hunt between December and February when the whales passed south, and from March to April when they returned north.[75]

Whaling activity, from all indications, declined in the early 1850s only to be revived by 1855. The *Herald* that year revealed movements on the part of whaling vessels in the area. A letter from the commander of the whaler *R. Adams* praised San Diego as the best port on the Pacific for the refitting of whaling ships. Ames, of course, agreed, and expressed the hope that in the future more whalers would stop in the town, as this would allow "the opening to us of a new and important brand of business, which we believe will center at this port." As Ames put it, "the easy access to our harbor, its perfect security, and the trifling expense at which repairs can be made, make this the most desirable port upon the Pacific coast for the recruiting and refitting of whalers."[76]

The *San Francisco Chronicle* disagreed and derided the idea of San Diego as a whaling port. An aroused Ames attacked the editor of the *Chronicle* for never visiting San Diego to judge for himself the value of its bay. He deplored the chauvinism of San Francisco. "Now it so happens that San Francisco," he wrote, "though claimed to be the entire Pacific coast, cannot be claimed as the whole world, and the rest of mankind."[77]

From 1855 to 1860, many small whalers visited San Diego for the purpose of capturing the grey-back whales found in the area. Heilbron in his history comments that "the lists of Yankee trading vessels calling at San Diego in the middle years of the last century include many a dirty old money making whaler." Nevertheless, whaling never became a predominant activity. It remained a limited one, although it continued to expand up to the 1880s when whaling rapidly declined due to new sources of oil.[78]

VIII

In the 1850s the wealthiest class of San Diegans were the Mexican rancheros. Although they had no political power, held only a minimal number of political offices, and played no role in the decision-making process, they possessed considerable economic resources. The Californios enjoyed a great deal of social prominence, but were quite willing to accept Anglo political dominance if it meant that their properties would remain intact. Unfortunately, they did not take into consideration the impersonal force of a market economy which brought depression to the Californios during the last half of the decade.

Depression had been far from the minds of the "ricos" in the early 1850s when they received high prices for their cattle from the hungry gold miners of the north. Regrettably for the Californios, this "boom" did not last long, and as historian Leonard Pitt points out, their spendthrift practices, encouraged by high profits, eventually put the rancheros in financial trouble. With the demand for cattle high in the early years, the Californios sold their herds as fast as possible and in great quantities without a care for the future. When a downturn in mining activities occurred during the middle and closing years of the decade and diminished the demand for beef, the rancheros found themselves overextended (15,452 head of cattle in 1860, as compared to 3,718 head in 1852)[79] and forced to give up some of their lands in payment of taxes and bills. The "Sheriff's Notice" of those with delinquent taxes listed in the *Herald* in December, 1854, included many of the prominent Californios, who, through public auction, lost parts of their property to Anglo ranchers and businessmen. By 1860 the economic downturn of the "ricos" became evident. The total value of real estate in San Diego that year was $206,400, and of this figure, the total value of land belonging to Mexicans had fallen to $82,700, while the value of Anglo lands rose to $128,900.[80] These are impresive figures, since in 1850 the Mexican had held the overwhelming amount of property.

This steady loss of land confronted the entire "rico" population in California, although there existed different circumstances between the north and the south. In the north the failure of a large number of Anglos in the mining regions, plus the insecurity of land titles, led many miners to engage in farming. In so doing, they encroached upon the large cattle ranches of the northern Californios. This produced what Pitt describes as a condition of "backyard guerrilla warfare with settlers bent on outright confiscation."[81]

As historian Paul W. Gates in his studies of land policy in California points out, Anglo-American settlers held to a tradition of pre-emption (the right of squatters who settled on unclaimed vacant and unimproved land to buy that land for a minimal price before it was publicly auctioned). They also believed in the right of occupants to their improvements. This attitude ran into opposition from many Mexican landowners who refused to allow squatters on their land. Those who did allow squatters refused to sell them land, only to lease it. Leasing, however, was unacceptable to the settlers. As Gates puts it: "Tenancy was barely a satisfactory position for an American brought up on the assumption that land in the United States was cheap and that everyone should have a piece of it and a share in the prosperity the future was sure to bring." Settlers, therefore, simply took over lands that belonged to Mexicans on the assumption they were opened to pre-emption.[82]

The squatter problem was intensified by the fact that contrary to policy in the territories, the federal government did not allow settlers in California homesteads of 400 to 600 acres. Not only did Congress fail to follow previous land policies in California, but it did not survey land there before settlers arrived. As a result, numerous disputes arose between squatters and Mexican landowners.[83]

This irritation deepened when settlers began to question the validity of land grants held by Californios. To settle these disputes, Congress passed the Land Law of 1851. The law provided for a three man Board of Land Commissioners authorized to determine the validity of land grants. Appeals could be made to the federal district courts and to the Supreme Court. If the Commission rejected claims or if land went unclaimed, the land became part of the public domain and settlers could purchase it. Senator William Gwin of California, who wrote the bill, later admitted he envisioned the law would force Mexicans off their lands by the encouragement it would provide squatters. The law, indeed, did lead to an increase in squatters and to a subsequent rise in violence. By 1853 every rancho around San Francisco had its squatters.

This was not the case in the southern part of the state as the so-called "Southern Cow Counties" remained undisturbed by the land law, and very few squatters appeared. "San Diego," it was reported, " also had a squatter by 1853, reportedly 'a good fellow and industrious and God-fearing.'" Northern ranches were not so fortunate as the Board of Land Commissioners took away, according to Pitt, one-fourth to two-fifths of the Californios' land.[84] It delayed the confirmation of land titles so that settlers continued to encroach on this land. From 1851 to 1856, the Land Commission considered over 800 cases involving close to twelve million acres. Of these, it approved 520 claims and rejected 273. The rest were either dismissed or withdrawn by the claimants.

In complying with the Board, the Californios, even though their lands were protected by the Treaty of Guadalupe Hidalgo (1848), faced great difficulties and heavy expenses to adjudicate their claims. They were at a disadvantage not knowing the laws of the United States or Anglo-Saxon legal procedures. The language difference also proved to be a problem, as well as the fact that many title documents had been lost or destroyed. Historian Robert Cleland points out that the validation of these claims, ironically, led to the loss of land, for to meet court costs and lawyers' fees the Californios paid in their major source of wealth—land.

The conditions of the Mexican landowners became so desperate by 1855 that some of them made a direct appeal to Washington:

> In view of the doleful litigation proposed by the general Government against all the land owners in California in violation of the Treaty of Guadalupe Hidalgo and the law of nations, which

year by year become more costly and intolerable, in view of the repeated falsehoods and calumnies circulated by the public press against the validation of our titles and the justice which supports us in this interminable litigation and which equally influences the tribunals of justice and prejudices our character and our dearest rights; in view of the injustices which have accumulated against us to carry out a general confiscation of our properties; and especially to adopt the most efficient means to assure the abrogation of the existing law which holds all titles acquired from the former government to be fraudulent and which were guaranteed us by treaty.[85]

This appeal proved useless and throughout the fifties Mexicans continued to lose their land through invalidation, to squatters, or forced sale to pay legal fees. In northern California this was especially true since this area bore the brunt of the early Anglo onslaught. Although such a critical situation did not exist in the south, what litigation and squatters failed to do in this area, mortgages, taxes, and personal expenses did. As a result of all this, plus the downturn in the market for beef, most Californios by 1860 retained only portions of their original land holdings.[86]

In 1860, José María Estudillo owned $10,000 worth of real estate, a far cry from the $30,385 worth of property he had possessed in 1850. The Argüello family during this time lost $24,000 worth of property. The most notable example of the Californios' depression was Juan Bandini who saw his vast lands which stretched from the Mexican border to present-day Riverside, pass into the hands of his Anglo sons-in-law. When he died in 1859, the *Herald* could only observe that "Don Juan was a prominent citizen of San Diego, and leaves a large circle of friends, who sincerely mourn his demise." The *Herald* could not have described any better the downfall of Bandini's realm; a downfall the prominent Californio sensed earlier than most of his "compadres." Commenting in 1855 on adverse decisions against Californios by the Land Commission, Don Juan had bitterly stated:

> Of the lands mentioned some have been in the quiet possession of the proprietors and their families for forty or fifty years. On them they have reared themselves homes—they have enclosed and cultivated fields—there they and their children were born—and there they lived in peace and comparative plenty. But now—our inheritance is turned to strangers—our houses to aliens. We have drunken our water for money—our wood is sold unto us. Our necks are under persecution—we labor and have no rest.[87]

Bandini's words were prophetic, although in 1855 the Californios still shared the naive expectation they could be accepted as partners by the Anglos in the exploitation of San Diego's wealth. This hope could only be justified to the extent that the Californios' numbers and landholdings allowed them some leverage with the Anglo-Americans. These assets, however, by 1860, had been dissipated. The census of that year shows a near parity between the Anglo and Mexican populations (217 to 220). With this changed condition, the symbiotic relationship of the "ricos" with the "Gringo" came to an end, and in the next thirty years the decline of the Californios became complete.[88]

Their decline resulted from the intense competition for land from Anglo miners, Anglo settlers, and Anglo speculators. It did not originate, as Pitt claims, from a clash of divergent cultures. Undoubtedly, differences in culture and race played a part, just as racial and cultural discrimination plays a part in economic exploitation today, but the essence of the decline was economic in nature. "If the history of Mexican grants of California is ever written," Henry George wrote in 1871, "it will be a history of greed, of perjury, of corruption, of spoliation and high-handed robbery, for which it will be difficult to find a parallel."[89]

Juan Lorenzo Bruno Bandini and his daughter Maria Ysidora Barbara Bandini de Couts

71

IX

By the mid-1850s, it became apparent to a number of San Diegans, principally the merchants, that the economy of the town needed stimulation. One solution was to develop San Diego's "Inland Empire" by establishing trade ties with the Mormon settlement at San Bernardino, but more importantly in the Great Salt Lake Valley. To establish this trade it was necessary to construct a road through the San Bernardino mountains.

As early as March, 1852, a party of San Diegans explored a new route to the San Bernardino Valley by way of San Luis Rey. "It is highly commendable," the *Herald* noted, "that our citizens are taking steps to make a good road to the valley as we know from reliable authority that there are several thousand immigrants who will arrive at San Diego this season in transit to the settlement at San Bernardino and the Great Salt Lake." [90]

This route, however, did not prove feasible, and for the next two years the matter lay dormant. In 1854, the matter again attracted consideration. At a public meeting at the courthouse on March 18, 1854, Colonel W. C. Ferrell delivered an address in which he pointed out how distressing it was that San Diego with all her natural advantages of climate and harbor still remained economically retarded. This could be alleviated, Ferrell concluded, by opening a road to the San Bernardino Valley by way of Temecula. The Colonel grandly attempted to prove that millions of dollars of trade would result if the Mormon settlers to the east could be induced to trade in San Diego. "Those enterprising and numerous settlers," Ferrell explained, "are seeking some outlet on the Pacific, and offer to us all the advantages, if we will make our own roads possible." [91]

Convinced by Ferrell's arguments, the public assembly organized a committee of seven to cooperate with the Colonel in exploring the possibility of building a road to Temecula. The committee included attorney Robinson, merchants Witherby, Rose, Morse, Jacobs, Franklin, Pendleton, and ranchero Bandini, and in about two weeks raised over $800 to fund the work of surveying and constructing the road. Pendleton attempted unsuccessfully to convince Davis to turn over to the Mormons some of his lots at New Town in the hope the Mormons would build a depot there. [92]

A short time later it became known that some influential Mormon settlers were coming to San Diego to transport a shipment of goods back to San Bernardino and the Salt Lake, and the committee expected to confer with them about the prospects of the new route. Of this development, Ames wrote:

> We are well convinced in our minds, that by the promptness of action which the call of Col. Ferrell has induced, there are better times in store for us, and the Mormons will meet with us with the liberality for which they are so eminently celebrated, till a regular, safe, and easy means of transportation will be completed from the port of San Diego to San Bernardino and Salt Lake. [93]

A week later the *Herald* reported that the Mormon merchants left San Diego pleased with the idea of a permanent arrangement whereby goods for the Mormon settlements would be shipped to San Diego and then transported inland to their several stores in the Utah territory. The road used in this trip passed through San Bernardino and then to Coal Creek in Iron County, Utah, and, finally, by wagon road to Salt Lake. Reliable information existed, however, according to the *Herald*, that an excellent road could be built from San Diego to mineral-rich Coal Creek that would reduce the distance considerably. These bright expectations led Ames to declare:

> The prospect for the rapid increase of business in San Diego is very flattering indeed. We find ourselves now only 400 miles from an immense mineral region now fairly tested, and on the eve of securing, permanently, an addition to our trade, with a community of seventy-five thousand people, and increasing 20,000 annually. The natural advantage of our city is great, and will soon be developed. At no other point can this trade arrive at the Pacific, or at San Diego. [94]

Despite these predictions the Committee organized to build the road ran into financial trouble. The matter became more urgent when a report arrived that the Mormons already were trading with Los Angeles; thus, San Diego faced the danger of losing the entire trade unless it moved quickly. Even though the Committee raised $2,000 to defray the cost of improving the San Bernardino road, no action occurred to carry out the improvements. "It seems to us," wrote a disturbed Ames, "that the merchants of this place, who will be the ones to reap the most immediate benefits . . . do not stir in this matter." Ames not only directed his criticisms toward the lackadaisical merchants, he also criticized the ranchers of the area for not contributing some of their money for the road. According to Ames, they would benefit by the road to the Mormon settlements as well:

> One thing is to our minds painfully evident, San Diego is going down hill as fast as possible, and will decrease in importance as a place of trade, unless men who have accumulated wealth in our midst employ their means in some manner tending to the development of the agricultural resource of the country, instead of quietly sitting down and loaning their money out on mortgages at 4 and 8 percent a month. The consequences of this is that the borrowers—who are mostly native Californians, who never having earned a dollar, have no idea of its value—spread their means in all sorts of extravagance without the slightest idea that pay day will ever come. They never lift a mortgage and do not seem to consider that in a few years all their fine ranches with their thousand head of cattle roaming over the plains, will be in the possession of strangers, and they and their children will be ejected from the fertile lands and happy homes which they inherited from their fathers.[95]

Ames' sharp criticisms failed to stimulate construction on the road, and by 1855 the San Diego merchants had their hopes on another form of inland transportation: the construction of a transcontinental railroad which would have its Pacific terminus at San Diego.

X

San Diegans, specifically the merchant class, understood that without such a railroad connection, San Diego had little hope of prospering and even less chance of becoming a great commercial center.[96] Ames wrote in early 1852, "we do not despair of seeing the day when the iron hands of a railroad shall link our young State with the Atlantic. Golden Years must pass away before that happy era in American history will be accomplished. Meanwhile, it is not for us idly to fold our hands and dream, thinking to wake, like Van Winkle, and find our visions realized."[97]

The first tangible steps toward accomplishing such a goal came on May 9, 1853, when the Anglo citizens of the town assembled at the courthouse and organized a Committee to investigate and report upon the best and most practicable route for a railroad to connect the Atlantic and Pacific Oceans. On the Committee sat the more prominent members of San Diego's Anglo "establishment": Colonel J. Bankhead Magruder, President; Vice Presidents: John Hays, William H. Moon, and Frank Ames; and secretary, J. Judson Ames. Other members included James W. Robinson, William C. Ferrell, J. J. Warner, Charles H. Poole, Cave J. Couts, and O. S. Witherby. A Committee of Correspondence also included the same people with the exception of Poole and the addition of E. B. Pendleton. After the organization of the factfinding group, the meeting adjourned until May 20 when the committee would report its findings.[98]

The Magruder report, as it was labeled, contained reasons why the southern route with San Diego as the Western terminus should be selected for the railroad: (1) from a physical standpoint, the southern route stood far superior to any other; it never would be snowbound, for example; (2) from a military perspective, the entire Mexican border would be protected; and (3) there would exist no obstacles to a cheap and fast construction of a railroad from El Paso to San Diego. (As early as 1848, John C. Calhoun had suggested the El Paso to San Diego route.)[99] The report, further, noted that the Mormons in Utah sought a railroad outlet, and favored San Diego as a Pacific terminus. The Committee recommended that the western line connecting the railroad with San Diego should be as follows: from El Paso to the Gila River, to Fort Yuma and across the Colorado desert to Vallecitos on its western rim, and from this point over the mountains to San Diego. It was also argued that San Diego would form a better outlet for the Pacific and Orient trade than San Francisco, for ships could reach China much faster from San Diego than from any other port on the Pacific.

In addition to these arguments, the Committee presented four resolutions. One of these called upon the President of the United States to authorize a survey from El Paso to the junction of the Gila and Colorado Rivers and from there to San Diego. The second key resolution stated:

> That an agent to represent the interests of the 'Southern location' and to make known to the public its real merits, be appointed, whose duty it should be to urge upon Congress and the Executive, a careful examination of the El Paso and San Diego routes, and to communicate with capitalists both in the United States, England, and on the continent of Europe, in relation to the same.[100]

To facilitate and promote San Diego's chances of becoming the western terminus, a number of citizens in November, 1854, organized the San Diego and Gila, Southern Pacific and Atlantic Railroad Company. "We the Undersigned," the Charter of the Company read,

73

SKETCH
of the
PORT OF SAN DIEGO
1850

Compiled from recent surveys

Average rise and fall of the tide, Six feet. Soundings are in fathoms at low water. Those on the bar outside were taken by officers of the U.S. Steamship Massachusetts and those inside of Port by A. B. Gray.

Explanations

Blocks in New San Diego are all numbered and generally 300 feet by 200 feet. Lots are lettered except those in blocks 18, 19 & 20 are projected for Wharf privileges. Lots in blocks 1½, 2½, 3½, 4½, & 5 are 50 by 140 feet. Lots numbered from 1 to 38 in blocks 18 & 19 are 75 by 50 feet except No's 7, 14, 25, & 32 of said blocks which are 75 feet square. Lots numbered from one to twenty-two and situated in block 20 are 100 by 50 feet; and those lettered H and G of blocks 8, 9, 10, 11, & 12 are 65 by 100 feet. Block 31 belongs to the United States, on which the Government has erected Buildings for depot etc. Block 39 belongs to the United States for Government purposes. Lots No's 1 to 19 inclusive in block 18 belongs to the United States and Front of said block, also for Wharf purposes etc.

Streets are 75 feet wide except Atlantic and Commercial, both of which are 100 feet.

hereby agree to form ourselves into a Corporation under the Laws of the State of California for the purpose of constructing a Railroad from a point on the Bay of San Diego running then Eastwardly through the County of San Diego, by the most direct practicable Route to the Colorado River at or near the mouth of the River Gila and for that purpose have found and agreed to the following Article of Association, and have signed the same and added to our Signature the amount of our subscription in the stock of said Company.[101]

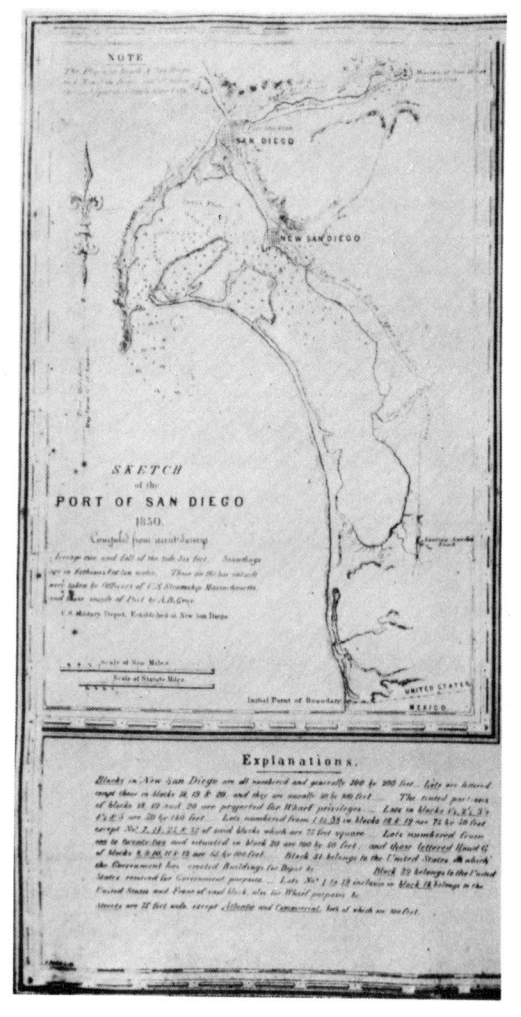

The articles of association stipulated that the duration of the Company be fifty years; that the capital stock be $4 million, to be divided into 40,000 shares of $100 each; that the Company go into operation upon the signing of the articles by holders of not less than $150,000; that at all elections of stockholders and at all meetings of stockholders, each share be entitled to one vote;

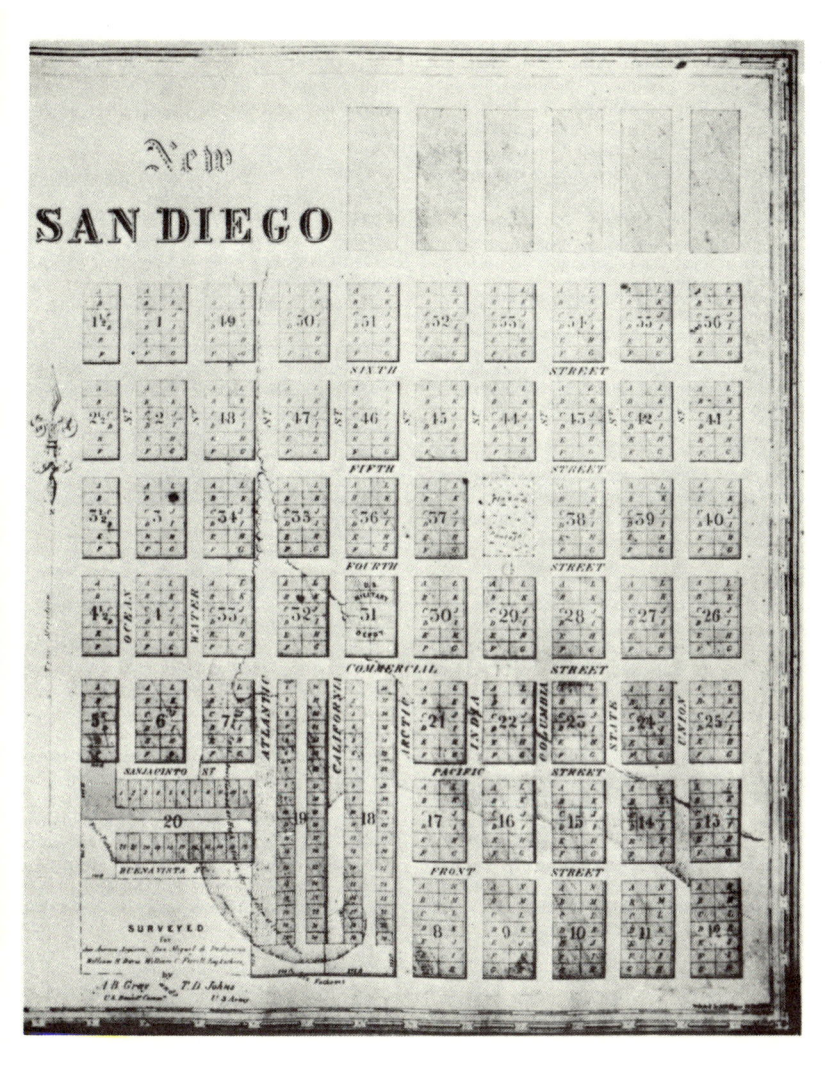

that the office of the Company be in San Diego, and that business be conducted by a Board of Directors composed of thirteen individuals which included prominent merchants such as Rose, Lyons, and Strauss. Not one Californio, incidentally, sat on the Board. According to the 1854 Treasurer's Report of the San Diego and Gila, the initial subscribers to the Company consisted of thirty Anglos, mostly merchants. Among them were E. B. Pendleton, who bought $500 worth of stock; George Lyons, $500; Louis Rose and J. W. Robinson each purchased $3,000 worth; Joseph Reiner $300; E. W. Morse $200; L. A. Franklin $500; William E. Terrill $2,000; and H. S. Burton $1,000. The total initial subscription came to $15,200.[102]

Later in November the state legislature

authorized a charter of incorporation, and the Company elected a set of permanent officers: J. W. Robinson, President, O. S. Witherby, Vice President, Louis Rose, Treasurer, and George P. Tebetts, Secretary. This attempt by the Anglo citizens of San Diego to take the initiative in constructing a line to the Gila River brought forth this comment from the *Herald*:

> Thus it will be seen that the Southern Pacific Railroad is no chimera—that it is deemed by rational, practical and cautious men, not only feasible, but easiest of accomplishment of all the routes proposed. The rancheros [not the Californios] and other property holders in the line between San Diego and the Colorado have declared their willingness to hypothecate half their lands and possessions to secure the payment of the loans necessary to complete the road.[103]

Part of this "hypothecation" came in the form of an election ordered by the Board of Trustees of San Diego on September 11, 1855 "to authorise (*sic*) the Trustees to convey to the San Diego & Gila Southern Pacific and Atlantic Railroad Co., two leagues of the Pueblo Lands to aid in the construction thereof." The returns of this election showed unanimous approval of granting the land, about 8,850 acres, to the Company which, according to Smythe, constituted "a gift which would have become of princely value had the railroad been built." The exact location of the pueblo lands turned over to the Company is difficult to determine. County tax records do not mention the specific lots, the 1856 "Map of the Pueblo Lands of San Diego" is not clear on this subject, nor do the Minutes of the Common Council and the Minutes of the Board of Directors of the San Diego and Gila provide any information. Nevertheless, as Smythe points out, this represented a significant amount of property.[104]

Another form of financing which the Company sought, with no success, included the attempt to persuade Congress to grant alternate sections of land for twenty miles upon either side of the road. In general, however, most of the funds available to the Company came from subscribers to its stock, who saw in this investment a chance at large returns. T. R. Darnall wrote in 1855 that he owned twenty shares of the San Diego & Gila, yet "besides the twenty shares in the Rail Road, I have invested every cent I have made, in city property, so I will sink or swim with old S. Diego on the issue of the railroad."

Moreover, Darnall purchased five acres at La Playa for $1,000 "which will be worth fifty thousand dollars the day that it is ascertained that San Diego will be the terminus of the road."[105]

Besides obtaining additional stockholders, the Company between 1855 and 1859 engaged in surveying the projected route, and attempting to convince Congress of the value of San Diego as a western terminus. A survey conducted by Colonel A. B. Gray reported the practicability of the southern route, and in 1856 news arrived of a report made by Secretary of War Jefferson Davis stating that the southern route stood as the best for military purposes. The *Herald* could not help but comment upon hearing of Davis' report that the Magruder Committee three years before had come to a similar conclusion:

> In alluding to these facts we would not presume to say that the Secretary has adopted the opinion of our Committee or of our Company, but it clearly shows the correctness and truthfulness of the views advanced by the leading advocates of this great Road in this city for the three years past. Truth is might and must sooner or later prevail where enlightened and important men investigate and decide.

The *Herald*, during the remainder of 1856 and the early part of 1857, ran a series of articles pointing out the advantage of San Diego as a western terminus. Additional support came in 1857 with the arrival of the first overland mail by the Butterfield Stage from San Antonio to San Diego in thirty-four days, which, according to the *Herald*, demonstrated the superiority of the southern route. In all of these arguments, the most consistent came to be the natural advantages of San Diego: its climate and location. "Let it once be enacted," Ames wrote on November 13, 1858,

> that a national railroad will terminate at the Colorado, and the various branches will take care of themselves—and if one of them don't find itself rapidly running into San Diego, then we will come to the conclusion, for the first time in our lives, that the Great Architect designs and contrives to no purpose, and that our beautiful bay was intended for a silina or fish-pond, and not for the magnificent ship harbor of a great and growing commerce.

However as in the case of other expectations during this decade, Ames and the rest of San Diego were disappointed in March, 1859, when the U.S. Senate voted down the Pacific Railroad Bill which authorized construction of the transcontinental railroad along a southern route. The defeat of the bill brought forth from the *Herald* this sad and bitter statement on March 12:

> The defeat of the Pacific Railroad Bill . . . has cast a melancholy gloom over our devoted little city. Everything is dreary, gloomy, and surrounded with the habiliments of woe. A nation's hopes have been signally blasted. Our expectations were great, and our disappointment may be measured in a corresponding ratio. We asked for bread and we have received a stone. . . .
>
> . . . Who is to blame? A great responsibility rests somewhere, and the people will not be slow to find it out. Let them scan the notes, search the records, and mark those who have trifled with the public weal—who have treated the Pacific side of the continent as if we were an alien people, and not deserving the fostering care of the Government.

Having received this "blow," the Board of Directors of the San Diego & Gila assembled on May 8, 1859, to decide the future course of the Company. The Board reiterated that the southern route with San Diego as its Pacific outlet was still the most feasible, and agreed with a Pacific Railroad convention held in Memphis in February, 1859, which adopted a report that the most practicable route to connect East and West by railway would be one from Memphis via Little Rock and Fulton to El Paso and on to San Diego.[106]

Nothing further could be expected of Congress concerning the Atlantic-Pacific route, and attention in September turned to a western railroad convention to convene in San Francisco on September 20. Delegates from California, as well as from Oregon, Utah, and Arizona would be present to discuss the construction of a transcontinental railroad and its western terminus. To participate in the conference, San Diego elected delegates, but, because boat passage could not be obtained in time, only Ames, who had moved to San Francisco, represented San Diego, along with another San Franciscan, George H. Ringgold. Again San Diego faced disappointment. The convention passed a resolution which called for the western terminus to be at San Francisco. Angered, the two-man San Diego delegation walked out of the Convention: "Has it thus really come to this?" Ames wrote back to the citizens of San Diego,

> . . . a Convention called by the Governor of a State; endorsed by the Legislature of the same; supported by the people at a general election; looked up to by the million inhabitants of a great and growing empire, meets and announces, not that it will have a road; not that the people who have poured into the lap of the Union $600,000,000, and twice saved the nation from bankruptcy, will no longer suffer their rights to be disregarded; but that the terminus of a road, the first sod of which has not yet been turned and to the completion of which not one cent has been subscribed, *shall* be located in the city of San Francisco!!!![107]

The defeat of San Diego's efforts to acquire the western terminus of the transcontinental railroad marked the climax of a decade-long attempt not only to diversify the economy of San Diego, but to make the town rival if not exceed Los Angeles and San Francisco as the great commercial center of the Pacific.

XI

San Diego's population had fallen from 650 in 1850 to 539 in 1860. Some of this loss, probably, came as a result of the demoralization that set in after the failure to acquire the rail terminus. The general economic downturn by 1860 must also be considered a factor in this loss of population. Further evidence of this condition can be seen in the 1860 census for the township of San Diego which shows that only eleven merchants remained; that only five farmers (as defined by the Census) could be found in San Diego, and only nine Anglo rancheros as compared to 25 Mexican rancheros. Twenty-four people were listed as "professionals," and 66 as skilled laborers (miners, teamsters, seamen, vaqueros) of which 43 were Anglos and 23 Mexicans. Finally, 30 persons fell in the category of unskilled labor (19 Mexicans and 11 Anglos).

These figures reflect the failures that characterized San Diego during the 1850s. The attempts by people like Davis, Morse, and Ames to transform San Diego as quickly as possible from the pastoral economy of the Mexican period to a more urban and commercial one proved to be too limited for such an undertaking. It would be two more decades before this transformation began. Nevertheless, the 1850s are representative of the modernization introduced into California by Anglo-American expansionism.

77

NOTES

1. William E. Smythe, *History of San Diego, 1542-1907* (San Diego, 1907), 96.
2. *Ibid.*, 98-100.
3. Max Miller, *Harbor of the Sun: The Story of the Port of San Diego* (New York, 1940), 133.
4. Ibid., 98-104; also see Lesley Burt Lesley, "The Struggle of San Diego for a Southern Transcontinental Railroad Connection, 1854-1891," (University of California at Berkeley Doctoral Dissertation, 1934), 5.
5. Smythe, San Diego, 105-106.
6. See U. S. Department of Treasury, *Manuscript Census*, 1850, San Diego (photostat copy), 1-19.
7. See *Taxpayers Roll*, San Diego, 1850, San Diego Historical Society Collections, Serra Museum, San Diego.
8. *Ibid.*; also see *Manuscript Census*, San Diego, 1850 and *Nathaniel Lyon MSS.*, Bancroft Library. Lyon was the Army quartermaster at New San Diego.
9. Andrew F. Rolle, "William Heath Davis and the Founding of American San Diego," *California Historical Society Quarterly*, Vol. 31 (1952), 33-34.
10. See Chapt. LXV in William H. Davis, *Seventy-Five Years in California 1831-1906* (San Francisco, 1929), 332-337; and W. H. Davis to Charles W. Lawton, New San Diego, July 10, 1850 and J. W. Raymond to Davis, New San Diego, Oct. 24, 1850, in *W. H. Davis MSS.*, (1840-1891), Cowan Collection, University of California, Los Angeles, Research Library.
11. No evidence exists that a study was made during the 1850s of the water depth of San Diego Bay. See *Senate Executive Documents*, Doc. 79, 33 Cong., 2d Sess. and *Checklist of United States Public Documents* 1789-1909, I (Washington, 1962). John S. Hittell, however, in his 1874 study of California reported the entrance of San Diego harbor as being only 25 feet deep at high water, "and calms off the coast frequently render it difficult for sailing vessels to enter or leave the harbor for days at a time...." See John S. Hittell, *The Resources of California* (San Francisco, 1874), 78. Lesley writes of the New Town location that "This particular spot was considered of great value by the interested parties, due to the fact that, next to La Playa, the channel comes very close to the shore there, making an ideal location for a wharf." See Lesley, "The Struggle of San Diego," 98.
12. Rolle, "Davis," 34-35.
13. Andrew F. Rolle, *An American In California: The Biography of William Heath Davis, 1882-1909* San Marino, California, 1956), 91; and San Diego County Tax Assessor, *Assessment Rolls, 1854-1860* (microfilm), San Diego County Building.
14. Rolle, *An American*, 98 and Thomas O. Johns to Davis, New San Diego, May 25, and 29, June 17, 1851 and George F. Hooper to Davis, August 6, 1851, in *Letters: San Diego Pioneers, 1850-1855*, California Room, San Diego Public Library. Hereinafter cited as *Letters*.
15. See "W. H. Davis Complainant (1881)," 2, California Historical Society, San Francisco; Rolle, "Davis," 35. Thomas R. Darnall in a letter to his brother in 1855 noted that the wharf cost $70,000. See Darnall to James Darnall, San Diego, Oct. 18, 1855 in *Thomas R. Darnall MSS.*, California Historical Society, San Francisco.
16. Charles H. Hill to Davis, San Francisco, Aug. 29, 1850, *Letters*.
17. Johns to Davis, San Diego, March 31, 1850, *Letters*.
18. G. H. Derby, Lt. Top. Engineers, to Col. J. J. Albert, Chief Top. Engineers, San Diego, Jan. 11, 1853, *G. H. Derby MSS.* (1849-1860), Bancroft Library.
19. Rolle, "Davis," 35. Gray, according to Rolle, advised Davis to add an additional structure to the wharf: "Davis, attach to your wharf—where it passes over the sand spit—a bathing house for ladies and gentlemen . . . this would be a great attraction and profitable also." See Rolle, *An American*, 96.
20. Rolle, "Davis," 37-38. No postal records concerning San Diego during this period are available. See *Preliminary Inventories No. 168: Records of the Post Office Department*, Federal Records Center, Los Angeles.
21. John G. Brown to Thomas Corwin, Sec. of Treasury, Wash., D. C., Feb. 10, 1852, *Davis MSS.*, UCLA. Brown served as an agent for Davis. Also see George F. Hooper to Davis, New San Diego, Oct. 8, 1852 in *Ibid*.
22. Rolle, "Davis," 38.
23. Other agents for Davis at New Town were George F. Hooper and William P. Toler, see *Letters*. Frank Ames to Davis, New San Diego, May 18, 1850, *Letters*. Ames and Pendleton to Davis, New San Diego, Nov. 22, 1852, *Letters*. Pendleton to Davis, New San Diego, April 19, June 9 and September 27, 1853, *Letters*. According to Pendleton, this was not the first time a ship had crashed into the wharf. Also see Rolle, "Davis," 41-42. Rolle states that further damage to the wharf occurred when two other steamers crashed into it. Rolle, *An American*, 101.
24. Hooper to Davis, New San Diego, Jan. 22, 1852, *Davis MSS.*, UCLA. "Tax Form of List of Property—Real and Personal of W. H. Davis, Subject to Taxation in the County of San Diego, State of California," in *W. H. Davis MSS.*, San Diego Historical Society Collections.
25. Rolle, *An American*, 93.
26. Rolle, *An American*, 97, 100.
27. *Ibid.*
28. Smythe, San Diego, 256-257.

29. City of San Diego, *Minutes of the Common Council of the City of San Diego, 1850-1868*, July 30, 1850, 36. Hereinafter, cited as *Minutes*.
30. *Ibid.*, Aug. 17, 1850, 55, Sept. 15, 1851, 176-179.
31. *Ibid.*, Nov. 8, 1850, 101, Nov. 19, 1853, 253; also see Jan. 6, 1853, 237-241; Feb. 1, 1854, 258-262; and Dec. 23, 1856, 297-299.
32. See the *San Diego Herald* from 1851 to 1860. Hereinafter, cited as *Herald*, especially March 13, 1852; Dec. 2, 1854, 2; June 2, 1855, 3; and June 19, 1855, 2.
33. See W. C. Ferrell to William L. Hodge, Acting Sec. of Treasury, San Diego, June 16, 1851, in *Letters Received by the Secretary of Treasury from Collectors of Customs 1833-1869* (M-174), Federal Records Center, San Francisco. Hereinafter cited as *Customs*.
34. See Thomas R. Darnall to James Darnall, San Diego, Oct. 18, 1855 in *Darnall MSS.*, California Historical Society.
35. *Herald*, May 29, 1851, 3.
36. *Ibid.*, June 28, 1852, 3.
37. *Ibid.*, June 5, 1851, 2. July 10, 1851, 3. Jan. 17, 1852, 3; May 15, 1852, 3. Aug. 7, 1852, 1. Aug. 26, 1854, 2.
38. *Ibid.*, July 31, 1851, 2.
39. *Eighth Census of the United States, 1860, Manufactures* (Washington, D.C.: Government Printing Office, 1865), 23-26.
40. See "Departures of American Vessels for American Ports from the District of Monterey, Cal., Port of Monterey during Quarter ending March 31, 1851" in *Customs*. Carl H. Heilbron, *A History of San Diego County* (San Diego, 1936), 80.
41. *Herald*, Sept. 4, 1851, 2. Oct. 22, 1851, 2. April 17, 1852, 2.
42. See Customs and *Letters Sent by the Secretary of the Treasury to Collectors of Customs at all Ports (1789-1847) and at Small Ports (1847-1878)* (M-175), Federal Records Center, San Francisco.
43. Mrs. Edwin T. Coman, "Customs House Survey," (San Diego [n.d.], unpublished manuscript and William Meredith, Secretary of Treasury, to James Collier, Collector of Customs for port of San Francisco, Washington, April 3, 1849 in manuscript entitled "Customs—U.S. Service Custom House 111.1," San Diego Historical Society Collections.
44. W. C. Ferrell to William R. Hodge, Acting Sec. of Treasury, San Diego, May 30, 1851, *Customs*.
45. This estimate, of course, was $20,000 below Davis!
46. John G. Brown to Thomas Carwin, Sec. of Treasury, Wash., Feb. 10, 1852, *Davis MSS.*, UCLA. Thomas Carwin to Ferrell, Wash., Feb. 20, 1852, *Ibid.* Ferrell to Carwin, San Diego, June 10, 1852, *Customs*.
47. San Diego, Oct. 30, 1852, *Ibid.*; also, see O. S. Witherby, collector, to James Guthrie, Sec. of Treasury, San Diego, Oct. 3, 1853, *Ibid.* David Michael Goodman, *A Western Panorama*, 1849-1875 (Glendale, Calif., 1966), 29.
48. *Herald*, March 11, 1854, 2; March 25, 1854, 2; April 15, 1854, 2; May 12, 1855, 2. *Eighth Census of the United States, 1860, Agriculture* (Washington, D. C.: Government Printing Office, 1864), 10-13.
49. *Eighth Census, Agriculture*, 10-13. *Ibid.*, *Seventh Census of the United States, 1850, and An Appendix*, "Population and Industry of California By the State Census for the Year, 1852" (Washington, D.C.: Robert Armstrong, public printer, 1853), 982-985.
50. *Herald*, May 31, 1856, 2.
51. *Herald*, Dec. 17, 1853, 2.
52. *Ibid.*, July 31, 1851, 2.
53. *Ibid.*, Sept. 17, 1853, 2, and Aug. 13, 1853, 2.
54. Elene C. Kendall, "Southern Vineyards: The Economic Significance of the Wine Industry in the Development of Los Angeles, 1831-1870," *Historical Society of Southern California Quarterly*, Vol. 37 (1959), 32-33; also see Vincent P. Carosso, *The California Wine Industry: A Study of the Formative Years, 1830-1895* (Berkeley, 1951); and Iris Ann Wilson, "Early Southern California Vine Culture, 1830-1865," *Historical Society of Southern California Quarterly*, Vol. 39 (1957), 242-250.
55. *Herald*, Aug. 13, 1853, 3.
56. *Ibid.*, Jan. 13, 1855, 2.
57. *Herald*, April 8, 1854, 2.
58. *Eighth Census, Agriculture*, 10-13.
59. Gerald D. Nash, *State Government and Economic Development* (Berkeley, 1964), 63, 69 and 124.
60. *Herald*, July 17, 1851, 2; Aug. 21, 1851, 3; Oct. 2, 1851, 2. also see William L. Taler to Davis, New San Diego, Aug. 14, 1851, *Letters*.
61. *Herald*, Dec. 4, 1852, 2.
62. *Ibid.*, May 15, 1852, 2.
63. Samuel P. Heintzelman, Quartermaster, to Thomas L. Jessup, San Diego, May 1, 1849 in *U.S. Quartermaster Dept. Correspondence, 1848-1857*. MSS. Bancroft Library. Davis to John Panott, New San Diego, June 17, 1850, *Davis MSS*, UCLA.
64. *Herald*, April 4, 1857, 2.
65. See U. S. Department of Treasury, *Manuscript Census*, 1860, Vol. V, San Diego (microfilm), Roll 64, 1-20.

66. A. B. Pendleton to Davis, San Diego, April 10, 1855, *Letters. Herald,* May 16, 1857, 2; July 25, 1857, 2; Sept. 19, 1857, 2.
67. *Herald,* July 25, 1857, 2; Aug. 1, 1857, 2; Aug. 22, 1857, 2; Sept. 12, 1857, 2; Dec. 5, 1857, 2. Rose already had spent a small fortune in unsuccessfully prospecting and working copper and silver mines in San Diego County. See also Thomas R. Darnall, "San Diego in 1855 and 1856," *Historical Society of Southern California Quarterly,* Vol. 116 (1934), 64; Darnall to his father and mother, San Diego, Sept. 13, 1857, *Darnall MSS.* E W. Morse, *Correspondence, Merchandise File (1857-1879)* San Diego Historical Society Collections.
68. *Herald,* Oct. 24, 1857, 2.
69. *Ibid.,* Sept. 12, 1857, 2.
70. *Ibid.,* Jan. 2, 1858, 2.
71. E. W. Morse, listing of Oct. 8, 1857 in *Day Book (1857-1858),* 1; also Oct. 20, 1857, 17; Nov. 9, 1857, 42; and Dec. 28, 1857, 104; See "Jesus Maria Mines Letters" in Morse, *Correspondence.* The dates for this correspondence are difficult to determine since no dates appear on some of them; however, those that do have dates are all for 1857, and presumably the undated ones are, also, for this year. All in San Diego Historical Society Collections.
72. Morse to Jesus Maria Mine, San Diego, Nov. 6, 1857 (?) Sept. 25 and Oct. 7, 1857(?) in *Ibid.* These dates appear, but it is not certain they are correct letter dates.
73. Samuel F. Black, *San Diego County, California: A Record of Settlement, Organization, Progress and Achievement* (Chicago, 1913), I, 113-114. *Herald,* Aug. 21, 1851, 3; and Dec. 4, 1852, 2.
74. *Herald,* Nov. 12, 1853, 2; Nov. 19, 1853, 3.
75. *Black, San Diego,* 116. For a brief description of whale hunting along the California Coast see Part III, Chap. 5 in Charles M. Scammon, *The Marine Mammals of the North-Western Coast of North America* (San Francisco, 1874), 247-251.
76. *Herald,* Aug. 18, 1855, 2.
77. *Ibid.,* Oct. 20, 1855, 2.
78. Heilbron, *San Diego,* 9.
79. *Seventh Census,* San Diego, 1850; *Eighth Census, Agriculture,* 10-13.
80. *Manuscript Census,* San Diego, 1860, 1-20.
81. Leonard Pitt, *The Decline of the Californios* (Berkeley, 1966), 108.
82. Paul W. Gates, "California's Embattled Settlers," *California Historical Society Quarterly,* Vol. XLI (June, 1962), 101.
83. Paul W. Gates, "Adjudication of Spanish-Mexican Land Claims in California," *The Huntington Library Quarterly,* Vol. XXI (May, 1958), 213.
84. Pitt, *Californios,* 86-106.
85. Robert Class Cleland, *The Cattle on a Thousand Hills* (San Marino, Calif., 1951), 38-42.
86. *Manuscript Census,* San Diego, 1860, 1-20.
87. *Southern Californian,* April 11, 1855.
88. *Manuscript Census,* San Diego, 1860, 1-22.
89. Cleland, *Thousand Hills,* 50.
90. *Herald,* March 19, 1852, 2.
91. *Ibid.,* April 1, 1854, 2.
92. Pendleton to Davis, New San Diego, March 20, 1854, *Davis MSS.,* UCLA.
93. *Herald,* April 8, 1854, 2.
94. *Ibid.,* April 22, 1854, 2.
95. *Ibid.,* May 12, 1855, 2.
96. See Lesley, "The Struggle of San Diego," and Lesley, "San Diego and the Struggle for a Southern Transcontinental Railroad Terminus" in *Greater America: Essays in Honor of Herbert Eugene Bolton* (Berkeley, 1945), 499-518.
97. *Herald,* Feb. 7, 1852, 2.
98. *Ibid.,* May 21, 1853, 1.
99. See Robert R. Russel, *Improvement of Communication with the Pacific Coast as an Issue in American Politics, 1783-1864* (Cedar Rapids, 1948), 14.
100. *Herald,* May 21, 1853, 1.
101. See San Diego & Gila Southern Pacific and Atlantic Railroad Company, *Subscription Blank and Stock Journal,* 1, San Diego Historical Society Collections.
102. See the "Treasurer's Report of the San Diego and Gila Southern Pacific and Atlantic Railroad Co.," (1854), 3-6 in Serra Museum.
103. *Herald,* Nov.18, 1854, 2.
104. *Minutes,* Sept. 11, 1855, 286; Oct. 30, 1855, 289. Smythe, *San Diego,* 353.
105. Darnall, "San Diego," 61.
106. *Herald,* April 16, 1859, 5.
107. *Herald,* Oct. 8, 1859, 2.

Charles Hughes, a native San Diegan, received his B.A. degree in History from San Diego State University in 1971, and his Master's degree in History from the same institution in 1974. For the past three years he has been doing research on the Californios in San Diego during the period between the Mexican War and the United States Civil War. An article entitled "A Military View of San Diego in 1847: Four Letters from Colonel Jonathan D. Stevenson to Governor Richard B. Mason," edited by Mr. Hughes was published in this *Journal* in Vol. XX, No. 3, Summer, 1974. His article published here is an edited version of his Master's thesis at San Diego State University. Illustrations are from the Historical Collections, Title Insurance and Trust Company, San Diego, and the San Diego Historical Society.

The Decline of the

CALIFORNIOS:

The Case of San Diego, 1846-1856

By
Charles Hughes

INTRODUCTION

In his widely read *Decline of the Californios*, historian Leonard Pitt sought to explain the rapid political and economic demise of the Spanish-speaking families who occupied and controlled California before the United States take-over in 1846. Pitt says the political demise of the Californios took longer in southern California compared with the rest of the state. Following statehood in 1849, Californios ran successfully for public offices in Santa Barbara and Los Angeles. Along with their political successes, Pitt argues that these Californios also reaped windfall profits from cattle sales during the early 1850s. They hastened their own economic demise, however, by profligating these profits, and by the 1860s their ranchos were either heavily mortgaged or in the hands of Anglo-Americans.

This case study suggests that San Diego does not fit the pattern for southern California as described by Pitt. Californios in San Diego had very little "declining" left to do by 1846. Far from enjoying an "Arcadian" era, the Californios were beleaguered and penniless landholders at the time of American occupation. The San Diego rancheros did not "decline." Their economic status was already nil in the Mexican period, and circumstances largely beyond their control prevented them from prospering in the 1850s, as Pitt says other rancheros did in the Los Angeles and Santa Barbara areas. Political affairs in San Diego reveals that Anglo-Americans controlled the city government much earlier than local historians have supposed, or that Pitt suggests was the pattern for southern California.

This study is based on contemporary newspapers and public documents. Few of the personal papers of the Californios in San Diego have been preserved. The memoirs and writings of Anglo-American residents of the community were used circumspectly, because their observations and recollections were strongly influenced by their racial and ethnic biases toward the Californios. Most of the research was done in San Diego and Sacramento, and only the first ten years following the American conquest is considered. Pitt has labeled the years 1850 to 1856 as the formative years of state government. Since the policies of the new state government caused the Californios many hardships, it is appropriate to study the community from the end of the American conquest through the formative years of state government.

Lack of sources prevented a systematic study of justice for the Californios under the new Anglo system. Government officials and local librarians believe that local court records from this period have been destroyed or lost. Available evidence, however, suggests that Pitt's arguments concerning a dual standard of justice, one for Anglos and one for Californios, seem applicable to San Diego during this era.

The terms "Anglo-American" (sometimes shortened to Anglo) and "Californio" are used to differentiate between two general groups. It is occasionally necessary to consider a Californio as any non-Indian with a Spanish surname, and born in California, Spain, or Latin America. Strictly speaking, however, Californios were those Mexicans who inhabited California prior to the American conquest, and the term also refers to their descendants. Anyone who had other than a Spanish surname and was Caucasian is considered to be Anglo-American for purposes of this study. These broad criteria are applied because of the difficulty in determining which individuals were citizens of the United States. Citizenship was automatically confirmed on the former citizens of Mexico who remained in California one year after the signing of the Treaty of Guadalupe-Hidalgo. Both the national census of 1850 and the California State Census of 1852 fail to indicate clearly whether a person was a citizen of the United States. The high degree of social mobility among early residents of San Diego constantly changed the makeup of both the Anglo and Californio communities. It is impractical to research more than seven hundred people to establish their citizenship and thus their status within San Diego. This study concentrates on those Californios who owned land grants, the same group whose decline Pitt studied.

Not included in this study are local Indians, who numbered several hundred more than both Anglos and Californios. During these years, Indians were confronted with a different set of problems from those which faced the Californios. Indians had to contend with hostilities from both Anglos and Californios. The new Anglo government extended in writing certain rights to the Californios which it denied to Indians. Rights guaranteed by the United States Constitution did not apply to Indians. They could not vote or own property. This study deals only with the two groups included in the new system of government, Anglos and Californios.

CALIFORNIOS AS "ARCADIANS," 1821-1846

Following the War of 1846, and up until the Civil War, Californios, or Spanish-speaking inhabitants of California, experienced a decline in economic status, political power, and social influence. With the coming of Americans, especially after the discovery of gold, Californios lost their dominance over the affairs of the state and the vast tracts of land they originally possessed. In part, this decline resulted from events occurring prior to American rule, during California's "Pastoral Era." This was especially true in San Diego. The secularization of the missions, Indian hostilities, and civil strife had all impaired the ability of the Californios to adjust to the changes initiated by the American government.

In describing the "Pastoral Era," most historians have emphasized the affluence of the Californios. Between 1826 and 1846, the Californios received approval for several hundred land grants from the Mexican government. After the secularization of the missions in 1833, these land grants included former mission lands. The Californios also acquired the large cattle herds that once belonged to the missions. These herds allowed the Californios to carry on a lucrative business with trading ships visiting the coast. In exchange for hides and tallow, Californios received manufactured goods and other luxury items. Along with the former mission lands and herds, Californios also inherited the labor force of the missions. After 1833 Christian Indians were relegated to positions of servitude by the Californios.

Because of these circumstances, one historian has argued that the Californios enjoyed a life similar to that of southern plantation owners in the antebellum South or feudal lords in the Middle Ages.[1] Although most historians find this description a bit exaggerated, they have accepted the arguments of Robert Glass Cleland, a prominent California historian. Cleland stated that "free from the pressure of economic competition, ignorant of the wretchedness and poverty indigenous to other lands, amply supplied with the means of satisfying their simple wants, devoted to 'the grand and primary business of the enjoyment of life,' the Californios enjoyed a pastoral, patriarchal, almost Arcadian existence...."[2]

Contrary to what Cleland and other historians believed, Californios in San Diego never experienced an Arcadian existence. In their studies, Cleland and others neglected to analyze the disruptive influence that the secularization of the missions had on San Diego's economy. They also failed to recognize the effect that the ouster of the Franciscans had on Indian and white relations.[3]

In 1830 San Diego consisted of about thirty houses located some three miles inland from the harbor, below the hill where the presidio was situated. The community's 520 residents were mostly retired soldiers and their families. Those living in town cultivated small gardens and grazed their cattle on communal lands. Before 1833 only seven land grants had been approved in the area. In 1823 Francisco Ruiz received Rancho Santa María de Peñasquitos and in 1829 José Antonio Estudillo was given ranchos Janal and Otay. In the latter year Santiago Argüello was also granted Rancho Tijuana, and four years later Rancho Melyo. In 1831 Pío Pico accepted a grant for the Jamul Rancho and the Silva family received Rancho San Dieguito.[4]

Under Spanish law, and under the Mexican constitutions after 1821, all land in California belonged to the state. A person could receive usufructuary rights to as much as 48,818 acres, if he met certain requirements. Franciscan missionaries, however, vigorously opposed the granting of land to settlers, arguing that it belonged to the Indians. Until 1833 the missionaries continued to control the best farming and grazing land in San Diego, as they did throughout the rest of coastal California.[5]

The missions in San Diego dated back to the arrival of the first Mexican colonists in Alta California. In 1769, Franciscan missionaries, accompanied by soldiers, came to San Diego with plans to settle in the territory and Christianize the Indians. Spanish officials had grown increasingly alarmed over Russian encroachment into Spanish territory. By using Franciscans and soldiers, these officials hoped to utilize the Indians to maintain control of their territory. The Franciscans had learned from previous experiences, however, that Indians required close supervi-

Rancho de la Cañada de los Coches,
showing the house, out-buildings, and some of its 28.39 acres. (1886)

sion to insure lasting Spanish influence.[6]

To solve this problem, the Franciscans created mission establishments that could support several hundred people. They built two missions in the San Diego Area, Mission San Diego de Alcalá in 1769 and Mission San Luis Rey de Francia in 1798. At these missions, Franciscans constructed blacksmith shops, tanneries, weaving rooms, and storerooms along with the churches. They planted crops, started vineyards, cultivated vegetable gardens, and raised livestock. Eventually both missions managed to provide for a large population. However, when the rainfall was slight and the crop yield minimal, the missionaries were forced to allow the Christian Indians to return to their villages to fend for themselves.[7]

In time the Franciscans acquired considerable wealth and land. Mission San Diego controlled land in the areas of El Cajon, Escondido, Santa Isabel, San Dieguito, and Rosarita Beach. The area south of San Diego was used by the presidio to graze government livestock. The lands belonging to Mission San Luis Rey stretched thirty-five miles from north to south and forty-five miles from east to west of the mission site. By 1800 the crop yield at Mission San Diego was from 2,500 to 10,000 bushels, and the livestock increased to more than 12,000. San Luis Rey Mission owned more than 16,000 animals and the crop yield exceeded 67,000 bushels in 1810.[8]

Despite these and other successes, the California missions came under increasing criticism after 1810. In theory, missionaries moved into a frontier region to convert and civilize the Indians. After being in an area for ten years, Hispanizing the Indians, missionaries were supposed to move on to a new region. The missions that were built, would be secularized—that is, a regular priest would take over the spiritual functions of the missionaries. The lands connected with the missions would be divided among the Indians, who would then farm on their own.[9]

In California this process was delayed. Franciscans argued that the Indians were not ready for secularization, even after forty years. The Franciscans believed that their wards, once freed, would return to their "pagan" ways. Franciscans also claimed that some Californios wanted the missions secularized to gain possession of the lands and to make slaves of the Indians. Both the Franciscans and the Californios who coveted Indian lands, charged one another with enslaving Indians. There is probably some truth to the allegations of each group.[10]

Throughout California, at this time, a strong anti-Spanish feeling existed among the Californios, creating attitudes which surely influenced the arguments of both groups. The Franciscans were probably correct when they stated that some Californios supported secularization to gain access to mission property.[11] Many Californios had lived in the territory for years, and had served in the military protecting the Franciscans and the missions. They had suffered hardships, and because of their service they probably expected some favors from their government. Up to the 1830s most of the Californios continued to live in coastal towns, on small lots granted to them; the missionaries monopolized most of the land and wealth of the province.

Critics, among them some Californios, were skeptical about the arguments of the Franciscans and doubted the efficacy of the mission system. Their thinking was influenced by the new philosophy of liberalism and its emphasis on humanitarianism and equal rights. These critics argued that Indians were equal to other Mexicans and entitled to equal rights. They opposed the absolute authority Franciscans had over the Indians and advocated the secularization of the missions. They proposed that Indians be granted the same rights as other citizens and suggested that they also be given land. Because of the profits and benefits accrued from their land, Indians would integrate into society. Critics also believed that Indians would eventually upgrade themselves and achieve social as well as political equality.[12]

After 1824 leaders of the new republican government in Mexico generally concurred with these liberal ideas, especially since many of them had some Indian ancestry. Their attitude, however, was also swayed by considerations of state. These new leaders were dissatisfied with the progress of the Franciscans in "civilizing" California Indians. This seemed particularly important to them since they feared Russian and American designs on the territory. In 1812 the Russians built Fort Ross at Bodega Bay in northern California to help supply food for their colony farther north. Mexican officials had heard rumors concerning a secret treaty in which Spain was to have ceded California to Russia. Officials realized that if Mexico wanted to retain California, she would have to occupy it effectively.[13]

Officials further recognized the necessity of making California independent of the national government and its exhausted treasury. Following the outbreak of the war for independence in 1810, the Spanish government stopped sending an annual stipend to the soldiers and missionaries in California. With the ouster of Spanish officials from Mexico in 1812, the new government failed to provide continuous support. Thus, soldiers in the territory forced the missionaries to provide them with supplies, and Franciscans were allowed to sell cowhides and tallow to trading ships stopping on the California coast.[14]

To remedy these unfavorable economic conditions, Mexican officials planned further colonization of the territory. As early as 1825 they started the practice of sending convicts to help populate the territory, over the protest of those already living there. To attract potential colonists, officials had to offer land, and the missions controlled most of the farming and grazing land along the coast. In the interior, non-Christian Indians hindered further colonization by Mexican farmers. Secularization of the missions, then, provided the only immediate way to make land available for further colonization.[15]

When the newly appointed Mexican governor, Lieutenant Colonel José María Echeandía, reached California in 1826, he brought orders to secularize the missions. He had been advised, however, to proceed with caution. Accordingly, he devised a plan to partially secularize the missions in the south to see how the Indians got along without Franciscan supervision. He proposed to grant land to those Indians who had been Christians for fifteen years, married, and no longer considered minors. These Indians also had to have a trade or a way to support themselves, and needed a favorable report from a Franciscan. Despite these stringent qualifications, the plan failed. The Indians who left the missions lost their property and ended up working for Mexican settlers, or were taken back by the Franciscans within a few years. Again, in 1833, another Mexican governor, José Figueroa, formulated plans for partial secularization of the California missions, but the national government's actions superseded his plans.[16]

In August 1833 the Mexican congress, cognizant of the complex problems involved, nevertheless approved legislation secularizing the California missions. The congress, however, failed to specify how this was to be done. Among other things, it neglected to establish regulations concerning the distribution of mission lands. Territorial officials did not know who was to have first priority, Indians, Californios, soldiers, or new settlers. The territorial assembly, consisting of Californios, and with the approval of the new government, finally devised a plan for secularizing the missions in June 1834. The missionaries were to be relieved of their temporal duties, but would remain at the missions until regular clergy were found to take over their spiritual functions. Civilian administrators were appointed to take over the economic affairs of the missions. They were required to take inventories of the property belonging to the missions. They were also to oversee the granting of land and other mission property to Christian Indians. The land remaining, after the Indians had received their allotments, was to be distributed among non-Indians. This plan was implemented tentatively until final approval came from the national government.[17]

In San Diego Mission San Luis Rey was secularized in 1834 and Mission San Diego the following year. With more land available for settlers, the national government expected the area to prosper. Within the next few years, new land grants were approved by government officials. Among them were Rancho Jolijol to José and Ignacio López, Rancho Jesús to M. J. López, and Rancho Temescal to Leandro Serrano; all granted in 1836. Secularization and the release of Christian Indians from the missions, however, brought disastrous consequences for the Californios in San Diego.[18]

After 1830 when secularization of the missions seemed assured, Indian hostilities increased throughout the San Diego area. In 1833 rumors spread that Christian as well as non-Christian Indians planned to unite and seize mission property. In the following year community officials reported numerous robberies committed by Indians. During 1835 citizens organized an expedition to put down a threatened Indian attack on Santa Isabel and San Luis Rey. That same year, authorities at San Luis Rey thwarted an Indian project to kidnap the governor when one of the planners revealed his intent. Throughout 1836 and 1837 Indian attacks reached new heights and forced the evacuation of ranchos, several times threatening San Diego itself. One of the more famous attacks occurred at the Jamul Rancho in April 1837. Indians killed several ranch hands and the foreman, and captured the foreman's two daughters. Californios' efforts to rescue the girls from their Indian captors failed. Shortly after the Jamul incident an Indian servant revealed a plan to attack San Diego and kill its residents. On the designated night, servants were to leave doors open to allow attackers to enter the houses and kill their occupants. After this project was uncovered, the residents apprehended its leaders and executed them.[19]

Indian violence continued through 1840 threatening the community and forcing the Californios to abandon their ranchos again and again. On several occasions Juan Bandini fled his rancho near Tijuana to seek safety in San Diego, and Silvestre de la Portilla and José Antonio Pico abandoned their grants, Rancho Valle de San José and Rancho San José del Valle, because of Indian pressure. Bandini eventually gave up his rancho near Tijuana and received a grant farther north.[20]

After 1842 and until the American conquest Indian hostilities subsided, never again reaching the intensity they did in the late 1830s. During these last few years before the conquest San Diego enjoyed some prosperity, and many new land grants were approved. Prior to 1842 twenty land grants were affirmed, and from 1842 until 1846 twenty-five more grants were issued. Some of these grants were the larger and more famous ones in the area. In 1845 Pío Pico, governor of California, gave the El Cajon Rancho, 48,799 acres, to María Antonia Estudillo de Pedrorena and the Cuyamaca Rancho, 35,501 acres, to Augustín Olvera. Pico also approved a grant for Rancho de la Nación, 26,631 acres, to his brother-in-law, Juan Forster. Despite these developments, Californios continued to worry about the threat of Indian violence in the San Diego area, and with some justification. During the American conquest, in December 1846, Indians surprised eleven Californios at a rancho, took them prisoners, and later killed all of them. The threat of Indian violence continued to concern San Diegans after the Mexican War.[21]

The outbreak of Indian attacks occurred for a variety of reasons during the 1830s. In the San Diego area, the non-Christian Indian population exceeded the white and Christian Indian population by several hundred. Although no exact figure is known for this period, non-Christian Indian population in 1847 numbered several hundred more than the other two groups. Prior to this time, the white population never exceeded six hundred, and declined drastically after the outbreak of attacks. The numerical superiority of the Indians must have influenced Californios' treatment of them. Franciscans reported that Indians received harsh punishments for minor infractions of the law. Evidently Californios tried to use the threat of severe punishment to teach the Indians to respect territorial laws. This kind of treatment must have created bitterness between the Californios and the Indians, which caused some of the violence. [22]

With the secularization of the missions, many of the Christian Indians joined other Indians in attacking the Californios. Christian Indians believed that the property of the missions belonged to them, and resented the Californios receiving any of it. They planned to kidnap Governor Figueroa to protest the approval of a land grant, which included land the Indians said belonged to them. Franciscans might have influenced this attitude of the Indians, since the missionaries used it in arguing against the breakup of the missions. [23]

Secularization also caused a significant decrease in military personnel in the San Diego area. The missions had been the main source of food and other supplies for the soldiers. Since neither the national nor the territorial government could afford to pay them, many soldiers left the army to avoid starvation. After their departure, the military force that remained failed to discourage Indian aggressions. Finally, Christian Indians cultivated crops to furnish their food supply, but in years of little rainfall they turned to taking cattle from the ranchos to avert starvation. Although rainfall amounts are not known for these years, this could have been an additional source of conflict. For example, in 1834 statistical reports for Mission San Diego and Mission San Luis Rey showed the lowest yield in crop production in recent years, while local authorities reported numerous robberies by Indians. [24]

The prevalence of Indian resistance during this period resulted in severe political and economic consequences for the Californios in San Diego. In the beginning of the 1830s, an estimated 520 non-Indians lived throughout the area. Up to this time, San Diego was a military town, with the presidio commander supervising community affairs. In 1834 residents petitioned the governor for self-rule, arguing that they possessed the population required by law, and that military rule violated the spirit of the Mexican constitution. Officials approved the petition, **and in** 1835 citizens in San Diego held elections to choose electors that would select a mayor, two councilmen, and a city attorney. Self-rule continued until 1837 when the mayor received a notice rescinding the city charter and making San Diego part of the Los Angeles district. In part, self-rule was withdrawn because of the ascendancy of centralism in Mexico, but more specifically because of the decline in population caused by the Indians. By 1840 only an estimated 150 people lived in San Diego. By 1846 the population had increased to 350, but prior to the Mexican War the city was far from its former population of 520. After the American conquest, this decline in population weakened the Californios' political strength significantly. [25]

The Indian attacks on San Diego in the 1830s also impeded economic development in a community already experiencing straitened circumstances. The descriptions of contemporary travelers visiting San Diego before the outbreak of hostilities emphasized the backwardness of the area. French traveler Auguste Bernard du Haut-Cilly wrote in 1827:

> Of all the places we have visited since our coming to California, excepting San Pedro, which is entirely deserted, the presidio at San Diego was the saddest. It is built upon the slope of a barren hill, and has no regular form: it is a collection of houses whose appearance is made still more gloomy by the dark color of the bricks, roughly made, of which they are built. [26]

Two years later, New Englander Alfred Robinson made a similar comparison when he wrote that "on the lawn beneath the hill on which the presidio is built stood about thirty houses of rude appearance, mostly occupied by retired veterans, not so well constructed in respect either to beauty or stability as the houses at Monterey...." [27] If we assume that the way people lived reflected their economic well-being, Californios in San Diego apparently were not as prosperous as the rest of their countrymen in the 1820s. Then, in the 1830s their circumstances were further reduced when secularization of the missions and the subsequent outbreak of Indian hostilities forced the San Diegans to abandon their ranchos and disrupted agriculture.

Historian Hubert Howe Bancroft has evaluated the impact of these attacks on the

Californios in the 1830s and after. He wrote that Indian depredations

> ...kept the country in a state of chronic disquietude in these and later years, being the most serious obstacle to progress and prosperity. Murders of the gente de razon [Californios] were of comparatively rare occurrence, but in other respects the scourge was similar to that of the Apache ravages in Sonora and Chihuaha. Over a large extent of country the Indians lived mainly on the flesh of stolen horses, and cattle were killed for their hides when money to buy liquor could not be less laboriously obtained by the sale of other stolen articles. The presence of the neophytes and their intimate relations with other inhabitants doubtless tended to prevent general attacks and bloody massacres, as any plot was sure to be revealed by somebody; but they also rendered it wellnigh impossible to break up the complicated and destructive system of robbery. Far be it from me to blame the Indians for their conduct; for there was little in their past training or present treatment by white men to encourage honest industry. [28]

Despite the prevalence of Indian hostilities and the abandonment of many ranchos, the hide and tallow trade seems not to have been significantly affected. Records left behind by American and English traders are, for the most part, silent about the break down in law and order. It appears that although the Californios had to leave their ranchos, they still managed to slaughter their cattle and sell the hides for manufactured goods. Conceivably, this trade might have sustained the Californios when they were unable to produce the food they needed. Juan Bandini, at one point, had to go north to sell his family jewels to provide for his family. Later, he had to write a friend in northern California to ask him to send food, so his family would not starve. [29] This seems to have been a common situation for other residents in the community. Alfred Robinson revisited San Diego in 1840 and observed that "everything was prostrated—the Presidio ruined, the Mission depopulated, the town almost deserted, and its few inhabitants miserably poor." [30] Under such circumstances, the Californios must have used the cattle they owned to provide for their families. The disruption of agriculture and the heavy reliance on the hide and tallow trade also explain the decline in the size of the cattle herds. When the missions were secularized, the herds exceeded 25,000, but by the beginning of the 1850s San Diego had less than 10,000. This meant that the Californios had fewer resources to meet the new demands placed on their ranchos after the Americans arrived. [31]

All of San Diego's economic woes, however, were not caused by the secularization of the missions and subsequent Indian hostilities. Some historians have emphasized the influence of civil strife in contributing to the economic problems of the territory. Others have argued that political upheaval in California during the 1830s and 1840s resulted in the disruption and decline of agriculture and trade throughout the territory. The main cause for confusion, and one which led to open revolt several times, was the failure of the national government to effectively govern its territories. After Mexico gained independence from Spain, the republic's new Constitution of 1824 failed to provide for the internal administration of the territories. Because of this failure, Mexican and territorial officials continued to use Spanish laws not in apparent conflict with the constitution to govern the territories. The resulting confusion concerning the laws of the territory created many political disputes. [32] Sectional rivalries, a struggle over the location of the capital and the custom house, and personal jealousies all added to the political divisions of the period. The controversy over a strong or a weak central government also increased the political divisions. [33] In San Diego in 1836 the decline of agriculture and trade, secularization, Indian hostilities, and the lack of local courts provoked the Californios to rebel against the territorial government. [34]

Evaluating the impact of two decades of political turmoil in California before the Mexican War, historians have agreed that it added to the declining fortunes of Californios. Historian George Tays wrote that armed conflict in California "caused the decline of commerce, the spoliation of the missions, and finally plunged the country into chaos." [35] In San Diego, these revolts had two specific consequences for the Californios. Northern Californios won control of the territorial government and sought to regulate trade for the benefit of the North. Hence, San Diego failed to become a legal port of entry for foreign trade. Ships involved in this trade had to go to Monterey and pay the import duties due on their goods there before doing business along the coast. A share in the revenue from import duties could have improved San Diego's commercial fortunes. More significant than the commercial impact, however, was the failure of the territorial government to aid San Diego with its Indian problem. Governors were more concerned with maintaining a sufficient military force in Monterey to insure their positions, rather than sending assistance to the South. With the American conquest in 1846 this proved to be a crucial matter.[36]

When the United States declared war with Mexico on May 12, 1846, American naval forces off the Pacific coast used the occasion to take possession of California. The initial occupation of San Diego and southern California occurred without any armed resistance by the Californios. On July 29 United States forces occupied San Diego, and on August 13 they seized control of Los Angeles. By the first part of October, however, some Californios forced the Americans to abandon Los Angeles and then, under the leadership of José Castro and Pío Pico, laid siege to American occupied San Diego. During this critical period, Americans enlisted the support of those Californios who opposed the actions of their countrymen. Efforts to maintain control of San Diego and retake Los Angeles included the participation of some Californios. Miguel de Pedrorena, a prominent San Diego resident, made a hazardous trip in an old whaling boat from San Diego to San Pedro, to get military assistance and supplies. In the reconquest of Los Angeles by an expedition under Commodore Robert Stockton, in January 1847, one military company was made up of thirty-one Californios.[37]

The loyalties of the Californios divided over the American conquest, partly because of the policy implemented by the conquering Americans. At first, the Californios appeared reluctant to resist the Americans, despite the urging by some who believed that as loyal Mexican citizens they had a duty to repel the American intruders. But the actions of Commodore Stockton and Lieutenant Archibald Gillespie in Monterey and Los Angeles also created angry resentments among the Californios. In Monterey, Stockton's arbitrary actions toward José Castro led to open resistance. Strict regulations imposed by Gillespie provoked the citizens of Los Angeles to expel the Americans.[38]

While the actions of Americans angered some Californios, others chose to accept the change in governments. Many supported the change because the Americans promised military protection against Indians and a stable government. Juan Bandini and Santiago Argüello issued a statement following the American occupation of San Diego which urged the local citizens to support the change. With protection and stability, they said, prosperity would follow. In accepting American rule, Californios believed California would become a territory of the United States. In the new territorial government, they expected to receive appointments to public office and retain some control over territorial affairs. At the same time, they would receive military protection and become part of an expanding commercial empire.[39]

Like the Indian attacks and the civil disorders, the American conquest resulted in the destruction and loss of property by some Californios. Historian George Tays declared that in reprisal to Californios' resistance, "Americans confiscated and robbed the peaceful population of its horses, cattle and other property."[40] In San Diego, some of the Californios who resisted the American aggressions incurred such losses. Lieutenant W. H. Emory recalled that when the United States military force he was with arrived at the Peñasquitos Rancho, they seized all the property they did not destroy because the owner opposed the Americans.[41]

During the "Pastoral Era" in San Diego, then, Californios experienced frustrations and setbacks while trying to improve their economic condition. Their efforts only began to succeed late in the period. The promise of economic prosperity as a result of secularization of the missions came after additional years of hardships. Although more Californios received land grants, the breakdown in law and order caused a decline in the political and economic fortunes of the community. The Californios had little opportunity to develop the resources of their ranchos. The decline in San Diego's population during Indian hostilities weakened the Californios politically after the arrival of the Americans, since political strength depended on numerical strength. Rather than being like feudal lords on princely estates, with vast herds and large retinues of Indian slaves, Californios in San Diego were impoverished rancheros struggling to survive in a hostile environment.

CALIFORNIOS AS IMPOVERISHED RANCHEROS 1846-1856

Following the outbreak of war between the United States and Mexico, Commodore John

SANTIAGO ARGÜELLO
(1792-1862)

D. Sloat seized Monterey, claiming California for the Americans on July 7, 1846. In a proclamation to the inhabitants of the territory, Sloat urged them to accept the American conquest and guaranteed protection and recognition of their rights and property. He predicted that California and her inhabitants would benefit from this change. Real estate values would increase as the territory became a part of an expanding commercial empire. In San Diego some Californios, such as Santiago Argüello and Miguel de Pedrorena, accepted Sloat's arguments and welcomed the American invaders. They pleaded with others to do likewise, stressing that with stability and protection the area would prosper. However, neither the Californios nor United States officials knew what the future held. No one could have predicted the great changes brought by the gold rush. [42]

By 1850 Californios consisted of less than 15 percent of the state's population. In the North where the gold was, Anglo-Americans supplanted the Californios, taking over the political affairs and seizing ranchos through legal and illegal means. In the South, however, historians have discerned a different pattern of events. [43]

Although the gold rush attracted thousands of immigrants to California, relatively few settled in the South, leaving the Californios and their ranchos unmolested. Rather than facing a threat to their ranchos, Californios in the South experienced a bonanza from the cattle trade. The throngs of immigrants arriving in the territory increased the demand for beef, and cattle prices soared. Before the gold rush Californios had sold cattle hides and tallow for a few dollars. By 1850, however, the price of cattle exceeded fifty dollars a head. Nevertheless, the enormous profits from the cattle trade led to the downfall of the Californios, according to some historians of the era. They have suggested that quick and easy wealth made the Californios extravagant and improvident. [44] Leonard Pitt put the matter squarely:

> More than any other factor, the Californio's spendthrift tendency, encouraged by windfall profits in the early cattle trade, put him in financial hot water and caused him to part with more land than he wished.
> ...Most rancheros simply spent cash prodigiously and mortgaged their future profits at usurious rates, in baseless expectation of a continuing boom in cattle. Recognition of deep economic trouble came in 1855, when out-of-state growers introduced new herds and toppled the established prices, but by then it was often too late for the rancheros to make amends, even if they cared to do so. [45]

Because of San Diego's peculiar circumstances, the boom in cattle prices brought only a few Californios very limited profits; rancheros in San Diego County had little with which to be improvident.

Along with improvidence, economic backwardness has also been suggested by historians to explain the demise of the Californios. This collateral argument asserts that the pastoral economy of Mexican California left the rancheros unprepared to cope with the Anglo-American free enterprise system. Californios lacked the initiative and drive to succeed in a capitalistic economy. But rather than being bewildered by free enterprise, Californios in San Diego during this early period seemed eager to take advantage of opportunities in their community. They participated in ventures to develop economic resources in the back country and the city in attempts to improve their economic condition. [46]

In the back country, most of the forty or more ranchos were vacant in 1846 because of war with the Americans and renewed Indian unrest. Hostilities between the Indians and rancheros continued through May 1848, by which time many of the Californios had departed for the gold fields. In 1849, however, San Diego began to undergo startling changes. The arrival of the boundary commission to establish a new border between the United States and Mexico and the presence of an increasing number of immigrants contributed to these developments. The *Daily Alta California* reported that:

> ...this port has taken quite a start, and is now rapidly growing. Quite a number of Americans have gone down there recently and established themselves in business for the winter. A number of frame houses are in the process of erection and many others are being shipped from this port [San Francisco]. The town is represented to us as being quite a bustling, lively, little place.[47]

Encouraged by San Diego's new prosperity, a group of men, including both Anglo-Americans and Californios, initiated efforts to relocate the town closer to the harbor. They believed San Diego would become a major commercial center because she had the best harbor south of San Francisco. It was deep, had a good entrance, and provided ample protection for ships. Up to this time, ships landed on the northwest side of the harbor at La Playa, where several hide houses stood, then passengers traveled by wagons to town. On March 16, 1850, William Heath Davis, José Antonio Aguirre, Miguel de Pedrorena, William C. Ferrell, Andrew B. Grey, and Thomas D. Johns formed a partnership and bought 160 acres for $2,304 near *Punto de los Muertos*, the foot of Market Street in downtown San Diego. These men recognized the necessity of moving the town closer to the harbor so ships could load and unload more easily. Soon a second group of men purchased land from the city between the two town sites hoping to make their site the new location of the town. On May 27, 1850, Oliver S. Witherby, William H. Emory, Cave J. Couts, Thomas W. Sutherland, Agostin Haraszthy, Juan Bandini, José M. Estudillo, Charles P. Noell, and Henry Clayton purchased 687 acres for $3,187. San Diegans called the original townsite Old Town, the site purchased by Davis and others New Town, and the site between the two Middletown.[48]

Along with efforts to relocate the town, Anglos and Californios also speculated in city lands, opened numerous businesses, and constructed new buildings. Many speculators believed the land around the harbor would be quite valuable once the community began to develop. They purchased lots from the common council for twenty dollars in 1850, but paid as much as five hundred dollars for lots owned by others. Many of these speculators also recognized the opportunity to earn a good profit by serving the needs of immigrants passing through the town. Immigrants coming by ship or overland along the Gila River, as well as miners from Mexico, paused in San Diego before going on to the gold fields. Between 1849-1851 some Anglos and Californios opened several new hotels, retail stores, and saloons to meet the needs of these travelers. In all, more than fifteen businesses operated in Old Town, New Town, and La Playa; Middletown remained unoccupied.[49]

Business from these immigrants also caused a building boom in the community during these years. At New Town, William Heath Davis constructed a wharf to accommodate the ships arriving in the harbor. He also built a general store and the

GEORGE F. HOOPER
another New Town merchant

Pantoja House, where he opened a billiard room and saloon. Two lots south of Davis's general store, Frank Ames and Eugene Pendleton built a structure to house their mercantile business. On the south side of New Town's plaza, J. Van Ness, Levi Slack, and E. W. Morse erected the Boston House and opened a general store and restaurant. The United States Army built a corral and barracks at this townsite after receiving land from its promoters. In Old Town, Juan Bandini constructed the Gila House, a two story structure, where he operated an inn and general store. This also seems to be the period when three hotels were constructed at La Playa: the Ocean House, New Orleans, and Playa House.[50]

By February 1851 San Diego's economy began to decline when gold was discovered 120 miles south in Baja California, and the flow of immigrants into the community subsided. In September George Hooper wrote to William Heath Davis that "with respect to the Pantoja House, everything goes on very quietly—indeed too quietly, for there is no business doing here or anywhere."[51] Efforts to relocate the city at New Town foundered because of this lack of business, opposition from Old Town residents, and the lack of water and fuel. By 1853 most of the community's residents lived in Old Town or La Playa with New Town nearly abandoned.[52]

Despite the languishing economy, some Anglos continued to speculate in city lots, still paying as much as five hundred dollars for a lot. The federal government wanted to build a transcontinental railroad, and these Anglos hoped San Diego would be the West Coast terminus. Lieutenant George Derby, a noted humorist and author who resided in San Diego during this period, commented on this paradoxical situation. He said that:

> ...from present appearances one would be little disposed to imagine that the Playa in five or six years might become a city the size of Louisville, with brick buildings, paved streets, gas lights, theaters, gambling houses, and so forth. It is not at all improbable, however, should the great Pacific Railroad terminate at San Diego....[53]

With merchants continuing their dominance of business affairs in the community, several unsuccessful enterprises and schemes were tried in order to revive the economy. The most significant undertaking, between 1852-1856, was the organization of the San Diego Gila, Southern Pacific, and Atlantic Railroad Company. In 1854 San Diegans formed their own company to construct a railroad to Yuma and join the transcontinental railroad that they thought would be built on a southern route. These plans never succeeded because the United States Congress could not decide on a route. Eventually the Civil War ended San Diego's chances for being the terminus of the transcontinental railroad. San Diegans formed another company in 1855 to mine coal deposits on Point Loma. These deposits, however, showed little profit. During this period some residents also contemplated building a road to San Bernardino, hoping to stimulate trade between San Diego and the Mormons in Utah. These plans never got beyond the discussion and planning stages. Trade with lower California also raised the hopes of the town merchants, but it lasted only a short time. In 1853 Louis Rose opened a tannery which employed about twenty workers. This venture proved profitable for Mr. Rose, but had a negligible effect on the community's economy. By 1855 some whaling ships from the Pacific fleet began to stop and buy supplies in San Diego. The community's economy, however, did not benefit substantially from whaling till about 1859.[54]

All these different enterprises, then, failed to revive the community's economy. Many of San Diego's Anglo and Californio businessmen experienced financial losses and hardships within a few years. Once the economy began to falter in 1851, William Heath Davis encountered one financial reversal after another, and at one point some of his property was sold for delinquent taxes. Juan Bandini needed the assistance of his son-in-law to pay loans he had contracted to finance his various enterprises. Delinquent tax lists for 1854 and 1855 indicate that other businessmen, such as William C. Ferrell, Andrew B. Grey, and Henry Clayton, also incurred financial difficulties. With the onset of this business slump, farmers and ranchers became the principal customers of Anglo and Californio merchants and the main support of the economy. During the decade 1846 to 1856, ranching showed meager profits and farming remained unprofitable.[55]

At the beginning of American rule forty-five Mexican land grants existed in the San Diego area; Californios possessed forty ranchos, Anglos four, and Indians two. These ranchos varied in size from a few acres to several thousand.[56] In the early 1850s, after the Anglo population began to expand, most owners retained control of their ranchos or sold them through their own volition. Pedro Carrillo sold Peninsula de San Diego Rancho to Capt. Bezer Simmons for $1,000 in 1849. Abel Stearns purchased the Guajome Rancho for $550 from its Indian owners, and later gave it to his brother-in-law, Cave J. Couts, as a wedding gift.[57]

Only one incident has been recorded in which a Californio's rancho changed owners through other than legal means in San Diego in the 1850s. Sometime during 1850 or 1851 Juan Forster, agent in charge of Rancho Santa Clara de Jamacha, allowed Captain John Magruder to use the ranch for grazing horses belonging to the United States cavalry detachment stationed in the community. About nine years later Magruder visited Apolinaria Lorenzana, the owner of the rancho, in San Juan Capistrano, hoping to buy the property. According to her recollection, she refused to sell or rent it to Magruder since she had never received any remuneration from him for his previous use of the property. After an angry exchange Magruder returned to San Diego and seized the property. Miss Lorenzana claimed that she never received any payment for her property and after being intimidated by Magruder never pressed her claim.[58]

Since Californios did not own all the usable land in the San Diego area, the problem of squatters never reached as serious proportions as it did in northern California. Anglo settlers moving into the community found land they could farm. Yet, contrary to what some historians have believed, squatting was widely practiced in the county. As early as September 1850 the common council found it necessary to pass an ordinance forbidding squatters from settling on city property. Indian agents in the county reported that Moses Manasse and others, sometime between 1847 and 1852, had moved into the San Pascual Valley and settled on Indian lands. Once the prosperity of the town declined after 1852 more settlers ventured into the surrounding country to take up ranching and farming. In 1853 Daniel Cline and William Moody settled in the Temecula Valley which was then a part of San Diego County. That same year the *San Diego Herald* reported that several individuals left town with plans to proceed to San Luis Rey to squat in that valley.[59]

By 1856 squatting had become quite common, especially on land belonging to Indians. Panto, "captain" of the San Pascual Indians, demanded that the government protect the Indians from squatters. One Indian agent published advertisements in newspapers warning squatters to stay off Indian lands. Explaining this action to his superiors, he wrote that:

> ...my reasons for advertising in English and Spanish wass [sic] ... at the date of my advertisement a great mania seized upon the people for acquiring lands ... these squatting operations were creating great excitement.... The object of my publication was to show and maintain the rights of the Indians to their lands and as far as possible to prevent collision between them and the squatters.[60]

Although squatting was widely practiced in San Diego, squatters were few in number because of the county's small population. Nevertheless, squatters did constitute a large percentage of the county's farming and ranching community. A comparison of statistics found in the United States National Census for 1860 and the county tax records reveals how widespread this practice was. Aside from the Mexican land grants and city property, the National Census for 1860 lists seventy-six persons with property. Of this seventy-six, thirty-six appear on the tax assessor's rolls for that same year, but only two paid taxes on the property that census records show they occupied. In other words, over half the ranchers and farmers in the community, including Anglos and Californios, resided on land they did not own.[61]

The large land holdings of the Californios and the boom in the cattle trade have caused many historians to believe that the Californios throughout southern California were quite wealthy. The flood of immigrants arriving in California after 1848 sent cattle prices skyrocketing as the demand for beef increased. Cattle that once brought only a few dollars, by early 1849 were worth fifty dollars a head and for awhile sold as high as five hundred dollars a head in some mining camps. For seven prosperous years, southern California ranchers drove their herds along the coast or through the San Joaquin Valley to the markets in northern California. During these years rancheros took between twenty-five and thirty thousand cattle annually out of Los Angeles alone to the northern markets. By 1855 the demand for southern California cattle began to decrease as a growing number of sheep from New Mexico and cattle from the Mississippi and Missouri valleys reached the California market. In 1848 California had only about twenty thousand sheep and three hundred thousand cattle, but by 1860 the state possessed one million sheep and three million cattle. As the market became more glutted, prices declined to about five or six dollars a head.[62]

Although some Californios reaped handsome profits from this cattle trade, in San Diego the decimation of the herds following the secularization of the missions in 1834 had left the Californios only a few thousand head of cattle. While rancheros in Los Angeles sold over 25,000 head of cattle a year during the boom, in San Diego cattle sales probably did not exceed 2,500 a year. The first assessment list for San Diego shows twenty-four persons owning 5,552 head of cattle in the county. Twenty of these twenty-four cattle owners were Californios, with 4,846 head of cattle. Four were Anglos with 697 head of cattle, or about 13 percent of the cattle in the county. Eight Californios out of twenty owned 3,870 head of cattle, about 79 percent of the cattle belonging to the Californios. In short, the small number of cattle in the county belonged to a few ranchers who derived profits from the cattle boom. Out of forty-five persons with land grants only fifteen rancheros, or less than 30 percent, owned cattle in 1850.[63]

Where twenty-four persons owned cattle in 1850, the California State Census of 1852 indicated only twenty individuals owning a total of 5,208 head of cattle in San Diego. The census showed that 252 head of cattle belonged to two Indians and seven Anglos possessed 458 head of cattle, or not quite 9 percent. Among the eleven Californio cattlemen, four of them owned about 87 percent of all cattle belonging to Californios. Out of all twenty cattlemen in 1852, only six owned land grants. The state census, then reveals the same type of trends that the first assessment list did. Within San Diego County a small group of persons owned the few thousand head of cattle in the area. Despite the high prices at the markets in San Francisco and Stockton, the Californios did not have the cattle to reap large profits that some historians believed they did.[64]

San Diego continued throughout this period to have only a few thousand head of cattle on its ranges. The Surveyor General's Report for 1855 shows only 8,100 head of cattle in the county. His report of 1856, however, indicates a dramatic increase, to about 18,000 head. This was probably not local cattle entirely. Judson Ames, editor of the *Herald*, explained that rancheros from Los Angeles were bringing their cattle down the coast because of ample grazing land in the county. Obviously, the fact that there was available grazing land in the area would indicate San Diego rancheros did not need all the grazing land available.[65]

Before and after the cattle market declined, some early Anglo residents recalled that Californios in San Diego neglected the agricultural potential of their ranchos. E. W. Morse, a prominent Anglo in Community affairs, claimed that the county had "literally no agriculture" in 1850. He said that most people believed the area was unsuitable for farming.[66] The San Diego correspondent to the *Alta California* noted in 1853 that a segment of the population opposed farming because it had never been done before and they were convinced it would never succeed. The county surveyor commented in 1856 that farming was neglected because of laziness among county residents.[67]

Contrary to what contemporaries stated, ample evidence exists which reveals that Californios and Anglos did pursue farming during this period. During the American conquest of San Diego John C. Frémont observed that "among the arid, brush-covered hills south of San Diego we found little valleys converted by a single spring into crowded gardens, where pears, peaches, quinces, pomegranates, grapes, olives and other fruits grew luxuriantly together...."[68] The agricultural statistics in the National Census of 1850 reveal that several individuals were actively engaged in farming. José Antonio Estudillo had 158 acres of improved land and 1,475 bushels of wheat, 165 bushels of Indian corn, and 1,650 bushels of barley. Santiago E. Argüello's farm included 100 acres of improved land with 275 bushels of wheat, 180 bushels of Indian corn, 13 bushels of peas and beans, and $200 worth of garden produce. Finally, the California surveyor general's report concerning agricultural statistics for 1856 indicated that over 17,000 bushels of wheat, barley, corn, potatoes, beans, peas, and sweet potatoes were produced in San Diego during that year.[69]

What most of the early critics of San Diego farmers were probably lamenting, however, was not the absence of agriculture but the failure to produce enough to meet San Diego's needs. For the most part, between 1846 and 1856 San Diego farmers failed to produce what the community required. Editor Ames declared in 1855 that it was "a disgrace to the people of this county that we are obliged to send to San Francisco for everything we eat except fresh beef and garlic."[70] Most of the Californios and Anglos who possessed land seem to have practiced subsistence farming or engaged in farming without the assistance of other workers. The small quantity of farm implements and the few acres under cultivation, as revealed by tax and census records, indicated that most Californios and Anglos with land carried on farming on a small scale.[71] They continued to farm on a small scale because they encountered problems and circumstances which hampered their efforts to develop agriculture, as well as the livestock industry.

One problem San Diego settlers faced rose from the geographical location of the county in relation to major centers of population in the state. The thousands of immigrants settling in California after 1848 created a demand for both beef and farm products, but the demand existed in the northern part of the state, more than five hundred miles from San Diego. The only means that San Diegans had of getting their goods to these markets was to ship them or send them overland. In 1856 the county assessor, realizing the effect of this problem on farmers, commented that "the distance of the county from the principal markets, [has] had a tendency to retard agricultural pursuits, and much land that might be advantageously cultivated, is now left for the free use of stock."[72]

Cattle owners drove their livestock overland to northern markets facing many hazards and dangers. Inclement weather, inefficient herdsmen, stampedes, great fields of mustard seed where animals were lost, and the lack of grass were some of the problems encountered on trail drives north. On one such arduous trip in 1853, John Forster suffered severe losses, and many of his cattle perished. Thieves and cattle rustlers presented another problem for cattle owners taking their livestock north. In 1852 Cave J. Couts reported to his brother-in-law, Abel Stearns, that he outwitted the thieves in Santa Clara, but some other San Diegans were not as fortunate. Couts reported that "they got about 100 head of Forsters, 50 from José Antonio Argüello, 70 of Machados, all of Castros and others in proportion."[73]

Besides their distance from the major markets, a gold rush inflated economy also

SANTIAGO EMIGDIO ARGÜELLO
(1813-1857)

hindered development of livestock and farming resources in the community. With thousands of immigrants arriving in California, prices soared as goods became more scarce. In May 1852 the *Herald* informed its readers that only a few members of the boundary commission were returning, "their salaries being absolutely too small to support them in the necessary expenses they are obliged to incur, at the exhorbitantly [sic] high prices of California, ..."[74] In San Diego prices exceeded those of San Francisco, the main commercial center, since merchants had to pay for shipping their merchandise down the coast. Editor Ames calculated that San Diegans paid between eight to ten thousand dollars a year in freight cost. These high prices made it impossible for farmers to produce their crops cheaply enough to earn a good profit. With labor, shipping, and other necessary expenses, commercial agriculture remained unprofitable during this period.[75]

High interest rates deterred many residents from securing a loan or mortgage to invest in agriculture. Throughout California during this era, a person had to pay usurious rates to borrow money. To finance some of his various ventures, Juan Bandini borrowed ten thousand dollars from a French gambler at 4 percent interest a month compounded.

Bandini eventually needed the assistance of his son-in-law to pay this debt. Interest rates such as this "...proved an enormous handicap to the state's prosperity and economic development; ... In southern California, especially, a complete dearth of capital caused general economic stagnation." [76]

Years of sparse rainfall constituted another serious problem confronting farmers and ranchers in San Diego between 1846 and 1856. Among the hills in the surrounding countryside, Californios and Anglos settled in valleys with streams passing through so they would have water to irrigate their crops. Over the rolling hills their cattle grazed on grass produced annually by the rains. Usually by the end of summer, these streams were dry and the grass supply exhausted. The ranchers and farmers depended each year on the rainfall to refurnish their water supply and produce more grass; several times during this period the rainfall was insufficient for their needs. Meteorologists who have studied rainfall patterns in southern California between 1850 and 1880 have noted that the facts "indicate a preponderance of dry years, with the result that the water supply of the period as a whole was undoubtedly considerably below normal." [77]

Rainfall statistics available for seven years between 1846-1856 show San Diego received less than ten inches in four of these years. In 1851 the *Alta California* reported "that the scarcity of water and feed of the present season [in southern California] has not been equalled in the last twenty-two years." [78] The sparse rainfall during the winter of 1856-57 resulted in even greater hardships for county residents. In the spring of 1857 the *Herald* reported that:

> Not one solitary blade of barley, wheat or other cereal is left. Every blade of grass this side of San Bernardino is parched up and withered, and our rancheros are selling off their cattle at any price that is offered. But for the money realized from the sale of stock, which will enable our farmers to purchase from abroad what, under other circumstances, they would produce at home, two-thirds of the rancheros in the county would be obliged to abandon their farms and seek a home in some more favored part of the State. What few cattle are left remaining here will have to be driven back into the mountains, where there is grass, and it will be a miracle if any escape the starving Indians,... [79]

Besides disadvantages created by their geographical location and problems caused by weather conditions and inflation, the lack of law and order throughout the entire region added further troubles to the precarious condition of county ranchers and farmers. During the American conquest of California, United States officials promised the inhabitants of the territory protection and security for their lives and property. Following the conquest in June 1847 citizens of San Diego petitioned the commander of the Southern Military District to have a force remain in the community. They informed the commander that renewed Indian attacks had forced the evacuation of local ranchos, and they expressed fear of an Indian attack on the town if the military was withdrawn. [80] Although a military force remained in the community, it provided little assistance to the rancheros. In a letter recommending the organization of a local militia, an officer informed the military governor:

> ...that almost daily places of deposit for cattle heads and other evidences of Indian depredations upon cattle are found by the people of the country between here [Los Angeles] and San Diego and for some 70 miles below and 'tis impossible to prevent it unless either the Alcaldes or myself are permitted to authorize the people of the country to unite for the protection of their property, a measure which in itself appears to me just especially as we cannot afford them the protection our government have [sic] promised. [81]

Further Indian resistance occurred in 1851 under the leadership of Antonio Garra, who planned to expel the Americans. The outbreak of violence started with an attack on the Warner Rancho in Agua Caliente and the killing of four persons. With renewed hostilities, most of the rancheros again evacuated their lands and sought safety in town until the uprising was quelled. [82]

Rancheros also had to contend constantly with attacks from Indians who poached on the ranch herds. The *Los Angeles Star* reported in March 1851 that Paiutes stole several hundred head of horses from area ranchos including Rancho Santa Margarita y Las Flores. Again in March and November of 1853 a group of Utah Indians raided several ranchos and stole several hundred head of livestock. At times circumstances beyond their control forced some Indians to steal livestock. In San Diego County Indians who did not work for whites supported themselves by growing their own food. During years of insufficient rainfall, however, Indians seized the rancheros' cattle to keep from starving. [83]

Although ranchers and farmers suffered severely from Indian thefts and attacks, historian Robert Glass Cleland suggested that bandits and other outlaws posed an even more serious problem.[84] Numerous accounts of thefts and robberies throughout this period exist and a few demonstrate the effect they had on agriculture and the livestock industry. In 1852, the *Alta California* reported that:

> Several different communications from Los Angeles have been received at San Diego, warning the citizens against a band of robbers who have left that vicinity for Lower California, and now said to be at Temecula. It has caused no little solicitude among the rancheros. They have brought their families into town, run their horses etc., into some private and secluded gorge of the mountains not easily to be found by the robbers, and fear themselves to return to their ranches. Those of them disposed to plant have lost the season entirely, by such stampedes. It appears that the place cannot rest in peace and quietude for a month at a time. These fears, which are too true and well-founded, not to be heeded, have seriously injured the agricultural portion of the community this season.[85]

Through 1856 lawlessness in the county continued unabated. In that year Cave J. Couts wrote to his brother-in-law that "the like in stealing as goes on at present we hardly ever knew of." Couts further stated that he was forced to kill his cattle to prevent thieves from getting them.[86]

Circumstances of their locality did not cause all the economic problems of the Californios. Laws affecting their property adopted by the new American government produced additional hardships for them. Concepts of land ownership and uncertainty concerning some land titles led to the passage of laws which brought distressing financial demands on their ranchos. Anglos settling in California after 1848 came with their own concept of land ownership, which collided with those of the Californios.[87] These Anglos believed they had a right to settle on public land, build a farm, and, after making a number of improvements, buy the land for a moderate price. They thought that the individual's right to own land was an essential ingredient for a democratic society. An article in the *Alta California* expressed this belief quite explicitly:

> For trade to flourish, for wealth to increase, for the establishing of good morals, and a virtuous and solid population, it is essential that the lands should be owned in small parcels by their cultivators. The very essence of Republicanism lies in this fact. A population that would properly exercise the right of sufferage must be free, and it cannot be free so long as the lands are held by great landholders, who rent them to their tenants, over whom they exercise an undue influence. It is against the very genius of our institutions that the lands be thus monopolized.[88]

Between thirteen and fourteen million acres belonged to grantees of Mexican ranchos in California. Under the former Mexican government, a person could receive as much as 48,818 acres provided he occupy the land, build a house on it, and raise cattle. During the Mexican period, officials employed very informal procedures for granting land which led to confusion after the Americans took over. When granting land, officials sometimes used objects of the natural terrain to mark boundaries and after a few years the tree, stream, or rock might disappear. Along with uncertainty about boundaries, many of the grantees were not careful about preserving legal papers that proved their ownership. Also, officials neglected to follow procedures established by law for approving land grants.[89]

The Treaty of Guadalupe-Hidalgo, ending the war between the United States and Mexico, guaranteed the inhabitants of California the right to their land. To clear up the confusion surrounding Mexican land grants, however, the Congress passed the Land Act of 1851, requiring the grantees to present evidence proving their ownership to a three member board of land commissioners. This act also allowed the federal government and the petitioners to appeal the Land Commission's decisions to the District Court, and from there to the Supreme Court. Historians have generally condemned this act because it placed the responsibility on the landowners to prove their ownership at considerable cost to themselves. William Heath Davis asserted that José Joaquín Estudillo paid over two hundred thousand dollars in litigation fees for Rancho San Leandro.[90]

Between 1852 and 1856 more than forty-five claimants in San Diego and other claimants throughout California presented their cases to the Land Commission. Paul Gates, one of the few historians to defend the land act, admitted that this lengthy legal procedure proved expensive for the Californios. Gates stated that lawyers' fees for presenting a claim before the Land Commission ranged from fifty dollars for small tracts to more than seventeen hundred dollars for larger grants.[91] Gates, however, did not discuss other expenses incurred by claimants while presenting their case before the Land Commission. Since most of the hearings were held in San Francisco, claimants had to pay to send witnesses and documents to substantiate their claim. One group of landowners claimed:

> ... that if the Government of the United States required them to proceed to San Francisco to have their claims settled, it would diminish the value of their lands at least one-third, and it would necessarily result that many just but ancient claims would be lost, owing to the impossibility of carrying all the witnesses there, and the impracticability of supplying the defect by taking testimony by deposition.[92]

For one of the few sessions held in Los Angeles, the San Diego Board of Trustees paid $1032.47 in lawyer's fees and for arrangements for a witness to appear. The latter expense exceeded the lawyer's fees by more than 300 percent; the lawyer's fees amounted to $250.00 and other necessary expenses totaled $782.47.[93] If the rancheros experienced similar expenses, many of their ranchos would indeed depreciate by one-third.

Along with expenses arising out of land grant litigation, the state government initiated a property tax in 1850 which placed further financial demands on property owners. The law obligated property owners to pay state, county, poll, and other taxes for special purposes. In 1850 on every hundred dollars worth of property, San Diegans paid fifty cents to the state, twenty-five cents to the county, and twenty-five cents for a new county court house. They also had to pay eight dollars in poll taxes to the state and county. Between 1850 and 1856 these tax rates increased twice. In 1854 on every hundred dollars of property, county residents paid sixty cents to the state and fifty-five cents to the county. The following year they paid $1.50 for every hundred dollars of property: sixty cents to the state, fifty cents to the county, a five cent school tax, and thirty-five cents special funding tax.[94]

Since state laws exempted much of the northern mining industry, the brunt of the property tax fell on the large property owners of southern California who were primarily Californios. Most of the state's population resided in the North and worked in the mines or in related occupations. Their representatives dominated state government and attempted to use taxation to break up the large land holdings.[95] Southern representatives, being powerless to modify state tax laws, sought to have the state divided, making southern California the "Territory of the Colorado." At a convention of delegates from southern California in Monterey in 1851, a resolution was approved stating that "the counties of the South do not feel able to support the expense of a State Government and are desirous of becoming a 'Territory,' to escape onerous taxation to which they are now subject."[96] In 1853 a State Senate Committee investigating these grievances claimed that large landowners desired light taxation "to retain their enormous possession to the detriment of progress and improvement."[97]

Not only did the large landowners and Californios suffer the brunt of the property tax, but maladministration appears to have been added to their plight. Judge Benjamin Hayes noted that:

> ... under the change of governments, the Californians have many cases of complaint. If the matter were examined into, it would doubtless be found that they could also make just and grievous accusations against their old system. Be this as it may, for half burthens they have borne and half the losses they have sustained from defective government of maladministration, since the year 1850.

He went on to cite the example of Juan Forster, owner of the San Felipe and Nación ranchos, as being taxed twice for the same property in 1856. Both Los Angeles and San Diego counties were taxing him for the cattle he owned because during the year the animals had been in both counties.[98]

Tax records indicate other areas of questionable action. There are reports of some city lots selling for as much as five hundred dollars during speculation booms, but tax records show most lots were valued below one hundred dollars. During the land boom of 1888, tax records reflect the inflated prices. On the other hand, while Californios did not have clear title to their land, they were required to pay taxes on the property. The assessments of their property seemed to fluctuate from one year to the next. In 1854 officials assessed the Agua Hedionda Rancho at $2,000 for 17,020 acres; the next year the ranch was worth $1,200 more when it had 3,820 acres less. Again, in 1854 José Aguirre's rancho was assessed at $15,000 for 85,000 acres; the following year the ranch was worth

$400 more when it had 23,400 acres less. Aguirre never received the patent to this ranch.[99]

While Californios were being assessed for their ranchos, most squatters were not being assessed for the land they used. Tax records of Moses Manasse, Daniel Cline, and William Moody show no assessment for real estate. In 1856, however, Lorenzo Soto, listed as squatting in San Pascual after 1848, was assessed three hundred dollars for improvements he made in the valley. Obviously, the manner of assessing property was less than equitable.[100]

Throughout the period 1846 to 1856 it was evident that San Diego residents continued to experience economic hardships and the Californios in the community met additional financial demands placed on them by the new government. Once the boom from the immigrants subsided, the town never recovered its prosperity as farmers and ranchers again constituted the main part of the economy. The small number of cattle, distance from the major markets, years of sparse rainfall, low prices for agricultural products, and inflationary economy, land litigation, and taxes combined to keep farmers and ranchers in straitened circumstances. Difficulties the Californios experienced stemmed from their situation and from policies initiated by the new government, not from improvidence or bewilderment with the new capitalistic system. Their adverse circumstances and government policies set the stage for the eventual loss of their ranchos. Finally, the promises and predictions of conquering Americans never came to pass. The guarantees of protection and security were never kept, and the prosperity predicted by American officials never occurred.

CALIFORNIOS AS POWERLESS POLITICOS 1846-1856

After the United States conquest of California in 1846 and the establishment of state government four years later, Anglo-Americans seized control of the state's political affairs, leaving the Spanish-speaking Californians without political influence. Leonard Pitt wrote that the exclusion of Californios from public office and the loss of political influence was especially acute in northern California with the arrival of thousands of Anglos, after the discovery of gold in 1848. On the other hand, in southern California, Pitt argued that Californios continued to win elections to local offices and managed to receive some of the spoils of office. Since fewer Anglos settled in this part of the state, Californios remained a viable political force during the formative years of state and local government, 1850-1856. The evidence Pitt used to support his arguments about southern California came from Los Angeles and Santa Barbara.[101] Available records regarding San Diego County, however, show that Californios there experienced less success than in Santa Barbara or Los Angeles.

During the ten year period 1846 to 1856 San Diego underwent several changes in the organization of local government. Following the cessation of armed resistance to the American conquest, the United States Army governed California until the National Congress decided the territory's status in 1850. Those laws which did not conflict with or were not specifically prohibited by United States' laws remained in force. Californios in San Diego and throughout the territory were allowed to keep their *alcalde* form of local government. With the organization of state government in 1850, the boundaries of the county were established and the city received a charter. Included in the boundaries of San Diego County were the present-day counties of San Bernardino, Riverside, Imperial, San Diego, and part of Inyo. The state legislature redrew boundary lines in 1851 giving a northern portion of the county to Los Angeles County. The Courts of Session looked after county business until the election of a Board of Supervisors in 1853. The new city charter called for the election of a mayor, city attorney, a five member city council, and several other officials to manage city affairs. Two years later, however, the exhaustion of city funds caused the state legislature to revoke the charter and set up a Board of Trustees to attend to city business.[102]

Following the conquest and during most of the military government period, Californios retained their political control of the community. With the arrival of the Americans in July 1846 most Californios refused to serve in public office; so Henry Delano Fitch, an American living in the community, was appointed *alcalde*. Because of pressing business matters, Fitch resigned in May 1847 and the military governor appointed Juan

JUAN MARIA MARRON

Bandini to take his place. In October 1848 bad health forced Bandini to resign and Juan María Marron, one of those who opposed the American conquest, won election as *alcalde*. By the end of 1849 the large number of immigrants in the community began to displace the Californios as the dominant political force. Poll lists show Anglo-Americans outnumbering the Californios by more than two to one.[103]

Once the new state government began to function after 1850, Anglo-Americans' control of civic affairs was never threatened. Out of more than 154 political offices available during the next six years, Californios held only eight positions. On April 1, 1850, the first county elections took place with Californios winning two of the eleven offices. San Diegans chose José Antonio Estudillo as their assessor and Juan Bandini as their treasurer. Bandini, however, never served in office; why he did not remains uncertain. One historian wrote that Bandini failed to qualify for office and another historian said that he refused to accept the office. Bandini's name appears on the poll list of the first precinct as having voted in the county elections of 1850. Under the new California Constitution, anyone who was eligible to vote was qualified to hold public office. In the city election held in June of that same year, Estudillo and Bandini again won election to office. With ten positions available, the citizenry elected Estudillo as treasurer and Bandini as assessor. Again Bandini failed to serve, but this time all the evidence indicated that he refused the job.[104]

The reason for Bandini's refusal remains uncertain. His personal affairs might have prevented him from accepting added responsibilities. He owned a large *rancho* near present-day Tijuana which might have required his close supervision. Bandini might also have thought it futile to serve in city and county governments that Anglos completely dominated. Other Californios throughout the state reached this conclusion, since Anglos managed to control different issues and exclude the Californios from the decision-making process.[105]

Californios did not serve in public office in San Diego during 1851, but in the following year they won election to four offices. José A. Estudillo served as both city and county treasurer, Francisco Alvarado as coroner, and Santiago Argüello as county assessor. In the elections between 1853 and 1855 one of José A. Estudillo's sons, either José María or José Guadalupe, tried twice to win election to office. In the 1853 election one of the Estudillo brothers sought to succeed his father in the county treasurer's office, but received only five votes out of 163. During the 1855 political campaigns one of the Estudillos tried to become the new superintendent of the schools, but again finished last, receiving nineteen votes out of 123. Little evidence remains concerning office seekers in 1856, and no Californios won election to public office.[106]

Thus, it appears that between 1850 and 1856 Californios did not seek political office, although ample opportunity appears to have been available since most of these elections suffered from a shortage of candidates. During this six-year period many candidates ran unopposed for office and some ran for more than one office at the same time. In the 1853 elections, for example, J. W. Robinson ran unopposed for district attorney and L. Stratiss won the post of coroner without opposition. Those running for sheriff, county judge, county surveyor, and coroner in 1854 all ran without opponents. P. H. Hoff campaigned for both justice of the peace and county judge in the 1853 elections, while G. P. Tebbets sought the offices of county judge and constable. In the following year William C. Ferrell sought election as the county's assemblyman and as a school commissioner. During the same election in the San Luis Rey Township, Cave J. Couts and a man named Cline both campaigned for positions of justice of the peace and school commissioner. In 1856 James Nichols won election as justice of the peace and county supervisor.[107]

Anglos monopolized county and city offices while Californios, for reasons yet unclear, never exploited this shortage of candidates to their own advantage. Failure to serve in more public offices, however, probably did not stem from a spirit of apathy. During this period a number of public meetings were held in San Diego to deal with community problems and Californios took an active part in these events.

In the 1850s, for example, southern Californians tried to separate themselves from northern California and establish a territorial government. Southerners resented the political domination of the northerners in state affairs and the property tax, which forced them to pay more taxes, since lands in the South still remained in large tracts. In seeking separation San Diegans held public meetings and formed several committees, which included some Californios as members. On August 28, 1851, the *Herald* cited the following Californios as being active in the territorial cause: José Estudillo, Joaquín Ortega, Juan Bandini, Juan Marron, and José Antonio Aguilla. Those who attended a public meeting on August 30 appointed a correspondence committee, with Joaquín Ortega and Pedro Carrillo as members, to petition Congress for territorial government.[108]

Besides being involved in efforts to divide the state, Californios also participated in attempts to build a road from San Diego to San Bernardino to develop trade with the Utah Territory. William C. Ferrell argued at a public meeting, held in April 1854, that San Diego possessed a fine harbor and with a good wagon road settlers in Utah would buy and trade their goods in this city rather than send their goods eastward by land. Most of the people attending this meeting agreed and a committee was established to study the feasibility of the proposal. The committee consisted of seven members: J. W. Robinson, E. W. Morse, O. S. Witherby, Lewis Rose, M. Jacobs, M. A. Franklin, and Juan Bandini. When a company was created to build this road Bandini became its treasurer.[109]

Even though Californios did not hold public office, these examples show that they did participate actively in public affairs when it was in their interest. Had the state become divided and the property tax lowered, a tremendous financial burden would have been taken off the Californios and their ranchos. Juan Bandini must have realized the potential benefits for San Diego and retail merchants such as himself in his efforts to build a road to San Bernardino. Californios, then, were not apathetic about participation in community affairs, but their reluctance to run for public office between 1850 and 1856 is difficult to explain without examining it in a larger context.

The large number of Anglo immigrants who came to California after 1848 provides one explanation for the Californios' loss of political power. When news of the 1848 gold discovery became known many people throughout the Americas and other foreign countries began to migrate to California. By 1850 California's white population had reached one hundred thousand with the Californios making up only 8 percent.[110]

During this period the population of San Diego more than tripled, despite its remoteness from the gold fields. In 1847 the military governor of California, William B. Mason, ordered a census taken in San Diego County. Captain D. C. Davis of the Mormon Volunteers carried out this order and reported a total of 248 white men, women, and children within the county. He set the total population of the county at 2,287 including whites, "tame" Indians, "wild" Indians, Sandwich Islanders, and Negroes. When the federal government took the

Old Town residence of Juan María Marron as it looked in 1874. Family members pose in front.

national census in 1850 the white population of the county had nearly tripled to 735.[111]

The 1847 census reveals very little information about the voting strength of Anglos and Californios. In the census Davis neglected to give a numerical breakdown of the two groups. From his figures there were possibly seventy eligible voters living in San Diego. With the national census a breakdown of eligible voters between Anglos and Californios can be determined. Out of a total population of 735, 311 were Californios and 424 were Anglos. In political terms the difference was more significant. The Californios had only seventy-eight eligible voters and the Anglos 266. Moreover, the figure for the number of Anglo voters is probably too low because the census fails to provide the ages of thirty-three soldiers stationed at San Diego. Out of the other fifty-eight soldiers listed on the census only one did not qualify to vote because of age. It would, therefore, seem reasonable to assume that most of these thirty-three men were over twenty-one and qualified to vote. Anglos, then, could marshal about 299 voters, four times as many as the Californios, even though they outnumbered the Californios by only 120.[112]

The explanation for this disparity lies, in part, in the nature of San Diego's Anglo population, which contained many soldiers and government employees. The United States government stationed ninety-one soldiers at the San Diego Mission in 1850, and the Quartermaster Department employed forty-two individuals in the city. Available evidence indicated that these soldiers could and did participate in community affairs and vote in local elections. Even without counting the soldiers, Anglos possessed almost three times as many eligible voters as the Californios. According to the census of 1850, Californios consisted of 78 men, 52 women, and 181 children, while 299 men, 39 women, and 86 children made up the Anglo population. Obviously, many of the Anglos coming to San Diego in the 1850s came without their wives and families. The fact that almost 75 percent of the Anglo population consisted of men over twenty-one years of age also accounts for the difference in the number of residents and voters between the two groups in the city.[113] This analysis clearly shows the voting superiority of Anglos in San Diego in 1850 and provides one of the reasons why the Californios lost political power.

The social attitudes of Anglos and Californios also played a significant part in the Californio loss of political power in San Diego in the early 1850s. Racist ideas appear to have influenced most San Diegans. Articles in the *Herald* make this quite apparent. When people discussed racial matters, they referred to individuals of different nationalities as belonging to separate races. Whenever an article in the paper discussed a social event in the city, for example, the writer usually mentioned the different racial groups present. In one article the writer compared the conduct of Californio and Anglo women:

> Suffice it to say, that the senoritas looked their prettiest and with their dangerous eyes shot bright glances clean through many a masculine waistcoat, while the American ladies present, appeared with that quiet grace and ease which belongs to their social character, . . .[114]

Articles about crimes committed in the city usually commented on the nationality of the individuals who committed these acts, informing the reader if the criminals were Mexicans, Indians, or Anglos. A typical article appeared in the *Herald* on August 6, 1853, and told the reader about a Mexican who had raped a little girl at Soledad. The listing of letters left in the post office, which appeared in the *Herald* periodically, also suggests the emphasis on racial characteristics. These lists always appeared with the different nationalities grouped under separate headings. In one list Anglos appeared in one group alphabetically, Californios in another, and Frenchmen in another.[115] If people did not stress ethnic backgrounds so strongly, all of the letters would have been cited in one large list. They did, however, and their attitudes must have influenced their political behavior.

When Anglos considered the racial background of the Californios, they divided them in two distinct groups. They thought of the upper-class Californios as Spaniards who had maintained the purity of their race. John Russell Bartlett, head of the Second United States Boundary Commission, wrote from San Diego: "there remain many of the old Castillian families here, who have preserved their blood from all mixture with the Indians."[116] Even so, most Anglos considered Spaniards inferior, known for cruelty and deceit. This was made evident in 1851 in events surrounding an Indian revolt in San Diego County. When Anglos apprehended the leader of this rebellion he implicated two upper-class Californios as his advisors, José Antonio Estudillo and Juan Ortega. Most of the citizens of San Diego dismissed these accusations, but on March 13, 1851, a letter appeared in the *Herald* commenting on them. The writer declared that he could "hardly believe the imputation cast upon these men, nor would [he] entertain it, but that it is possible they are illustrations of the refined and subtil [*sic*] treachery that has so long characterized the race from which they are descended."[117] Another example of Anglos' belief in Spanish cruelty appeared in an article in the *Herald* in May 1855. The writer described a recent execution in Havana, emphasizing the enjoyment Spaniards took in the event and calling it a brutal murder.[118]

Whereas Anglos believed upper-class Californios to be cruel and treacherous, they considered the lower-class Californios, whom they termed "greasers," even more inferior because they were of mixed blood. One early Anglo traveler described a "greaser" as exhibiting "much of the Indian character; the dull suspicious countenance, the small twinkling piercing eye, the laziness and filth of a free brute, using freedom as the mere means of animal enjoyment."[119] Lt. Cave J. Couts, a prominent San Diego resident, declared that when you have met a "greaser," you have met a thief and a robber. Upper-class Californios even made this fallacious distinction, separating their class racially from the lower-class Californios, whom they termed *cholos*. Modern scholarship demonstrates that both classes had mixed blood and suggests slight racial differences between upper- and lower-class Californios.[120]

The important point, however, is not the existence of this belief about upper-class racial purity, but its manifestations. One of the significant manifestations of class divisions among Californios occurred over the conflicts with the administration of justice. Many Californios believed that a dual system of justice existed, one for Anglos and a harsher one for Californios, Mexicans, and Indians. Yet, some upper-class Californios

Jose de Guadalupe Concepción Estudillo
(1838-1917)

joined with Anglos and supported the Anglo system of justice. In San Diego, José M. Estudillo served as a member of the 1854 Grand Jury. The report of the jury talked about the problem of justice when the system had to deal with people of a lower order. The members of the jury, apparently including Estudillo, believed that the presence of Mexicans and Indians in San Diego made the enforcement of the law more difficult. One political repercussion of this division among Californios is the fact that Californios running for public office could not win a majority of even the Californios' votes. In the 1855 election, for example, poll lists show that Californios cast forty-one votes. One of the Estudillo brothers, running for school superintendent, won only nineteen votes, less than half of the Californios' votes.[121]

Besides racial attitudes, other feelings developed from a cultural conflict between Anglos and Californios which affected the political fortunes of the Californios. In 1854 and 1855 articles appeared in the *Herald* about the new American Party, popularly known as the Know-Nothings. Those who belonged to this party worried about the threat of the Catholic Church to the United States. They looked upon Catholic priests and bishops as instruments in a popish plot to gain control of the country. One article in the paper discussed this plot and suggested actions that could be taken to defend against it.

> This Know-Nothing Movement will have one good effect, we think, in the Western States, where some denominations have attempted to interfere with, and get control of our public schools. By being prescribed and debarred from holding any office of honor, profit or trust, for a few years, they will learn to conduct themselves as republicans should, and keep Church and State as far asunder as possible.[122]

In the first half of the 1850s the Know-Nothing party gained little support at the polls in San Diego, but some Anglos agreed with their ideas about Catholicism. One writer believed that the growing Catholic population threatened America and declared that the Catholic world planned to gain control of the country. The author appealed to the patriotism of the readers to resist this threat.[123] In another issue of the paper the editor condemned a Catholic priest for interfering in local affairs because the priest told Catholics of the community not to participate in the St. John celebration of the Free Masons. The writer criticized the priest for stirring up discord among the people "who have long been taught to consider the Romish Church as the most corrupt and wicked institution ever organized since the creation of the world."[124]

Some contemporary observers in this period have revealed other explanations for Californios' loss of political power. John H. Richardson, in an interview in the *San Diego Union*, on July 16, 1876, described the apparent lack of strict enforcement of residency requirements and election regulations. He recalled that when he arrived in San Diego in the summer of 1849, after traveling around Cape Horn, some men came out to the ship and asked the Anglo passengers if they would like to vote in the local elections. These men offered to take the passengers into town and if they did not want to do this, the men told them to write their choices down on paper and they would take their ballots to the polls.[125]

This incident demonstrates the importance of two points which allowed Anglos to dominate political affairs over the Californios. First, election regulations created by Anglos allowed other Anglos the privilege of voting and holding office after being in California for only a short period of time. In the election of 1849 the military governor of the state declared that every free male citizen of the United States and Upper California who was twenty-one years of age could vote, if they were residents of their electoral district.[126] The lack of time qualifications with residency requirements enabled almost all Anglo adult males to vote. After the state constitution went into effect in 1850, these regulations changed making it necessary for voters to be residents of the state six months prior to any election and a resident in a voting district for thirty days before an election.

For the first city and county elections the state legislature declared that all persons eligible to vote were eligible to hold public office. Californios under these regulations became citizens and eligible to vote if they gave up their Mexican citizenship as required by the treaty signed by the United States and Mexico ending the war of 1846.[127]

All of these regulations enabled Anglos to quickly assert their dominance over California to the disadvantage of the Californios. Anglos coming to California in tremendous numbers during these years received the right to vote with little delay and also the right to hold public offices. On the other hand, Californios remained relatively fixed in the numerical size of their group after they became citizens of the United States, and the flood of Anglo immigrants eventually overwhelmed them. In time regulations governing voters and office seekers became stiffer, but only after a large number of Anglos had lived in the state for five or six years. In the first half of 1855 the state legislature modified some of the laws pertaining to qualifications for office holding. The assembly and senate both approved an amendment to the state constitution requiring candidates for the legislature to be citizens of the state for two years and of their district one year prior to their candidacy.[128]

The shipboard episode described by Richardson also suggested that the operation of elections functioned under Anglo control. Little evidence remains about early election procedures in San Diego, especially since the city did not have a newspaper to cover them until 1851. Because Richardson and his traveling companions cast ballots in the election of 1849, it seems reasonable to conclude that Anglos took charge of the local elections and controlled the different precincts.

After 1851 the *Herald* reported information about local elections which included the names of judges and inspectors appointed to watch over the elections. Through an examination of these appointments the extent of Anglo control over these affairs becomes evident. In the 1853 election for city trustees, Judge Benjamin Hayes appointed E. M. Morse as inspector and Julian Ames and Albert B. Smith as judges. In this election San Diegans elected Morse as a trustee; evidently no one thought he would have a conflict of interest acting as an inspector while running for office. During the 1853 electoral activity Judge Hayes appointed two Californios to serve as judges for the precinct at San Luis Rey, Ramón Osuna and Jesús Machado. Anglos filled the remaining positions of judges and inspectors throughout the county. Of the five elections during this period in which records do exist, this is the only time Californios were given appointments. One practice, however, did repeat itself in 1853. William H. Moon served as an inspector for the precinct at New San Diego while running for the office of public administrator.[129]

In the 1854, 1855, and 1856 elections, Anglos filled all the positions of inspectors and judges in the different precincts. Again, individuals served as inspectors and judges while running for office. In the first election Cave J. Couts, the county judge, appointed J. S. McIntire as one of the judges at the Township of Agua Caliente while McIntire sought election as justice of the peace. Couts also appointed John S. Barker, a candidate for justice of the peace, as a judge for the precinct at New San Diego. While Couts was making all of these appointments, he was running for offices of justice of the peace and school commissioner in the San Luis Rey Township. This pattern repeated itself in the 1855 election, with Anglos filling all the positions as inspectors and judges. Julian Ames served as a judge in New San Diego and also ran for superintendent of public instruction. In 1856 James Nichols acted as an inspector at New San Diego, while winning election as justice of the peace and county supervisor.[130]

25

County resident, Jose Antonio de Jesus Serrano, born at the San Diego Presidio 1814.

The way election judges and inspectors could influence an election is revealed in an editorial in the *Herald* by Judson Ames, calling for election reform.

> The present slow-coach process of counting the votes, delays the knowledge of the result until the officers of the polls (who may be always honest, but are not invariably,) choose to declare it. In the meantime, as is the notorious practice in San Francisco, the wrong tickets may be stolen from the box, the right ones stuffed in, and any candidate made sure of his election.
>
> The judges or inspectors of the election, who reads off the tickets, in the process of counting, may without detection, substitute in the reading, another name in the body of the tickets, for the one that is there, if he wishes to help out a friend of his, or a political candidate of his own faith.[131]

These charges leveled by Ames were not without some substance. After the new members of the Common Council took office in 1851, Charles Haraszthy, a member of the previous council, contested the election of Councilman J. Jordan. After prolonged debate, the council decided that Jordan should be removed from office because his election was invalid. The next year, some San Diegans sent formal protests to the state legislature contesting the election of their representative to that body. They charged that many people were allowed to vote who were not qualified.[132]

Besides voting procedures, contemporary observers also indicated language as a reason for the weakened political strength of Californios. George Derby, a lieutenant in the United States Army and a popular writer, described one of the elections and noted that an Anglo translator explained the ballot to the Californios who wished to vote. Judson Ames, editor of the *Herald*, commented on one occasion that the language barrier made it difficult for Californios and Anglos to understand each others' ways. Significantly enough, election notices, appearing in the *Herald*, were printed in English, while tax notices were published in Spanish and English.[133]

Benjamin Hayes, a county judge during the 1850s and a sympathetic observer, noted that the Californios' lack of political experience put them at a disadvantage. Prior to the coming of Anglos, Californios in San Diego had seldom participated in local elections. Only briefly, in the 1830s did the Mexican government grant San Diego civil rule and permit elections to be held. Otherwise, San Diego was under a military government. The populace did choose their representatives to territorial and national government occasionally in the Mexican period. Thus, although the system of government instituted by the Anglos was not entirely new to the Californios, they had little experience with it. Judge Hayes declared further that the Californios never took full advantage of the new Anglo system of government. The Californios, he thought, were too reserved in their manners and did not know how to use the system to their full advantage. He remarked that Anglos would seek political office or try and force those in office to do what they wanted. The Californios only voiced their grievances in private.[134]

The reluctance of Californios to run for public office in San Diego, and their subsequent loss of political power, between 1849 and 1856, occurred for a variety of reasons. Americans from the beginning dominated political affairs of the community through their numerical superiority and control of election laws. Racial biases and cultural conflicts created attitudes which also made it difficult politically for Californios. The lack of unity among the Californios added further to their political weakness. Language differences and cultural patterns made it difficult for Californios to compete successfully with Anglos at their own game, under their rules. This experience of Californios in San Diego contrasted sharply with the experiences of Californios in other parts of southern California. In the formative years of state and local government, from 1850-1856, Californios in Los Angeles and Santa Barbara apparently remained a viable political force while in San Diego Anglos took charge almost immediately.

GEORGE PARRISH TEBBETS
Early Anglo Merchant

NOTES

1. Nellie Van de Grift Sanchez, *Spanish Arcadia* (Los Angeles: Powell Publishing Co., 1929), pp. 195-97.
2. Robert Glass Cleland, *The Cattle on a Thousand Hills: Southern California, 1850-1880*, 2d ed. (San Marino: Huntington Library, 1951), p. 31. Most historians have accepted Cleland's arguments. For example, see Leonard Pitt, *The Decline of the Californios: A Social History of the Spanish-Speaking Californians, 1846-1890* (Berkeley: University of California Press, 1969), p. 12; Cecil Robinson, *With the Ears of Strangers: The Mexican in American Literature* (Tucson: University of Arizona Press, 1963), pp. 29-30; Richard F. Pourade, *The History of San Diego: The Silver Dons* (San Diego: Union-Tribune Publishing Co., 1963), pp. 61, 68-69; John W. Caughey, *California: A Remarkable State's Life History* (Englewood Cliffs, N. J.: Prentice-Hall, Inc., 1970), pp. 113-16; Andrew F. Rolle, *California: A History* (New York: Thomas Y. Crowell Co., 1969), pp. 112-19; and Warren A. Beck and David A. Williams, *California: A History of the Golden State* (Garden City, N.Y.: Doubleday & Co., 1972), pp. 80-86.
3. Although most historians have agreed with Cleland, some have not. For example, see Jessie Davis Francis, "An Economic and Social History of Mexican California, 1828-1846," 2 vols. (Ph.D. dissertation, University of California, Berkeley, 1936), 2:755-61; and Raymond V. Padilla, "A Critique of Pittian History," *El Grito*, 6 (Fall 1972): 8-15.
4. Hubert Howe Bancroft, *The Works of Hubert Howe Bancroft: History of California*, 7 vols. (San Francisco: History Co., 1884-90; reprint ed. Santa Barbara: Wallace Hebberd Publisher, 1970), 3:611-12.
5. Robert G. Cowan, *Ranchos of California: A List of Spanish Concessions 1775-1822 and Mexican Grants 1822-1846* (Fresno: Academy Library Guild, 1956), p. 148; and Bancroft, *Works: California*, 3:309.
6. Herbert E. Bolton, "The Mission as a Frontier Institution in the Spanish-American Colonies," in *Wider Horizons of American History* (Notre Dame: University of Notre Dame Press, 1967), p. 117.
7. Richard F. Pourade, *The History of San Diego: The Time of the Bells* (San Diego: Union-Tribune Publishing Co., 1961), pp. 108-9.
8. Zephyrin Engelhardt, *San Diego Mission* (San Francisco: James H. Barry Co., 1920), pp. 204, 221-23; and Idem, *San Luis Rey Mission* (San Francisco: James H. Barry Co., 1921), 41, 218-22.
9. Bolton, "The Mission," p. 115.
10. C. Alan Hutchinson, *Frontier Settlement in Mexican California: The Híjar-Padrés Colony, and Its Origins, 1769-1835* (New Haven, Conn.: Yale University Press, 1969), pp. 145-46, 228-29.
11. *Ibid.*, pp. 133-34.
12. C. Alan Hutchinson, "Mexican Government and the Mission Indians of Upper California 1821-1835," *The Americas*, 21 (April 1965): 340-45.

13. Hutchinson, *Frontier Settlement*, p. 178.
14. *Ibid.*, pp. 89-93.
15. Hutchinson, "Mission Indians," p. 343.
16. Hutchinson, *Frontier Settlement*, pp. 128, 224-29.
17. Bancroft, *Works: California*, 3:336-37, 342-44.
18. *Ibid.*, pp. 611-12, 620-23.
19. *Ibid.*, pp. 613-14; Raymond S. Brandes, trans., "Times Gone by in Alta California: Recollections of Señora Doña Juana Machado Alipaz de Ridington (Wrightington)," *Historical Society of Southern California Quarterly*, 41 (September 1951): 203-7; George Harwood Phillips, "Indian Resistance and Cooperation in Southern California: The Garra Uprising and Its Aftermath" (Ph.D. dissertation, University of California, Los Angeles, 1973), pp. 62-63; Martin Cole and Henry Welcome, eds. *Don Pío Pico's Historical Narrative*, trans. Arthur P. Botello (Glendale, Calif.: Arthur H. Clark Co., 1973), pp. 86-87; and William Ellison and Francis Price, eds. *The Life and Adventures in California of Don Agustín Jassens, 1834-1856* (San Marino: Huntington Library, 1953), pp. 93-105.
20. Bancroft, *Works: California*, 3:611-15.
21. *Ibid.*, 4:618; and Cowan, *Ranchos of California*, passim.
22. Bancroft, *Works: California*, 3:611-12, 4:617-18; Carl H. Heilbron, ed., *History of San Diego County* (San Diego: San Diego Press Club, 1936), p. 76; and Sherburne Friend Cook, *The Conflict between the California Indians and White Civilization: I. The Indian versus the Spanish Mission* (Berkeley: University of California Press, 1943), pp. 133-34.
23. Bancroft, *Works: California*, 3:361; and Ellison and Price, *Life and Adventures*, p. 103.
24. Bancroft, *Works: California*, 3:609, 619, 356-57; *Daily Alta California*, September 10, 1856; and *San Diego Herald*, April 11, 1857.
25. Lucy Lytle Killea, "The Political History of a Mexican Pueblo: San Diego from 1825 to 1845," *The Journal of San Diego History* 12 (July and October 1966): July, 24-32.
26. Charles Franklin Carter, trans., "Duhaut-Cilly's Account of California in the Years 1827-1828," *California Historical Society Quarterly* 8 (June, September, and December 1929): 218-19.
27. Alfred Robinson, *Life in California: During a Residence of Several Years in That Territory* (San Francisco: Doxey, 1897: reprint ed., with an Introduction by Andrew F. Rolle, Santa Barbara: Peregrine Publishers, 1970), p. 12.
28. Bancroft, *Works: California*, 3:361-62.
29. Pourade, *History: Silver Dons*, pp. 24-25.
30. Robinson, *Life in California*, p. 128.
31. William E. Smythe, *History of San Diego 1542-1908* (San Diego: History Co., 1908), p. 255. Bancroft (*Works: California*, 3:349) also revealed that missionaries at San Luis Rey, anticipating the secularization of the missions, ordered the killing of thousands of cattle. Christian Indians at San Luis Rey also destroyed some cattle (same vol., p. 346).
32. Hutchinson, *Frontier Settlement*, pp. 122-23.
33. Killea, "Mexican Pueblo," October, 33-34.
34. *Ibid.*
35. George Tays, "Revolutionary California: The Political History of California from 1820 to 1848" (Ph.D. dissertation, University of California, Berkeley, rev. ed., 1934), p. iv.
36. As late as 1846, San Diego remained closed to foreign trade. Bancroft, *Works: California*, 3:548, 5:618.
37. Rolle, *California*, pp. 196, 201-2; Samuel Francis DuPont, *Extracts from Private Journals-Letters of Captain S. F. DuPont while in Command of the Cyane during the War with Mexico, 1846-1848* (Wilmington, Del.: Ferris Bros., 1885), pp. 40-42; James Millar Guinn, *Historical and Biographical Records of Southern California, Containing a History of Southern California from Its Earliest Settlement to the Opening Year of the Twentieth Century* (Chicago: Chapman Publishing Co., 1902), pp. 104-9; Muster Rolls of the Native California Co., December 22, 1846, Pierson B. Reading Collection, California State Library, Sacramento, Calif.; and Bancroft, *Works: California*, 5:386.
38. Pitt, *Decline of the Californios*, pp. 28-34.
39. Pourade, *History: Silver Dons*, pp. 83-84; and U.S., President, *California and New Mexico*, H. Ex. Doc. 17, 31st Cong., 1st sess., 1850, p. 680.
40. Tays, "Revolutionary California," p. xiii.
41. William H. Emory, *Lieutenant Emory Reports: A Reprint of Lieutenant W. H. Emory's Notes of a Military Reconnaissance* (New York: H. Long and Bro., 1848; reprint ed., with an Introduction by Ross Calvin, Albuquerque: University of New Mexico, 1951; also in paperback edition by the same publisher, University of New Mexico, 1968), p. 174.
42. John Caughey and Laree Caughey, *California Heritage: An Anthology of History and Literature* (Los Angeles: Ward Ritchie Press, 1966), pp. 160-62; and Pourade, *History: Silver Dons*, pp. 83-84.
43. Rolle, *California: A History*, p. 217; and David J. Weber, ed., *Foreigners in Their Native Land: Historical Roots of the Mexican Americans*, with a Foreword by Ramón Ruiz (Albuquerque: University of New Mexico, 1973), p. 148.
44. Cleland, *The Cattle on a Thousand Hills*, p. 102.
45. Pitt, *The Decline of the Californios*, pp. 108-9.
46. Rodman W. Paul, "The Spanish Americans in the Southwest, 1848-1900," in *The Frontier Challenge: Response to the Trans-Mississippi West*, ed. John G. Clark (Lawrence, Kan.: University of Kansas Press, 1971), pp. 41-42.

47. *San Francisco Daily Alta California*, December 22, 1849.
48. Andrew F. Rolle, "William Heath Davis and the Founding of American San Diego," *California Historical Quarterly* 31 (March 1952): 33-34; and *San Francisco Daily Alta California*, February 26, 1850. Clarence Alan McGrew, *City of San Diego and San Diego County: The Birth Place of California*, 2 vols. (New York: American Historical Society, 1922), 1:70-71.
49. *San Francisco Daily Alta California*, January 22, 1850; and Pourade, *History: Silver Dons*, p. 163; Pitt, *Decline of the Californios*, p. 111; and Pourade, *History: Silver Dons*, pp. 170-72.
50. Pitt, *Decline of the Californios*, p. 111; Pourade, *History: Silver Dons*, pp. 170-72; and *San Diego Herald*, September 25 and October 6, 1851.
51. *San Francisco Daily Alta California*, February 27, 1851; and Pourade, *History: Silver Dons*, p. 172.
52. Rolle, "William Heath Davis," pp. 39-41.
53. Smythe, *San Diego*, p. 243; and *San Francisco Daily Alta California*, July 6, 1854. An account book of the county treasurer listed more Anglo and Californio merchants than newspaper records indicated were here. In 1855 eight Californios and twenty-four Anglos paid license fees to "vend goods and wares." (All those with Spanish surnames were considered Californios, and the others listed were counted as Anglos.) Evidently, some of these merchants chose not to advertise in the local paper. San Diego County, Calif., Treasurer's Office, Cash Book of the Treasurer of San Diego, 1854-1855, Ephraim W. Morse Collection, California State Library, Sacramento, Calif.
54. Marjorie Tisdale Wollcott, ed., *Pioneer Notes from the Diaries of Judge Benjamin Hayes, 1849-1875* (Los Angeles: Privately printed, 1929), p. 128; William M. Kramer and Norton B. Stern, "The Rose of San Diego," *The Journal of San Diego History* 19 (Fall 1973): 32; Pourade, *History: Silver Dons*, pp. 204-8, 234-37; and *San Diego Herald*, April 1, 1854, August 18, 1855, and September 15, 1855.
55. Pitt, *Decline of the Californios*, p. 112; Rolle, "William Heath Davis," p. 42; and *San Diego Herald*, December 23, 1854 and December 1, 1855.
56. Cowan, *Ranchos of California*, passim. Cowan listed three other ranchos as being within the county, but they were either in Orange County or Baja California. Historical research on the number of ranchos in the San Diego area is incomplete. Most of the literature on the subject listed only those ranchos approved by the 1851 Land Commission. Bancroft, Cowan, and newspaper accounts revealed that other ranchos existed in San Diego but were either not presented to or rejected by the commission. Since Cowan examined all the land grant papers, I relied on his research for deciding how many ranchos were in the area.
57. Iris Wilson Engstrand and Thomas L. Scharf, "Rancho Guajome: A California Legacy Preserved," *Journal of San Diego History* 20 (Winter 1974): 2-3; and Cecil R. Moyer, *Historic Ranchos of San Diego*, ed. Richard F. Pourade (San Diego: Union-Tribune Publishing Co., 1969), p. 95. Also Captain George W. Hamley probably acquired Rancho Guejito y Canada de Palomia sometime during this period.
58. *Memorias de la Beata* by Apolinaria Lorenzana, March 1878, Bancroft Library, Berkeley, Calif. Bancroft concluded that she lost the rancho "by some legal hocus-pocus" which she never understood (Bancroft, *Works: California*, 4:718). Most other historians have accepted Bancroft's conclusions. A Federal Writers' Project book about San Diego, however, has a third explanation for Miss Lorenzana's loss of the rancho. They described how some men induced her to sign over the rancho, while she believed she was signing a statement about the census. Federal Writers' Project, *San Diego: A California City* (San Diego: San Diego Historical Society, 1937), p. 56.
59. Kurt Van Horn, "Tempting Temecula: The Making and Un-Making of a Southern California Community," *Journal of San Diego History* 20 (Winter 1974): 29; City of San Diego, Calif., Common Council, Minutes of the Common Council, Serra Museum and Library, San Diego, Calif., August 31, 1850; Marjorie McMorrow Rustvold, "San Pasqual Valley: Rancheria to Greenbelt" (Master's thesis, San Diego State College, 1968), pp. 88-89; and *San Diego Herald*, November 19, 1853.
60. Letter of H. S. Burton to E. D. Townsend, January 27, 1856 and letter of Adam Johnson to Thomas J. Henley, July 10, 1856, "Letters Received by the Office of Indian Affairs, 1824-1881," Microcopy No. 234, roll 35, National Archives, Washington, D.C.; and Rustvold, "San Pasqual," p. 89.
61. U.S., Census Bureau, *8th Census, 1860, Population Schedules: San Diego, Calif.*, Washington, D.C., photostat copy; and San Diego County, Calif., Assessor's Office, Assessor's Rolls 1860, San Diego Public Library, San Diego, Calif.
62. Caughey, *California*, p. 198; and Cleland, *Thousand Hills*, pp. 103-10.
63. San Diego County, Calif., Auditor's Office, Tax Book 1850, Tax Files, Serra Museum and Library, San Diego, Calif.
64. California, State Legislature, State Census of 1852, Agricultural Production Statistics for San Diego County, State Archives, Sacramento, Calif. This analysis is not an exhaustive review of all available statistics about this problem. Cursory examination of other statistics, such as the Assessor's Appraisement List for 1852, revealed the same kind of trends. San Diego County, Calif., Assessor's Office, Assessor's Appraisement List 1852, Tax Files, Serra Museum and Library, San Diego, Calif.
65. California, State Legislature, Assembly, "Annual Report of the Surveyor General," Doc. No. 5, *Appendix to Assembly Journals*, 6th sess., 1855, p. 78; California, State Legislature, Senate, "Annual Report of the Surveyor General," Doc. No. 5, *Appendix to Senate Journals*, 7th sess., 1856, pp. 296-97; Wollcott, *Pioneer Notes*, p. 114; and *San Diego Herald*, April 26, 1856.
66. Smythe, *San Diego*, p. 241.
67. California, State Legislature, Senate, "Surveyor General Report, 1856," p. 297; and *San Francisco Daily Alta California*, September 8, 1853.
68. John Charles Frémont, *Geographical Memoirs upon Upper California in Illustration of His Map of Oregon and California*, with an Introduction by Allan Nevins and Dale Morgan (San Francisco: Book Club of California, 1964), p. 35.

69. California, State Legislature, Senate, "Annual Report of the Surveyor General," *Appendix to Senate Journals*, 8th sess., 1857, pull out page between page twenty-eight and twenty-nine; and U.S., Census Bureau, 7th Census 1850, Agricultural Production Statistics; San Diego County, Calif., California State Library, Sacramento, Calif.
70. *San Diego Herald*, January 13, 1855.
71. See tax records for the years 1850 through 1856, the United States Census for 1850, and the California State Census for 1852. They all show small amounts of improved land, as well as the value of farming implements.
72. California, State Legislature, Senate, "Surveyor General Report, 1856," p. 296.
73. Cleland, *Thousand Hills*, pp. 104-5; and *San Diego Herald*, May 21, 1853.
74. *San Diego Herald*, May 15, 1852.
75. *San Diego Herald*, May 31, 1856.
76. Cleland, *Thousand Hills*, pp. 111, 115; and Pitt, *Decline of the Californios*, p. 111.
77. Henry Baker Lynch, *Rainfall and Stream Run-Off in Southern California since 1769* (Los Angeles: Metropolitan Water District of Southern California, 1931), p. 13.
78. Ford A. Carpenter, *The Climate and Weather of San Diego California* (San Diego: San Diego Chamber of Commerce, 1913), p. 36; and *San Francisco Daily Alta California*, October 28, 1851.
79. *San Diego Herald*, April 11, 1857.
80. Letter to Captain Jesse D. Hunter from Miguel de Pedrorena et al., July 2, 1847, Records of the Tenth Military Department, 1846-1851, 7 rolls, Microcopy No. 210, National Archives, Washington, D.C., roll 2.
81. Letter to Col. R. B. Mason from Col. J. D. Stevenson, May 16, 1848, Tenth Military Department, roll 3.
82. Pourade, *History: Silver Dons*, pp. 177-80.
83. Cleland, *Thousand Hills*, p. 67; and *San Francisco Daily Alta California*, March 31 and November 22, 1853. *San Francisco Daily Alta California*, September 10, 1856.
84. Cleland, *Thousand Hills*, p. 70.
85. *San Francisco Daily Alta California*, February 14, 1852.
86. Cleland, *Thousand Hills*, p. 302.
87. Paul W. Gates, "Adjudication of Spanish-Mexican Land Claims in California," *Huntington Library Quarterly* 21 (May 1958): 216.
88. *San Francisco Daily Alta California*, December 26, 1853.
89. Cleland, *Thousand Hills*, p. 23; and Gates, "Land Claims," p. 217.
90. Cleland, *Thousand Hills*, p. 294; and Weber, *Native Land*, p. 159.
91. Gates, "Land Claims," pp. 233-34.
92. *San Francisco Daily Alta California*, March 8, 1852.
93. Common Council, Minutes to the Common Council, August 2, 1854.
94. California, *Statutes Passed at the First Session of the Legislature* (1850), pp. 135-44. San Diego County, Calif., Clerk to the Board of Supervisors, Minutes to the Board of Supervisors, County Administration Building, San Diego, Calif., July 30, 1853 and July 10, 1855.
95. Cleland, *Thousand Hills*, pp. 122-23.
96. *San Francisco Daily Alta California*, September 8, 1851 and March 1, 1852.
97. *San Francisco Daily Alta California*, January 28, 1853.
98. Wollcott, *Pioneer Notes*, pp. 113-14.
99. San Diego County, Calif., Assessor's Office, Assessor's Rolls 1886, 1887, and 1888, County Administration Building, San Diego, Calif. San Diego County, Calif., Assessor's Office, Assessor's Records 1854, California State Library, Sacramento, Calif.; and San Diego County, Calif., Assessor's Office, Tax Book 1855, San Diego Public Library, San Diego, Calif.
100. San Diego County, Calif., Assessor's Office, Tax Book 1856, San Diego Public Library, San Diego, Calif.
101. Pitt, *Decline of the Californios*, pp. 131-37.
102. Theodore Grivas, *Military Governments in California, 1846-50: With a Chapter on Their Prior Use in Louisiana, Florida, and New Mexico* (Glendale, Calif.: Arthur H. Clark Co., 1963), pp. 102-3; California, *Statutes 1850*, pp. 58-59, 121-24; Pourade, *History: Silver Dons* pp. 159, 174, and 198; and Heilbron, *San Diego County*, p. 407.
103. Letter to Stephen Kearny from Henry Fitch, May 2, 1847, Election Results for the Office of the *Alcalde*, October 1847, Tenth Military Department, rolls 2 and 6; and U.S., California Military Governor, San Diego Election Poll List, San Diego Election Files, State Archives, Sacramento, Calif.
104. Heilbron, *San Diego County*, p. 82. Smythe, *San Diego*, pp. 230, 427.
105. Pitt, *Decline of the Californios*, pp. 139-46.
106. Smythe, *San Diego*, pp. 427-35; *San Diego Herald*, September 27, 1853, September 15, 1855 and November 8, 1856.
107. *San Diego Herald*, September 27, 1853, September 9, 1854, and November 1, 1856.
108. *San Diego Herald*, August 28, 1851 and September 4, 1851.
109. *San Diego Herald*, April 1, 1854 and April 22, 1854.
110. Rolle, *California: A History*, pp. 213-18.
111. Heilbron, *San Diego County*, p. 76. This total remains uncertain because he listed thirty-one males between the ages

of twenty and thirty, and there is no way of knowing how many were twenty and, therefore, below the minimum voting age of twenty-one.
112. U.S., Census Bureau, 7th Census, 1850, Population Schedules: San Diego, Calif., National Archives, Washington, D.C., photostat copy.
113. Smythe, *San Diego*, pp. 230-31. Comparing the poll list in the 1850 county election with the 1850 census disclosed evidence that soldiers had cast ballots. U.S., Census Bureau. 7th Census, 1850. The California State Census of 1852 showed the same type of trends as the national census. California, Legislature, California State Census, 1852, San Diego Public Library, San Diego, Calif.
114. *San Diego Herald*, December 10, 1853.
115. *San Diego Herald*, August 6, 1853 and November 4, 1854.
116. John Russell Bartlett, *Personal Narrative of Exploration and Incidents in Texas, New Mexico, California, Sonora, and Chihuahua, Connected with the United States and Mexican Boundary Commission during the Years 1850, '51, '52, and '53*. 2 vols. (n.p.: Appleton, 1895; reprint ed., Chicago: Rio Grande Press, 1965), 2:104.
117. Robinson, *With the Ears of Strangers*, pp. 67-68, 190-95; and *San Diego Herald*, March 13, 1852.
118. *San Diego Herald*, May 19, 1855.
119. Thomas Jefferson Farnham, *Travels in California* (New York: n.p., 1844; reprint ed., with a Foreword by Joseph A. Sullivan, Oakland: Biobooks, 1947), p. 140.
120. Cave Johnson Couts, Unpublished Diary, San Diego Public Library, San Diego, California, p. 70. Manuel P. Servín, "California's Hispanic Heritage: A View into the Spanish Myth," *Journal of San Diego History* 19 (Winter 1973): 2; and Jack D. Forbes, "Black Pioneers: The Spanish-Speaking Afroamericans of the Southwest," in *Minorities in California History*, ed. George E. Frakes and Curtis B. Solberg (New York: Random House, 1971), pp. 29-33.
121. *San Diego Herald*, June 24, 1854 and September 15, 1855; and San Luis Rey Election Poll List 1855, Election Files, Serra Museum and Library, San Diego, Calif.
122. *San Diego Herald*, December 2, 1854.
123. *San Diego Herald*, July 30, 1853.
124. *San Diego Herald*, June 28, 1852.
125. *San Diego Union*, July 16, 1876.
126. California, Constitutional Convention, *Report of the Debates in the Convention of California, on the Formation of the State Constitution, in September and October, 1849*, by J. Ross Browne (Washington, D.C.: J.T. Towers, 1850), p. 4.
127. *Ibid.*, Appendix, p. iv; and California, *Statutes 1850*, p. 121.
128. *San Diego Herald*, June 30, 1855.
129. *San Diego Herald*, August 20, September 3, and September 27, 1853.
130. *San Diego Herald*, September 2 and September 9, 1854, August 25 and September 15, 1855, and November 1 and November 8, 1856.
131. *San Diego Herald*, September 8, 1855.
132. City of San Diego, Minutes to the Common Council, January 30, 1851; and *San Francisco Daily Alta California*, November 16 and November 30, 1852.
133. *San Diego Herald*, September 10 and October 15, 1853, and September 8 and November 17, 1855.
134. Killea, "Mexican Pueblo," October, 33. Wollcott, *Pioneer Notes*, pp. 113-14.

AGUA MANSA

and the

FLOOD OF JANUARY 22, 1862

SANTA ANA RIVER

San Bernardino County

Flood Control District

California

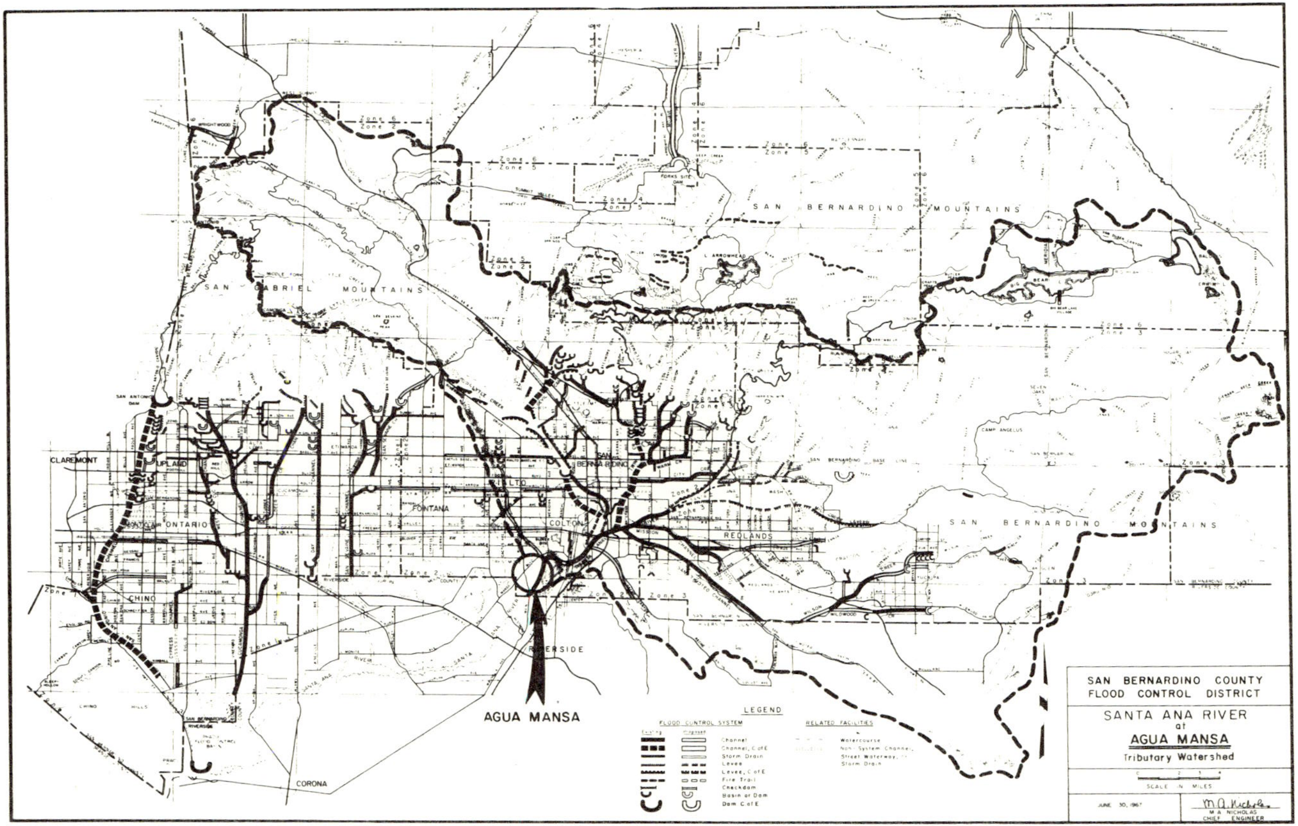
SAN BERNARDINO COUNTY
FLOOD CONTROL DISTRICT
SANTA ANA RIVER
at
AGUA MANSA
Tributary Watershed
SCALE IN MILES
JUNE 30, 1967
M A NICHOLAS
CHIEF ENGINEER
LEGEND
FLOOD CONTROL SYSTEM
Existing
Proposed
Channel
Channel, C of E
Storm Drain
Levee
Levee, C of E
Fire Trail
Checkdam
Basin or Dam
Dam C of E
RELATED FACILITIES
Watercourse
Non-System Channel
Street Waterway, or Storm Drain
AGUA MANSA
SAN BERNARDINO MOUNTAINS
SAN GABRIEL MOUNTAINS
CLAREMONT
UPLAND
ONTARIO
CHINO
FONTANA
COLTON
REDLANDS
RIVERSIDE
CORONA
CHINO HILLS
CAMP ANGELUS
L. ARROWHEAD
SAN BERNARDINO BASE LINE

SANTA ANA RIVER
San Bernardino Valley
History of Floods

SAN BERNARDINO COUNTY FLOOD CONTROL DISTRICT

SANTA ANA RIVER FLOODS

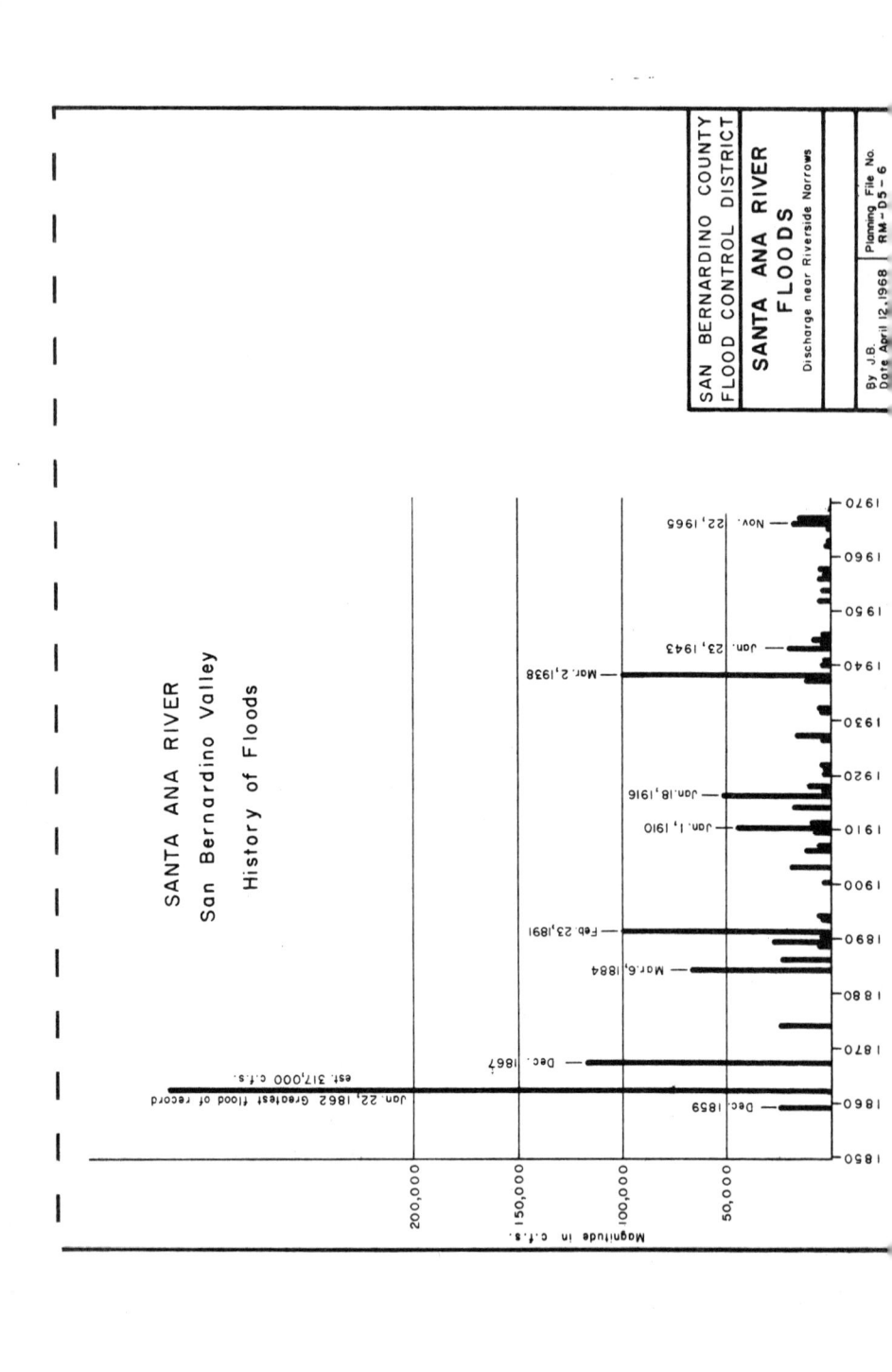

Discharge near Riverside Narrows

By J.B. | Date April 12, 1968 | Planning File No. RM-D5-6

- Dec. 1859
- Jan. 22, 1862 Greatest flood of record est. 317,000 c.f.s.
- Dec. 1867
- Mar. 6, 1884
- Feb. 23, 1891
- Jan. 1, 1910
- Jan. 18, 1916
- Mar. 2, 1938
- Jan. 23, 1943
- Nov. 22, 1965

Magnitude in c.f.s.: 50,000 / 100,000 / 150,000 / 200,000

Years: 1850, 1860, 1870, 1880, 1890, 1900, 1910, 1920, 1930, 1940, 1950, 1960, 1970

DELUGE, PRECIPITOUS RAINFALL, FLOOD! In some regions, these words have considerable impact. From past relationships or experiences therewith, they incite instant fear and alarm.

This is not true in Southern California or its San Bernardino Valley, where popular concepts of the region are likely to instill a more comfortable, semi-arid feeling of perennial sunshine. Even the crisp white rim of the San Gabriel and San Bernardino Mountains in close proximity, rising upwards to 11,000 feet, and capricious as they may be, are looked upon by the populace only as a pleasurable retreat or scenic backdrop to the sub-tropical valley.

There is an apparent incongruity between these popular concepts and the considered opinion of those who peer into a limited heritage of historical data and the arts or sciences of climatology and hydrology. In view of this, it is apparent that there is a need to quiet or clarify many of the misconceptions, and to provide as factual a portrayal of flood potential as we can on the Upper Santa Ana River in the San Bernardino Valley. It is to this end that this paper is devoted.

It is our purpose to discuss the greatest flood known in the upper reaches of the Santa Ana River Basin, and so far as practical, to remove the conjectural and legendary aspects heretofore attached. The flood occurring on January 22, 1862, is generally acclaimed as the greatest flood of record in the Upper Santa Ana River Basin following the entry of the white men in 1772. Many glowing accounts of the flood of 1862 have been documented and passed down through history. Of importance are those which directly bear on the community of Agua Mansa on the banks of the Santa Ana River about two miles southerly of the present City of Colton. The significance is that at this specific location there has been established the only high water mark on the Santa Ana River for the flood of 1862. It is also believed that this is the only high water mark established in Southern California, or even in the entire State of California, for that great flood.

Excerpts from the book "Pioneer Days in San Bernardino County" by Mrs. E. P. R. Crafts paint a vivid picture of that flood:

"The fall of 1861 was sunny and dry and warm until Christmas Day. The year of 1862 was a year to be remembered by the settlers of the San Bernardino Valley. This was the year of the great flood which culminated on the night of January 22, 1862, and wrought great destruction and desolation. It rained continuous for fifteen days and nights.
The gentle Santa Ana River became a raging torrent which, washing, swirling, and seething, swept everything from its path. The settlers awoke in alarm. The inhabitants of La Placita rushed to the Cerro de Harpero - the hill west of Loma District; those of Agua Mansa took refuge in the little church (Capilla San Salvador), which seemed to offer a place of safety. The church and the house of Cornelius Jensen, opposite the church, were the only buildings on high ground and the only ones that escaped the destruction in the flood.

"When morning came -- a scene of desolation. The Village of Agua Mansa was completely washed away, and where trees had been planted, a waste of muddy turbulent water met the gaze. Nothing remained of the little village but the church which stood on higher ground, some distance from the river. The settlers were left entirely destitute and some assistance was sent them from Los Angeles to help them build their homes upon higher ground far enough from the river to escape future damage from its overflow. The settlement again flourished, but never did the people trust the river which twice treacherously deceived them and wrought destruction to the work of their lands."

The San Bernardino correspondent of the Los Angeles Star reported on January 22, 1862 - "The Agua Mansa, a beautiful and flourishing settlement, is destroyed and not a vestige of anything left to denote that such a place even existed."

The following accounts are taken from the "Heritage of the Valley", by George William and Helen Pruitt Beattie:

"In January, 1862, came the memorable flood that harassed all California, and to which we have referred at length in the chapter on Agua Mansa. Mrs. Eliza P. R. Crafts, the widow of Ellison Robbins and later the wife of Myron H. Crafts, wrote of this flood many years after, describing it as follows: 'The fall of 1861 was sunny, dry, and warm until Christmas, which proved to be a rainy day. All through the holidays there continued what we should call a nice, pleasant rain...This... lasted until the 18th of January, 1862, when there was a downpour for twenty-four hours, or longer. All the flat from the Santa Ana River to Pine's Hotel (corner of present Third Street and Arrowhead Avenue) was under water, inundating the Valley for miles up and down the river; and Lytle Creek came rushing down D Street, across Third, finding an outlet through an open space into Warm Creek. Many families fled in the night to higher ground, losing everything they had stored away for the winter. There were so many families rendered homeless that there was not a house in San Bernardino with only one family in it. Some sheltered three or more. The constant rain on the adobe houses turned them to mud, and of course they fell to pieces.'"

"The location of the settlements on the Donation was apparently ideal. The Santa Ana flowed through it in a well-defined channel, the lands on either side being forested with alders, sycamores, willows and cottonwoods. No serious flood had interfered with their growth for centuries, as the rich bottom land testified, and the seepage from the river encouraged the growth of lush grass. Where irrigation was needed, water from the river was easily available. The settlers had the privilege of cutting firewood and fence material on Bandini's adjoining lands. Their sheep, cattle, and horses had free range in the river bottom for miles. There was every evidence of prosperity, modest though it was.

"But in January, 1862, after seventeen years of steady growth, dire disaster visited Jurupa Valley. Long-continued, warm rains followed an exceptionally heavy snowfall in the mountains, and the fast melting snow swelled the waters of the Santa Ana and its tributaries into a flood that came upon the settlement unexpectedly. One writer says there were 'billows fifty feet high.' The waters from the vast drainage area found themselves forced abruptly into a narrow channel, and just above Agua Mansa the river filled the entire Valley from bluff to bluff, reaching almost to the little church. For years two posts before it indicated the point to which the waters rose. The greatest rush came in the night. Father Borgatta, then the pastor, heard the roar in the distance, rang the bell frantically, and the people fled to high ground. Some of the last ones had to swim. Fortunately no lives were lost.

"Peter C. Peters, of Colton, told how he stood on the bluff by the cemetery the next morning and watched the adobe houses melt down in the flood and disappear. Trees were uprooted and carried along bodily, the land was cut and washed, and the fertile fields were buried under deposits of coarse sand and gravel. Only the church and a house near it remained."

It is the steps of this church and the rude marble posts referred to above which form the basis for establishing the high water mark for the flood of 1862.

In 1937, the County of San Bernardino's program of flood control and water conservation was guided by an Engineering Advisory Committee on Flood Control appointed by the Board of Supervisors. This committee consisted of P. B. Hasbrouck, George S. Hinckley, E. T. Ham, Charles L. Foulke, R. V. Ward, and Howard L. Way, the County Surveyor and ex officio member.

In 1937 Mr. Ward, in conjunction with the committee, undertook to recapture the high water mark of 1862. It was firmly established through the records that the waters had reached almost to the steps of the church and that later two rude marble posts were set in the earth to show the levels to which the waters rose. Photographs and artists' sketches of the church, steps and posts were yet in existence, though the adobe church had collapsed many years before. Only the adobe mound existed with the site pockmarked by numerous diggings, the result of those hunting rumored treasure buried at the old site.

Mr. Ward was able to locate the adobe step shown in the photographs, which elevation was equivalent to the top of the pipe base to an El Camino Real Association Mission Bell marker previously set on the northerly side of Agua Mansa Road. With this as a base mark, he surveyed the cross section and slope of the Santa Ana River. Mr. Al Reed, presently with the San Bernardino County Road Department, served on this original survey party. Mr. Ward's computation was summarized by the following data:

Santa Ana River drainage area	720 square miles
Cross sectional area	35,620 square feet
Wetted perimeter	3,420 feet
Hydraulic radius	10.38 feet
Slope	0.0041 feet per foot
Manning 'n'	0.050
Discharge using Kutter's formula	314,000 c.f.s.

It might be noted that Mr. Ward originally computed the flow at 338,000 c.f.s. but later recomputed it at 314,000 c.f.s.

The committee accompanied Mr. Celso Rubidoux to the site of the Agua Mansa Church. Mr. Rubidoux was the grandson of Louis Rubidoux, original settler of the present Riverside County area. He identified landmarks which had been pointed out to him in his childhood by his parents, which landmarks then showed evidence of the flood of 1862. He told of the sweeping away of the settlement and cultivated lands, evidences of what he saw in his boyhood. He corroborated the high water level of the flood at Agua Mansa as determined by the advisory committee through other sources.

Considerable dispute has ensued over the years concerning this large flood flow figure, primarily centering on the question of just where stream bed elevation actually was during the flood of 1862. If the stream bed had degraded since the flood, then this measurement would obviously be high. Many have expressed opinion that this is the case. Mr. Ward himself touched on the problem in his comments given below:

"It may be (perhaps rightly) contended that, due to the heavy load of debris which the river was undoubtedly carrying at the time, that a larger value should have been assigned to 'n' -- say .100 instead of .050 as used. On the other hand, it should be remembered that the bed of the Santa Ana River opposite Colton has silted up five or six feet within the past forty years and doubtless more since 1862. The profile of the river would indicate that a similar silting has occurred at Agua Mansa, less than two miles below Colton. Thus, a section taken just after that flood would have shown a greater cross-sectional area than at present. Furthermore, the fact that during a peak flood along an alluvial channel the section is always greater than the one taken just after the flood, would indicate that the discharge as shown is little, if any, in excess of the actual flow for that flood."

Consequently, the 1862 flood flow at this point on the Santa Ana River over the ensuing thirty years following 1937 has been subject to question and doubts and not heretofore been afforded official recognition.

In July of 1967 and as the result of conferences between Marion Scott of the United States Geological Survey and representatives of the San Bernardino County Flood Control District, it was concluded that a determined effort should be made to settle this question and if possible, officially establish the high water mark for the flood and the discharge. As the direct outcome, Mr. Scott undertook to evaluate and attempt to establish the 1862 stream bed. The Flood Control District undertook to verify or re-establish the cross section originally made in 1937. The latter was necessary, inasmuch as arbitrary datum had been assumed in the 1937 survey, part of the notes were found to be missing, and the El Camino Real bell post used as a bench mark no longer existed.

Mr. Scott undertook research of irrigation diversion works in the vicinity, and based upon elevations of certain early diversions, evidence of which still exists, concluded that the stream bed in the immediate vicinity was essentially as it exists today. This fact had been strongly suspected by those watching the river over a period of years.

With regard to the river cross section, it was necessary once again to locate the old adobe church and hope to find the all-important church steps. The site of the old church had long ago been cultivated over and there was no visible evidence of its existence. Only an undulating countryside remained. A review of County Surveyor records, however, produced an old Agua Mansa Road survey, marking and fixing the location of the El Camino Real pipe post and bell. Excavation at the exact location of the sign produced the actual enameled sign buried beneath the surface where it had fallen apparently when the post was uprooted many years ago in past road improvement work. The sign was turned over to the San Bernardino County Museum.

With the sign location established, and by the use of old artists' sketches, the residual mound of the old adobe church was quickly established. Trench excavation work was under the direction of Joseph Cowan, Field Engineer for the Flood Control District. The excavations revealed the actual foundation stones for the outer church walls. The foundation stones for the all-important church steps were also located. In addition, the approximate floor level of the old church was established through the finding of a stratum of white calcium material. It was concluded that this layer was the whitewashed surface of the inner church wall which toppled onto the floor. Also uncovered were decomposed cedar beams forming sills at the rear of the church building.

Thus the step elevation was again established and new profiles and sections made of the river under the direction of Al Bernatow, Flood Control District Surveyor. Upon plotting these, they duplicated with marked similarity the profile made by Mr. Ward in 1937.

All survey data was afforded to the U. S. Geological Survey for computation. The following hydraulic properties were computed:

    Cross sectional area   35,560 square feet

    Wetted perimeter   3,405 feet

    Hydraulic radius   10.4 feet

A survey of the recent flood of December 6, 1966 (20,000 c.f.s.), was made at the same site on October 10, 1967, by the U. S. G. S. The channel slope was computed as 0.00471 ft. per foot, and the water slope was computed from poor high water marks as 0.00305 ft. per foot. On the basis of this, and Mr. Ward's 1937 survey, the slope of the 1862 flood has been assumed to be 0.004 ft. per foot.

It was further determined from historical reports of the river channel in 1862 that the 'n' value determined by Mr. Ward was reasonable, and there was no sound basis for changing the value.

Based on the foregoing evaluation, the discharge for the flood of 1862 was computed by the U. S. G. S. with Manning's formula as follows:

$$Q = \frac{1.486}{n} R^{2/3} S^{1/2} A$$

$$Q = \frac{1.486}{0.050} \times 10.4^{2/3} \times 0.004^{1/2} \times 35,560$$

$$Q = 317,000 \text{ c.f.s.}$$

As the direct result of this, the United States Geological Survey has approved the computations and will enter the following maximum discharge statement into the records for the Santa Ana River at Riverside Narrows:

"Flood of January 22, 1862, about 320,000 c.f.s., result of slope-conveyance study at site 9.3 miles upstream. Stage at that site was about 5 feet higher than that of March 2, 1938."

The importance attaching to the formal establishment of this discharge can not be over-estimated. It means that in the Upper Santa Ana River Basin there is a new maximum flood of record to reckon with, over three times the magnitude of the heretofore accepted record flood of 1938, estimated at 100,000 c.f.s.

If, in 1938, there was a loss of 14 lives and $12,000,000 in direct flood damages in San Bernardino County, the question is posed as to what might be expected today with a re-occurrence of an 1862 flood peak with a fivefold population and tenfold valuation. To compound the effect, note must be made of the extensive encroachments into floodways since 1938 and tremendously increased areas exposed to flood hazards.

Thus, the need for a second look at flood potentials and measures in the Upper Santa Ana River Basin area is readily apparent.

W. A. Sidler
March 1968

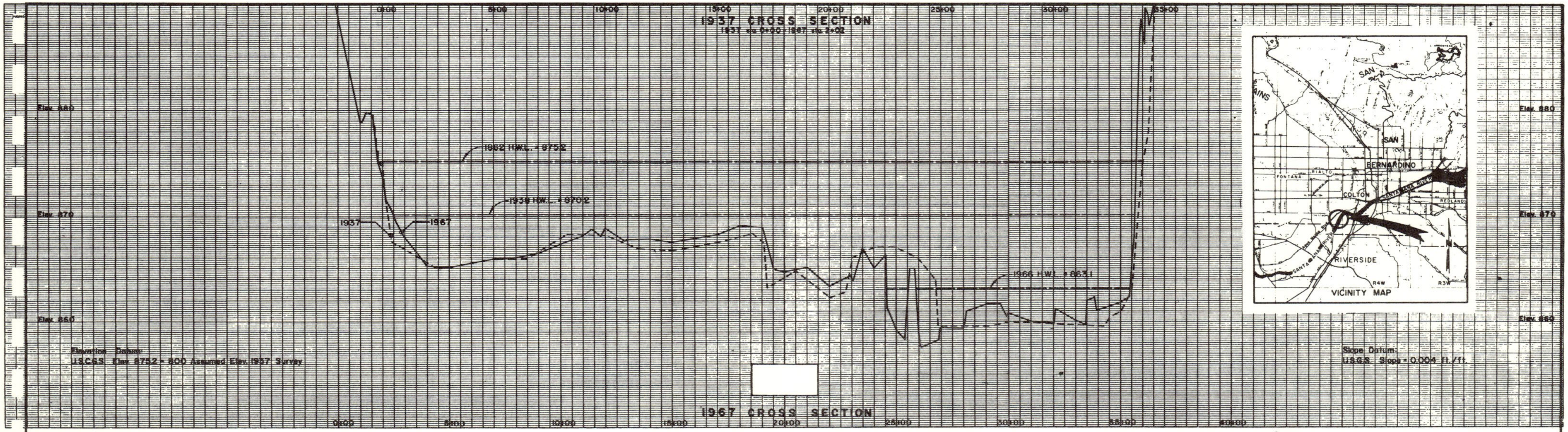

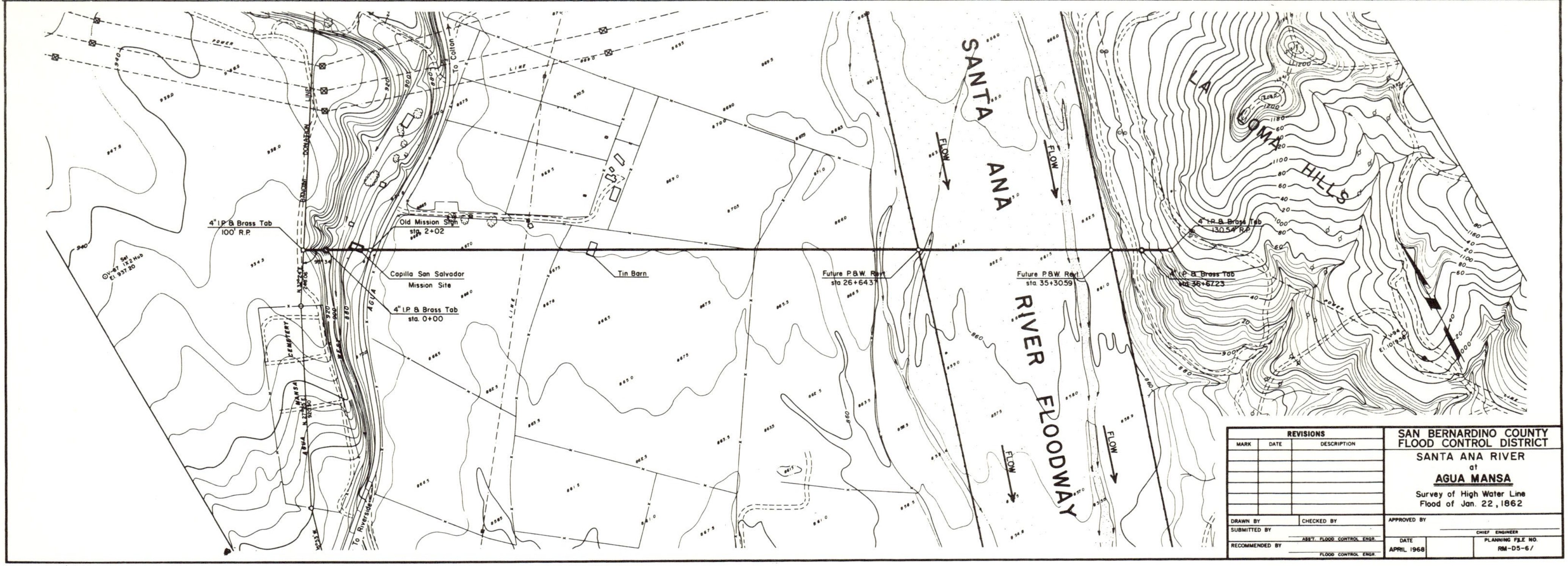

REVISIONS		
MARK	DATE	DESCRIPTION

SAN BERNARDINO COUNTY
FLOOD CONTROL DISTRICT

SANTA ANA RIVER
at
AGUA MANSA

Survey of High Water Line
Flood of Jan. 22, 1862

DRAWN BY | CHECKED BY | APPROVED BY
SUBMITTED BY | ASS'T. FLOOD CONTROL ENGR. | CHIEF ENGINEER
RECOMMENDED BY | FLOOD CONTROL ENGR.
DATE: APRIL 1968 | PLANNING FILE NO. RM-D5-6/

DON BERNARDO YORBA

Bernardo Yorba

Don Bernardo Yorba

By
TERRY E. STEPHENSON

GLEN DAWSON   LOS ANGELES

*Two hundred seventy-five copies
printed by Tom Williams at
The Fine Arts Press, Santa Ana
for Glen Dawson, June, 1941*

*Six hundred copies reprinted
by Edwards Bros., Ann Arbor, 1963*

TABLE OF CONTENTS

Chapter Title	Page
Introduction	1
On the Rio Santa Ana	4
California's First Farmers	8
Bernardo's Brothers	11
The Young Bernardo	18
Life on Rancho San Antonio	31
Mexican War Period	45
Before U. S. Land Commission	48
Land Transactions	52
The Chapel and the Cemetery	60
The Will is Written	66
Distribution of Estate	72
Anaheim and Water	79
A Hundred Years Ago	91
Purchases by J. W. Bixby	97
The Contests of 1896 and 1916	104
Today Where Bernardo Lived	110

ILLUSTRATIONS

Don Bernardo Yorba, his picture, his signature
. . . . Frontispiece

> This picture is from a painting by the French artist Penelon, who was in California in the 1850's. It is from a photo by C. C. Pierce of the original painting, now in the possession of Mrs. Ana Begue Packman. Two copies, one or both of which Penelon made, are in the Bowers Museum, one loaned by Mrs. Herman Locke, one by Arnold Domínguez.

Roads, Ditches and Anaheim in 1860 . . . 21

Adobe San Antonio about 1895, with insert showing ground plan in 1859 28

Adobe San Antonio in 1905 and 1925 . . . 52

INTRODUCTION

IN the romantic history of California appear the names of men whose lives covered many years under the Spanish flag, many years under the banner of Mexico, and eventually years under the Stars and Stripes. Don Bernardo Yorba was one of those men.

It has seemed to me that students of history too often are prone to select for research the doings and affairs of men whose lives were marked by violence rather than by quiet achievement such as have characterized the solid and lasting development of our State. Don Bernardo Yorba was not a man of violence. He was not a man of battle. However, in the substantial development of southern California, in his life as a ranchero, he was an outstanding man of his time.

This particular study in California history was begun for the purpose of presenting the historical background of one of California's newer and most interesting institutions, the Rancho Santa Ana Botanic Garden of the Native Plants of California, established and endowed by Mrs. Susanna Bixby Bryant as a memorial to her pioneer father, John W. Bixby. The Garden is located in the Santa Ana Cañon eight miles east of Placentia on land that was once a part of the old Rancho Cañon de Santa Ana, granted by the Mexican government to Don Bernardo Yorba in 1834. The bit of research involved led to unfolding the story of the life of Don Bernardo, and it seemed to me that the story was one worth telling to those who are interested in the history of our State. So, this book is being published as a contribution to the annals of southern California. Equally, it is offered as a contribution to the color and lore that, as the years go by, will gather about the institution that is devoted to the trees and shrubs and flowers of California. It comes from one who, for some years, has had the privilege of serving the Botanic Garden as a member of its advisory board.

Don Bernardo Yorba was born at San Diego, learned to read and write under the instruction of the Franciscan padres of the Mission San Diego, and in early manhood established himself as a ranchero on the banks of the Santa Ana river. The men of the Yorba and Peralta families pioneered in irrigation. Their use of the gravity flow of the river eventually, long after the second generation of Yorbas had died, became the basis of the division of the waters of the river.

There were four Yorba brothers, José Antonio, Tomás, Teodocio and Bernardo. The activities of any one of the four would prove deeply interesting, illustrative of the life that was led by those who had settled upon this fringe of Spanish civilization. José

Antonio and Tomás died before American occupation. Teodocio lost his vast possessions. It was Bernardo who held his ranchos together through the trying years of the '50's, and by many students of California history he may be chosen as a prime, perhaps the most outstanding example of the ranchero of California's golden age of rancho romance.

It is with gratitude that I acknowledge my indebtedness to Thomas Workman Temple III, of San Gabriel, foremost authority on the genealogy of California's old families, to William McPherson of Orange, whose extensive library of Californiana was a valuable source of information, to the Orange County Title Co., for generous access to its records, to those charming daughters of old California, granddaughters of Don Bernardo Yorba, Miss Mary Scully and Mrs. Martina Pelanconi, and to my wife, whose interest in and patience with my adventures in California history are highly appreciated.

TERRY E. STEPHENSON

Postscript

Twenty-three years have passed since Terry Stephenson wrote the above introduction. During those years many things have changed. The Santa Ana Botanic Garden has been moved from the high hills of the old Yorba ranch to a more accessible location north of Claremont Colleges; sub-divisions have crawled toward the place where Don Bernardo lived, and many of the landmarks that were vestiges of old California in Santa Ana canyon have disappeared. Although the landscape is changed the romance and history of the Yorba country is still alive in the writings of Terry Stephenson.

Terry wrote four books about the country he knew so well. In "Caminos Viejos," "The Shadows of Old Saddleback," "Forster vs. Pico" and in the present volume he rescued from oblivion a multitude of details that add warmth and color to cold history. He was a successful newspaper man who was keenly aware of his environment. He searched the records for facts, then laced them with sympathy and understanding. He was steeped in the lore of his homeland, he was generous with his information and modest about his great knowledge. As a companion and guide on the trails of local history he was an excellent mentor.

Bernardo Yorba and Terry Stephenson had much in common. Both were men who loved the land on which they lived; both were dreamers yet practical individuals. One built the tradition of gracious living, the other extended it to future generations. One created the facts and flavors of old California; the other preserved them for posterity. Both were important in southern California. The book "Don Bernardo Yorba" was Terry Stephenson's last published contribution to local history. He had other works in mind, but unfortunately they were never written. In May 1943 Orange County lost its greatest antiquarian.

This new edition is issued with the cooperation of the Charles W. Bowers Memorial Museum in Santa Ana.

Don Meadows.

Santa Ana
May 1963

ON THE RIO SANTA ANA

INDIANS were living on the banks of the Santa Ana river when Governor Portolá and his band of soldiers, muleteers and padres arrived on July 28, 1769. Diaries tell the story of Portolá's progress through what is now Orange County. It is a familiar story and need not be repeated here, further than to refer to the fact that it was an incident of that march that brought the name of Santa Ana to the valley.

It was on St. Anne's day, July 26, that the explorers, starting the day with a celebration of the mass marking that holy day, came in view of a broad valley. The name of St. Anne, the mother of Mary, was applied to the valley and eventually was attached to the river as we know it today. However, a terrifying earthquake that occurred while Portolá was camped at Olive, caused the river, for a time, to be called Rio Jesús de los Temblores. That name was used by padres over a period of years, but its use soon passed and the name of Santa Ana remained.

Early Spanish references to the Santa Ana river area indicate that the Indians who lived there were distinguished for just one attribute, and that was their color. Governor Fages in his report in the '70's stated that the Indians were white. Other Indians along the southern coast were described as dark and swarthy in color. Not so, these Santa Ana Indians. Fages made no guess as to why the distinction existed. At this late date we may surmise, if we wish, that a band of shipwrecked sailors at some early date made their homes among the fore-parents of the villagers as Fages found them.

Too, one may enter conjecture upon the fact that in this same Santa Ana river area, archaeologists have found several scores of so-called cog-stones, known as one of the unexplained relics of Indian occupation. But few have been found elsewhere in California. The late Senator S. C. Evans of Riverside gathered data far and wide, photographed and studied every cog-stone he could locate, and was ready to publish the result of his studies when death ended his work, and his theories went with him.

Once the name Santa Ana became attached to the valley and river, it persisted. It came on down through the slow decades of the development of the California missions. It came through the meager settlements along the river during the early half of the century, down through the rancho period and down through the fast-moving years of American development. It became a part of the names of four ranchos, Santiago de Santa Ana, San Juan Cajón de Santa Ana, Cañon de Santa Ana, and Santa Ana del Chino. In 1869, a hundred years after Portolá passed this way, Santa Ana was the name selected by William H. Spurgeon for the city he founded.

Sixty or more years ago John W. Bixby gave the name, Rancho Santa Ana, to his 6,000-acre property in the Santa Ana Cañon, and that name was used when in 1934 his daughter, Mrs. Susanna Bixby Bryant, dedicated Rancho Santa Ana Botanic Garden of the Native Plants of California to his memory.

With Portolá was a youthful Spanish soldier, José Antonio Yorba, later stationed at Monterey.

In 1797, after some twenty-five years or more of service as a soldier, Yorba was retired as a "sargento invalido" (invalid sergeant) at San Diego, where in 1789 he had established a home. There, too, was his father-in-law, Don Pablo Grijalva, who had come to California as a right hand man of Don Juan Bautista de Anza when that distinguished colonist had brought his band of settlers from Sonora and across deserts and mountains to California.

While still in army service at San Carlos, Yorba had married María Josefa Grijalva, while her sister, María del Carmen, became the wife of another soldier, Don Pedro Peralta. This Peralta seems never to have become a resident of the south end of the state.

Grijalva and Yorba together entered into a cattle growing business somewhere along the Santa Ana river and Santiago creek, probably earlier than 1800. No definite record of a right to use of the land appears, however, until the year 1810 shows a Spanish land grant to José Antonio Yorba and his nephew,

Juan Pablo Peralta. Grijalva had died, and though he had passed from the scene, his widow gave consent to the grant. She made her home on the rancho with her grandson, Juan Pablo Peralta, even before 1810, and died there a few years later. Dreaming her last days away in an adobe on the banks of the Santa Ana river, what a story of pioneership that old lady could have told! She had come from Mexico with Anza, bringing her family with her; she had lived years among the missions and presidios, and on the ranchos. She came to the end of her days, one may hope, in quietude and contentment.

The grant of land to Yorba and Peralta was for a rancho definitely fixed as lying south and east of the Santa Ana river. Whatever one may conjecture as to earlier occupation and use of the land, the date of 1810 is rather fixed in history as the time of the beginning of the settlement of the rancho.

As the years went by, the Yorbas and Peraltas, while united closely by kinship and friendship and occasional inter-marriages, seemed by common consent, to enter into a division of homestead areas. The Peraltas occupied the east side of the Santa Ana river in the section that we now know as Peralta, while the Yorbas who had the advantage of numbers of adult members in the family, ready and anxious to become active in affairs, settled along the southeast side of the river from Olive southward for three or four miles.

CALIFORNIA'S FIRST FARMERS

UPON El Camino Real, Don José Antonio Yorba built his adobe home, brought up his family, and in 1825, there he died. He was buried at San Juan Capistrano mission. His partner, Juan Pablo Peralta, outlived him by only a few years. His death was in 1829. The rancho that had been theirs was first known as Rancho Santiago, then as Rancho Santa Ana, and finally, when the claims were presented to the United States Land Commission in the 1850's, as Rancho Santiago de Santa Ana, by which name the old rancho appears on title records of today. Within the boundaries of that rancho Santa Ana, Orange, Tustin, El Modena and Olive today are located.

The Yorbas might well be chosen as southern California's pioneer farmers, outside the missions. It has generally been believed that Don Manuel Nieto, who in the 1780's under a Spanish permit to use the land, settled at the place we know as Los Nietos, near Whittier, planted some fields and vineyards. His activities in that regard may have predated the early, primitive development along the Santa Ana river, but there is no evidence to show that his farming covered more than a very few acres. Nobody knows when José Antonio Yorba and Juan

Pablo Peralta dug their first ditches and planted their first fields and vineyards. Testimony given about 1882 by Juan Pablo Peralta, son and namesake of Peralta, was to the effect that they had ditches prior to 1825. Just as pertinent as that testimony, is the record left in the will of José Antonio Yorba, written at San Juan Capistrano a short time before his death in 1825. In that document Yorba listed as property owned by him, a house on the outskirts of the Presidio at San Diego, a house on the rancho where he lived together with orchard and vineyards, evidently walled, 800 neat cattle, 16 yokes of tame oxen, 250 sheep and 19 pack mules with pack saddles and leather bags.

We are not especially concerned in this story over whether the honor of being California's first farm should go to the Yorba-Peralta ranch on the Santa Ana river. The matter, however, can be cited as of current interest for the reason that in Reuben L. Underhill's interesting new book, "From Cowhides to Golden Fleece," published a few months ago, the author gives to John A. Sutter, who did not arrive in California until 1838, special mention for his early efforts in irrigation. This book says on Page 41, that John A. Sutter "unfolds to Larkin plans to build a dam across the American river in order to divert water from a stream by ditches to his wheat fields. This established him as the pioneer in the utilization of stream-flow for irrigation. True, the padres, years before had had their gardens and small plots of vines watered either by hand labor or through furrows leading from a spring; but even that primitive practice had disappeared with the decadence of the missions. And more elaborate irrigation had been employed in southern California. But Sutter was the first in California to convey the river waters by gravity to broad fields in the manner which today keeps vast areas productive and the great interior valleys in other than semi-desert condition."

A bit of research may convince one that the Yorbas and Peraltas with their brush dams and "tomas" (entrances to canals) were diverting water from the Santa Ana river, perhaps twenty-five years before Sutter's arrival, and using it for the irrigation of several hundred acres.

BERNARDO'S BROTHERS

WHEN José Antonio Yorba died in 1825, his adobes along the Santa Ana river were the homes of his four sons. However, down through the decades into the '40's the old family home at the point of the hill in Olive seems to have been a central living point. There Tomás and Teodocio lived most of their lives, rearing their families almost under the same roof. There, too, lived Bernardo as a young man and for a dozen years after his marriage.

The eldest, José Antonio, namesake of the original Yorba, was born at Monterey in 1785, the first born of the Yorba marriage to María Josefa Grijalva. Probably before his father's death, this eldest son had built his own adobes near the Santa Ana river, identified today as a mile and a half directly west of Orange. That place became known as Santa Ana Abajo, Lower Santa Ana, and many travellers between Los Angeles and San Diego in the first half of the century took this alternate "el camino real" crossing the valley, rather than the more travelled "el camino real" that touched the Yorba settlement at Olive, then known as Santa Ana.

This particular Yorba later built an adobe for himself at the southwest edge of what is today Santa

Ana. This place became somewhat famous as the rancho home of Don José Sepulveda. It was known as El Refugio. Several sons and daughters of this Yorba settled at San Juan Capistrano, and became the founders of the mission branch of the Yorba family. Nearly every old resident of San Juan Capistrano, today, has Yorba blood coming down from this José Antonio. One of the best known of his immediate family was his daughter, Soledad, wife of Don Juan Avila, and mother of Mrs. Marcos Forster and Mrs. Rosa Pryor. A mission record indicates that this José Antonio died in 1844 and was buried at San Gabriel.

Of all the brothers, the one who at all times, and persistently took an interest in the growing of crops, was Bernardo. It can be surmised that in his interest in the land he was in accord with his father's activities, for it was Bernardo who was chosen by the father as an executor of his will.

It seems a reasonable surmise that after the death of the first José Antonio Yorba in 1825, it was young Bernardo who carried on the growing of crops on the old rancho. The second José Antonio and Tomás were interested primarily in cattle. In fact, there is record to show that Tomás took no interest in farming until after his marriage in 1834, and at one time John J. Warner said he did not see that José Antonio had been successful in his farming. In the middle '30's José Antonio was past 50 years of age, so that

Warner referred to him as an old man. The same term was used by Warner concerning Bernardo, who was 57 when he died. These references indicate that in those days old age came earlier than it does in our day. Perhaps in his advancing years José Antonio found it impossible to become much interested in farming. Not so with Tomás, for from 1835 to 1845 Tomás farmed extensively, his fields located beside those of his brother Teodocio.

In September 1834, at the age of 47, Tomás married Vicenta Sepúlveda, aged 20, a sister of Don José Sepúlveda and a woman destined to long life and prominence, a reputation for beauty, hospitality and leadership. Tomás died in 1845, leaving Doña Vicenta with four children: Juan Francisco Santo, who became the husband of Isabel Serrano of El Toro; Josefa, who became the wife of John S. Smythe, long a leading citizen of Anaheim; Ramona, who became the wife of her cousin, Marcos, son of Bernardo, and later the wife of Juan de la Guerra, who died recently, the last survivor of the Union troops of California; José Antonio, educated at San Jose, who was never married. Owing to the multiplicity of José Antonios among the Yorbas, it is impossible to determine at this late date, whether he was the José Antonio Yorba who was the perpetrator of a huge joke at a Los Angeles dance. The story is told in Bancroft's "Pastoral California". The pride of every caballero's heart was the fine appearance of his horse, and the tail of his horse was braided until it curled. To trim the tail of a fine horse was sacrilege. The night of the dance, José Antonio Yorba trimmed the tails of all of the horses, including his own, and when the heinous deed was discovered, he feigned great anger.

After the death of Tomás, Doña Vicenta managed the affairs of the estate, as detailed in William Heath Davis' "Sixty Years in California". She was praised by Davis for her great beauty, business ability and gracious hospitality. In 1847 she married the well known Ramón Carrillo, active during the Mexican War. He was pictured by Major Horace Bell in his "Reminiscences of a Ranger" as one who, armed only with a knife, fought grizzly bears to their death. He was a ranchero and cattleman in the '50's, forefather of the Carrillos of Yorba, Santa Ana and El Toro, and of Miss Esperanza Carrillo, a supervisor of education in Los Angeles. The death of Ramón Carrillo by an assassin's bullet at Cucamonga in 1862 furnished one of the major tragedies and mysteries in the blood feuds surrounding the history of that area and period.

Doña Vicenta was again left a widow. For years she was active in looking after affairs left in her charge. Her old age was spent at Anaheim with relatives. Her stories of the old days were cherished by those who knew her and especially by her descendants. She died May 8, 1907, at the age of 94.

Teodocio, the youngest of the brothers, born at San Diego in 1809, was never content to live the quiet life of a ranchero. As a young man be became "compadre" of the turbulent Picos, Pio and Andrés, and throughout the remainder of his life his affiliations with them were close. He took sides with Don Carlos Carrillo against Governor Alvarado in the revolution of 1838 and was taken prisoner at the close of the battle at San Buena Ventura Mission. His friendship with the Picos may account for the fact that during the years when Pio Pico, the last of the Mexican governors, was handing out land grants freely, Teodocio was granted Rancho Lomas de Santiago, which included the Santiago canyon and which today is a part of the Irvine ranch. Teodocio through a grant from Governor Alvarado, May 8, 1840, already had eleven leagues of land in Amadór and Sacramento counties. There Teodocio and Andrés Pico built a log house, (that is one instance where Spanish Californians used logs instead of adobe), and ran horses and cattle on the property. Indian hostilities seems to have been partly responsible for failure of any extensive development of this rancho. Teodocio's interest in that rancho terminated when he deeded it to Andrés Pico, October 4, 1852. In his flight from California in 1846, Pio Pico found refuge the first night at the home of his friend, Teodocio. It was a narrow escape for Pico, for that same night General Fremont, Kit Carson and their band of frontiersmen were camped at Santa Ana Abajo, three miles away.

Teodocio was at times associated with the Picos in horse racing events around Los Angeles. He appeared in 1852 with Pio Pico as one of the backers of Sarco against Black Swan, owned by Don José Sepulveda. Sarco lost, and those who had pinned their faith to him were out thousands of dollars and hundreds of cattle. The race itself is easily classed as the greatest horse race of those early horse-racing days. The story of it has been told and retold many hundreds and thousands of times. In the Bowers Museum at Santa Ana is a fine Spanish shawl that the wife of José Sepúlveda threw over the sweating back of the great and victorious Black Swan.

Teodocio was always attached to the soil. Much of his farming was done through rentals to Sonorians, yet his own operations were extensive for his day. He had a ditch of his own that took water out of the Santa Ana river and around the point of the hill at Olive, and out upon the plains lying below Olive. Descendants of Teodocio today blame Pio Pico for the declining fortunes of Teodocio, in the late '50's. The story is that Teodocio gave Pio Pico a power of attorney, which, used injudiciously, put Teodocio in a bad financial situation from which he never recovered. Eventually, the Rancho Lomas de Santiago was deeded by Teodocio to William Wolfskill, thus terminating a troublesome mortgage, and in a few years it passed from Wolfskill to a new sheep-growing firm, Flint, Bixby and Irvine. In 1863, Teodocio, for some years ill, died a poor man at the home of a daughter in San Gabriel. Those who knew him, and I have in mind among them, the late J. E. Pleasants, spoke of him always as a man of fine appearance and courteous and kindly manners.

For some years, parts of the old Teodocio holdings at Olive were looked after by Teodocio's son-in-law, Desiderio Burruel. So closely was this son-in-law identified with the area that early settlers of the Santa Ana valley called the place Burruel's Point, a name that was abandoned by promoters of the Olive Heights townsite during the boom of the 1880's. The name of Olive was chosen because a grove of gnarled old olive trees grew upon the point of the hill. Some of those old trees remain today. Tradition has it that they were planted by Teodocio Yorba, perhaps in the '40's or '50's.

THE YOUNG BERNARDO

DON Bernardo Yorba, the third son in point of age, was of an industrious temperament. While of pure Spanish blood, he had Yankee thrift and Yankee acquisitiveness and Yankee independence. Since the early history of the area in which we are especially interested in this study centers largely around the life of Don Bernardo, and since these attributes of character had much to do with his career, it seems well to point them out. They were unusual among the dons of his day. Far too many of the rancheros were careless of their rights, too free with their spending and too quick to mortgage and sell their ranchos.

Throughout his life, Bernardo seems to have been a devout Catholic. Certain it is that he was punctilious in the matter of baptisms and family records. Whether upon his insistence does not appear, but certain it is that in the mission records at San Juan Capistrano, no greater detail is given for anyone than is given for the baptisms of Bernardo's children. For instance, there is the record for the baptism of María Dolores Francisca Yorba, February 2, 1829, the "legitima hija" of Don Bernardo Yorba and María de Jesús Alvarado. "conj abuelos paternos el Sargento retirado Dn. Antonio Yorba natural de

Saturnino and Bishipado de Catalina en la Antigua España, y la Señora María Josefa Grijalva, y maternos el Sergento retirado Don Francisco Xavier Alvarado natural del Presidio de Loreto en la Baja California, y la Señora Igancia Amadór, natural del mismo Presidio de Loreto."

"José-Tomás Yorba, hermano de Bernardo," is named as "padrino" (godfather), and María Josefa Grijalva, the child's grandmother, as godmother. That there is an error in the name of the godfather is apparent. Bernardo had a brother José Antonio and one named Tomás Antonio, but no José Tomás.

The record is signed by Fra. Geronimo Boscana, one of the leading figures in the history of the mission, and author of "Chinigchinich", recognized as the most striking and most authentic record we have of the religion and customs of any Indians of California.

The fact that many of the family records are to be found at San Juan Capistrano indicates that Don Bernardo's church affiliations were closer with that mission than they were with San Diego or San Gabriel. In fact, as this book will tell, there was some shadow of dispute with San Gabriel mission over Bernardo's land grant, and perhaps that had something to do with the ranchero's devotion to San Juan Capistrano.

The mission records, now in the possession of Father Hutchinson, begin showing Yorba entries as early as June 20, 1818. On that date baptism was given José Miguel Yorba, son of José Antonio Yorba and María Antonia Verdugo de Yorba, residents, "de el Rancho Sta. Ana." This may indicate that earlier family affiliations were almost entirely around San Diego. The Yorba records at Mission San Juan Capistrano run down through the deaths, baptisms and marriages to this day. Certain it is that all, or almost all of Bernardo's children born in the '20's and '30's were baptised by the priests of San Juan Capistrano, which fact rather causes a question to arise as to the correctness of the oft-repeated assertions, that the Yorba settlements along the Santa Ana river were stations of Mission San Gabriel.

The great wedding of Leonor Yorba, daughter of Bernardo, with its accompanying fiesta at Rincón, referred to by Judge Benj. Hayes, in his "Pioneer Notes," is recorded in the marriage register. The señorita married "Juan B. Roland" (John B. Rowland) on Feb. 5, 1853. Witnesses of record are Leonardo Cota, Anastacio Botiller, Antonio Vilel, Santiago Rios and Manuel Feliz.

Interesting though they are, this is no place for further study of mission records, and we must return to the story of Bernardo and his activities upon the rich lands along his beloved "rio de Santa Ana."

While Bernardo seems to have had the use of all the land he wanted for farming along the Santa Ana river between Olive and West Orange, the desire

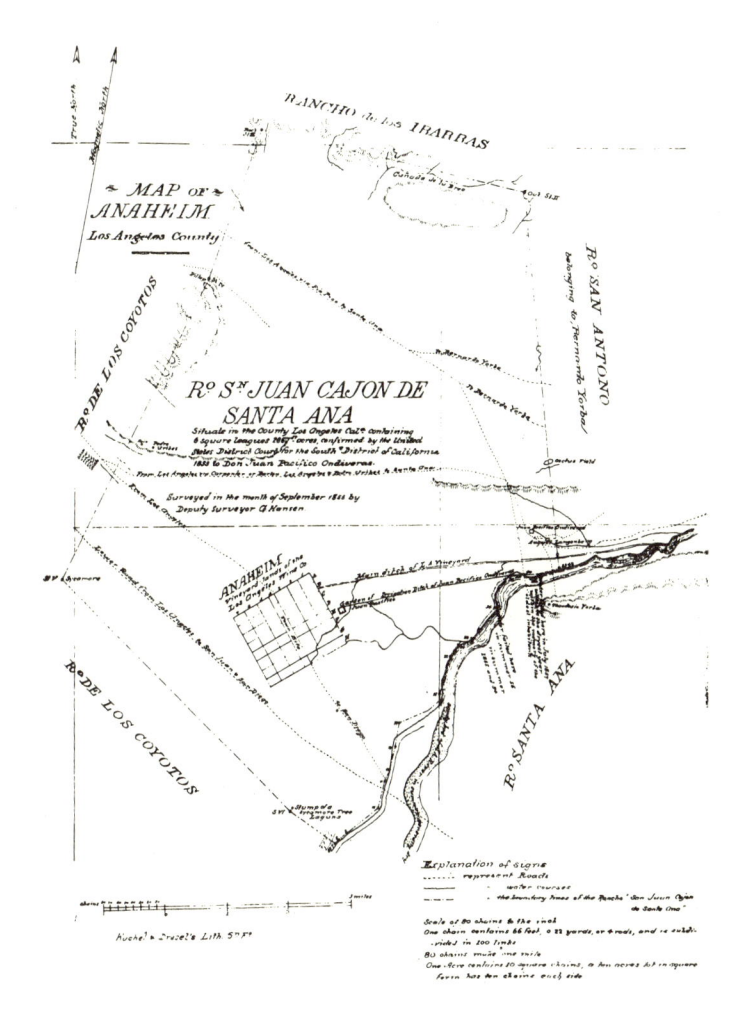

ROADS, DITCHES AND ANAHEIM IN 1860

This map showing Rancho San Juan Cajón de Santa Ana was recorded in Los Angeles, February 9, 1860. It shows no strip of public lands between Rancho San Juan Cajón de Santa Ana and Rancho San Antonio (Rancho Cañon de Santa Ana). Rancho Santiago de Santa Ana is here shown as Ro.SantaAna.

for a rancho of his own and for a home of his own, seems to have brought a decision on his part to secure the property that is known today as Rancho Cañon de Santa Ana, lying entirely north of the Santa Ana river.

On that side of the river were rolling foothills and small canyons branching from the Santa Ana. In that beautiful land Don Bernardo visualized the development of his own hacienda.

Early in the '30's the secularization of the missions was under way. Younger Californians were just beginning to take advantage of the fact that the Mexican government was taking the use of lands from the missions and giving ranchos to men who would develop cattle ranches. It was the beginning of an important period in California's history. An old mission policy was being given up, and a new land program was under way.

One of the first to take advantage of the change was Don Bernardo Yorba. His family was growing. His first wife, María Jesús de Alvarado, had died in 1828, and his second wife, Felipa Domínguez, had presented him with the first of the numerous children born to her. The opportunity for acquiring a rancho of his own whereon he could raise his family was at hand.

Bernardo made formal application for the Rancho Cañon de Santa Ana. Immediately came a protest from the Mission San Gabriel. That mission, not yet under secularization, declared that the area north of the river had been used always for pasturage of mission herds, that the mission had a rancho station there, and that Bernardo's petition for a grant should be denied.

Bernardo replied, that the mission had abandoned the use of the property. Bernardo seems to have had the best of the argument. The government policy of granting land to individuals was getting along. There was no hesitancy in acting upon Bernardo's petition. The records show that Governor José Figueroa, in 1834, granted Bernardo three leagues of land, more or less. The usual formalities of giving possession were gone through, and Don Bernardo became a Mexican rancher with a domain all his own, still in a position, of course, to carry on his farming on the opposite side of the river, on the old Yorba-Peralta rancho, the Santiago de Santa Ana.

Even as Bernardo was acquiring this three-league rancho, he was building his adobe, making it his home, putting a "toma" in the river, and building ditches for irrigation water. As the years went by, he enlarged his house, and eventually there was constructed a fine two-story adobe, which with its wing and nearby adobes is reputed to have been one of the best in southern California. This fine structure was known throughout Bernardo's lifetime as San Antonio.

It seems likely that the houses built by Bernardo

were covered with brea, hauled in from Brea canyon. In that regard, the construction differs from the kind of roofing used on many ranch houses built during the years the missions were on the down grade. Some of the ranch houses were covered with red tiles taken from mission buildings. Mission tile covered Santiago Argüello's adobe on the Trabuco Mesa, and to this day, quantities of them are to be found in the adobe ruins. Within the past half dozen years floor tiles were dug from the mounds of the old Juan Forster adobe at Mission Viejo and taken to make a walk at Rancho Santa Margarita in San Diego county. No doubt there are tiles on the Santa Margarita buildings today that came from Mission San Luis Rey.

There are no bits of mission tiles found on the site of San Antonio, and it is easy to conclude that Bernardo built without their use. The oldest pictures obtainable show the two-story building covered with shakes, and the oldest of the Yorbas today remember it with that kind of covering. When the peaked roof with shakes was put on cannot be determined. Probably in Bernardo's time the roof was flat. Construction of that kind was the commonest architectural detail in Los Angeles during the '50's, where brea (a tar) and tules were used on the roofs.

The right to the use of brea, which in early days was found in ledges on the surface of the ground in Brea canyon, has been one frequently referred to by old-timers of the Yorba family. The story was first told to me by Mrs. T. S. Grimshaw of Anaheim, a daughter of Daniel Kraemer. Mrs. Grimshaw's early life was spent on the Pioneer Ranch at Placentia, where today a portion of the old Ontiveras adobe still stands.

"I have always heard," said Mrs. Grimshaw "that Bernardo Yorba's descendants have a perpetual right to go into Brea Canyon and get brea."

By long experience, I should have taken Mrs. Grimshaw's word for it. I know of no real old-timer whose memory is so keen as hers, whose faithfulness to facts is so true. I admit that I was incredulous. Yet there is basis in the records for the story:

It was about 1863 that Juan Pacífico Ontiveras decided to sell all his holdings in Rancho San Juan Cajón de Santa Ana, and move to San Luis Obispo. He carried out that plan. Of the 26,632 acres in the rancho, he had already sold 1,398 acres to the founders of Anaheim and others who took land near Anaheim. Moreover, he had deeded 3,900 acres to his sons, Patricio and Juanito, who had sold the land to August Langenberger, a son-in-law of Juan Pacífico, and Ben Dreyfus. These two on April 27, 1865, sold the 3900 acres to Daniel Kraemer for $4600, land that today lies south of Placentia and between Placentia boulevard and the village of Atwood. In 1863 all that was left, 21,572 acres, Ontiveras sold to Abel Stearns of Los Angeles for $6,000. This was one of the last rancho purchases made by Stearns before the great drouth of 1864 brought financial ruin to him. That deed from Ontiveras to Stearns carried with it the plain reservation of "all such rights as the parties of the first part (Ontiveras and his wife) granted to Bernardo Yorba to use the brea in the Cañada known as Cañada de la Brea." The deed to Stearns is dated May 22, 1863, five years after Bernardo's death.

Brea today, of course, is of no value. In Bernardo's time it may have been used not only for roofing, but also for flooring and for fuel. Today scattered along on the bare ground where Bernardo built his home one can find flat pieces of brea, and a few yards disstant where "la casa de Julian Manríquez" stood is a wide streak of brea that might have been part of a foundation, more likely the floor of a corridor. Certain it is that the settlers of the '70's and '80's in the Santa Ana Valley sometimes drove their lumber wagons into the canyon, loaded up with brea and hauled it home. Attorney Horace C. Head of Santa Ana, whose parents settled in Garden Grove in 1876, well remembers journeys of that sort. As a matter of pure speculation, one might wonder how far Rancho Santa Ana of today would get were it to go among the oil fields of Brea Canyon and demand the exercise of that ancient right to gather brea and haul it away.

Bernardo's home was built during the time that

adobe was used everywhere in southern California. Years passed before wood became available or popular. In fact, even into the '50's lumber was not only scarce and hard to get but was not looked upon with favor. Pio Pico, testifying before the United States Land Commission at the hearing on the petition of Teodocio Yorba for confirmation of his grant to Rancho Lomas de Santiago, made a distinction between the two kinds of construction, a wooden building was designated as temporary, an adobe as permanent.

The walls of Bernardo's "casa" were of thick adobe, covered with heavy coatings of whitewash. The floor of the second story was, no doubt of wood, brought down probably from the San Bernardino mountains where a mill in which for a time Bernardo had an interest was located. Brick tiles found upon the ground today indicate the probability that they were used on the lower floor and in a fireplace. To some of them are attached bits of plaster, to others bits of brea.

Concerning the size of the Adobe San Antonio much has been written with inaccuracy. Perhaps the most exaggerated account proclaimed the great mansion to have had 200 rooms. Other accounts in round figures have put the number at 80 or 90 or 100. Perhaps the most reliable statement to be had at this time as to the number of rooms is that found in an article printed in the World's Fair edition of the

Santa Ana Daily Blade, June 1, 1893. The article was written by Amelia L. Davila, daughter of Andrea Elisalde de Yorba de Davila, Bernardo's widow. Without doubt Amelia got her information from her mother, with whom she lived. She wrote:

"His (Don Bernardo's) residence proper was a two-story building of adobe (in those times all houses were made of adobe) part of which is still extant, and contained, with the wings, thirty rooms, this not counting schoolrooms, harness and shoemakers' rooms, which, together with all the rooms occupied by servants or dependants of Don Bernardo, made twenty rooms more.

"The trades and people working here," continued Miss Davila, "were as follows: Four woolcombers, two tanners, one soapmaker, one butter and cheese man, who every day milked (or servants under him) from fifty to sixty cows, one harnessmaker, two shoemakers, one jeweler, one plasterer, one carpenter, a blacksmith, a majordomo, two errand boys, one head sheepherder, one cook, one baker, two washerwomen, one woman to iron, four sewing women, one dressmaker, two gardeners, a schoolmaster, and the man that made the wine. Very fine Angelica, Port, and other wines were made. Whiskey, brandy, etc., were also distilled here."

Following Bernardo's death the adobe was occupied for a time by his widow and the unmarried children. Then the widow, married to Pioquinto

Davila, moved into a near-by adobe that her husband had bought from Andrés. Thereafter, the big house was occupied by other Yorbas. By 1890 the old buildings were falling into disrepair, and finally, soon after 1900 were abandoned. For years the ruins stood beside the road, with doors and windows gone, a sleeping place for tramps and a place into which sight-seers, enamored of old adobes, climbed and looked about. Fearful that someone might be hurt in the ruins and that he might be held for damages for having "maintained an attractive nuisance," Samuel Kraemer, husband of Bernardo's granddaughter, Angelina, then owner of the property, had it torn down. That was perhaps twelve years ago.

Further evidence, if any is needed, to show the size of the old "casa" in the day of its prime is to be found in an old survey map, No. 14, in the archives of the Orange County Title Co., at Santa Ana. This survey was made by George Hansen January 25 and 26, 1859, during the probate of Bernardo's estate.

Hansen's ground floor survey does not show the number of rooms. It does show in links outside measurements of all the buildings. (A link is 7.92 inches). The big casa was in the shape of a capital T, with the upper part of the T being the front. The house measured 176 links across the front, about 115 feet. A porch 15 links deep ran entirely across the front. Without the porch, the house from the front

DON BERNARDO YORBA'S ADOBE

This picture of San Antonio adobe was taken about 1895. To the right is main building, with rear "wing" barely showing in the center. To left, is the adobe designated as "otra casa vieja," separate from the main building but used as a part of the family habitation. Insert is part of sketch made in 1859 by George Hansen showing shape and location of adobes.

wall down the stem of the T was 125 links, about 82.5 feet. There is nothing to show whether the rear part of the house was two-story. It measured 37 links wide.

The front part, which was two-story, had a 36-link wall at the east and 20 links on the west with a porch 16 by 78 links built against the rear of the west arm of the T. It is believed that the two rear open spaces were enclosed with adobe walls.

Northwest of the main building at a distance of about 50 feet was another adobe standing alone. It measured 29 links wide by 69 long. No doubt this adobe is the one described in an inventory of Bernardo's estate as "otra casa vieja en usal estado continguo a la principal." Still further to the northwest and some 60 feet from this "otra casa vieja" the surveyor showed a smaller adobe, 24 by 32 links.

To the west a few yards away was located the old Julian Manríquez house, occupied by José de Jesús at the time of his father's death, and adjoining it was the adobe built for Andrés. The Manríquez adobe was 59 feet long with a porch the full length.

Between the big house and "la casa de Julian Manríquez," was an adobe corral. Often Spanish Californians had corrals built against their houses for horses that might soon be used. In the old Rodríguez adobe west of Orange the back door opened into the corral; the well was located inside the corral. Hansen's survey showed that Bernardo's big house, together with the yards at the rear, occupied .36 acre, the corral .17 acre.

Mrs. Martina Pelaconi, who spent many happy hours visiting in the old adobe when a girl, remembers that there were three interior stairways in the main building, one at each end and one at the center.

LIFE ON RANCHO SAN ANTONIO

WITH his adobe San Antonio as headquarters, Bernardo carried on a widespread stock business, largely in cattle, with horses, mules, burros and sheep as of secondary importance. The need of the burro on a rancho of the day should not be overlooked. He was a much used beast of burden, and though slow, no doubt furnished faster transportation over difficult ground than was furnished by the old wooden-wheeled carretas drawn by oxen, with yokes bound to their horns with rawhide.

Bernardo acquired lands far up the Santa Ana river in what is now Riverside and San Bernardino counties. These lands were called the Ranchos Sierra and Rincón. As an heir, he owned a one-seventh of one-half of Rancho Santiago de Santa Ana, and in 1849, he bought an added interest. That purchase was from Don Juan Pablo Peralta, son of the grantee of the same name. Altogether Bernardo's holdings constituted one of the largest cattle properties ever known in Southern California. He could run his herds as he willed over a vast territory that reached practically from Riverside to Newport Bay.

A story has come down to Bernardo's grandchildren to the effect that at the time of his death in 1858, Bernardo had practically completed negotiations for the purchase of Rancho Santa Ana del Chino in San Bernardino county. Had that purchase been completed and had Bernardo lived a few years longer, the course of history might have been changed. He, instead of Don Abel Stearns, might have become the owner of other ranchos, including Rancho San Juan Cajón de Santa Ana, and he, instead of Stearns, might have become the central figure in the great crash of cattle properties as a result of the drouth of the middle '60's.

Whatever plans for increasing his cattle empire Bernardo may have had, certain it is that he was high among the successful cattlemen of his day.

Bernardo's interests were not confined to stock growing. Far from it. Under irrigation he grew crops of corn, wheat, beans and other annuals. He planted vineyards and fruit trees. Two of his vineyards were walled with adobe, not to keep out thieves, but to prevent damage from his own cattle.

"I was quite intimately acquainted with Don Bernardo Yorba," testified John J. Warner, in a law suit of the 1880's. Warner came to California in 1831. He gave his name to Warner's Hot Springs and Warner's ranch in San Diego county. "I became so acquainted with him in 1834. I was frequently at his ranch in 1835, '36, and '37. He was a stock raiser and cultivated more extensively than any person upon the river. He did this mainly for his own consumption, and for that of his employees and servants, of whom he had a large number.

"He was remarkable for the employment of laborers, and had most of the cultivable lands of the Santiago de Santa Ana under cultivation.

"From the early part of 1844, or the latter part of 1843, up to the close of 1846, I was very frequently at his home, I bought cattle from him at different places.

"He cultivated land in parcels along the river for four or five miles above his house, and nearly up to the Sierra and Rincon: large fields, wherever there was a piece of level land upon which he could get water. He also planted some vineyards about that time.

"From 1846 to 1857 I was not there very much. In the latter year I came through for a day or two, and the old gentleman was still cultivating his lands. Going to Warner's ranch I always went that way, unless I had business to take me elsewhere. It was the nearest road between Los Angeles and my ranch, and he and I were always friendly and liked to see each other.

"I became pretty intimate with that section of the country (meaning the Santa Ana) in 1835. I had a young lady in that part of the country to whom I was paying some attention."

Bernardo's farming was done in primitive fashion, with oxen and old-fashioned Mexican plows, yet it was extensive as things were in California during his lifetime. In later years, describing changes that had taken place on the rancho, one of his sons remarked upon the fact that in the '60's, American made plows were used. That was after Bernardo's death.

Hides and tallow were hauled by carreta from the rancho to the ports of San Pedro and San Juan Capistrano, where they were traded with Yankee skippers who brought American goods around the Horn and Oriental goods from China. Bancroft in his "California," says that Bernardo kept a stock of 100 patterns of fine cloth in chests for the trousseaus of his daughters. There is no way of knowing where Bancroft got his information. When Bernardo died there was no evidence of any such an accumulation of dry goods, as we shall see later in this review, yet the story is one that has always been accepted, for there was a magnificence about Don Bernardo and his great adobe that cannot, and should not be decried. Heirlooms among his descendants today, some of them on exhibition at the Bowers Museum in Santa Ana, in themselves are deeply interesting mementos of the romantic days of Bernardo's occupation of Rancho Cañon de Santa Ana. Fine textures and beautiful handwork characterize garments worn in Bernardo's household.

Upon his rancho, Bernardo carried on activities almost independent of the rest of the world. He had his tannery, his distillery, his metal shops, his saddlery, his soap vats, his weaving, his store and his grist mill.

For years, it had been tradition that an early survey in the Yorba section gave as a corner "the hill on which Bernardo Yorba sits on horseback." This bit of picturesque description has often been quoted as indicative of the loose descriptions found in Mexican archives. On the face of this story, it would appear that at the time of the survey, Bernardo was sitting on horseback on some hill. As a matter of fact, the hill was one well known locally as the one to the top of which Bernardo rode almost daily, that he might look out over his fields. It was thus a fixed point.

From this hill, located northward of the old adobe home, Bernardo could see nearby fields and grazing lands, his ditches and his vineyards. There were no pasture fences. Here and there would be an adobe corral, or a brush corral for sheep, or a bit of fence, "live" or dry," around a field. Pasture fences did not come into use in southern California until the '60's and the '70's, after Bernardo was in his grave, and barbed wire was not invented until later. In Bernardo's time, cattle roamed at will from canyon to canyon and from hills to plains. Once a year, or once in two or three years a rodeo was held, and a great occasion it was. Rancheros whose cattle might be found in the area, were invited to come with their families. The "gente de razon" gathered at the ranch house for feasting and dancing. Camps of the vaqueros were marked by cooking fires and by fires for feasting festivities. Blankets were spread upon the ground for gambling.

Cattle were driven together, and separated into herds according to ownership. The great man of the rodeo was the "juez del campo," the judge of the plains. His word was law. His keen eye told him when a half-grown calf belonged to a particular cow. On his decision, the owner of the cow would brand the calf. If there was no cow to which the younger animal seemed attached, it was declared to be an "orejano," and it went to the owner of the rancho on which the rodeo was held.

Often Bernardo served as "juez del campo". Probably no man among them was better qualified for the job.

With the coming of the Americans, Bernardo's position as a substantial ranchero was rapidly enhanced. Cattle values advanced. No doubt, some of Bernardo's herds were driven to the gold fields, others to San Francisco.

During the hectic '50's, many of Bernardo's countrymen fell by the wayside, some of them through inability to withstand losses by horse racing and other gambling, some through inability to meet the changing conditions of the period, some by fraud, though losses by fraud, it appears likely, have been romantically exaggerated in these later years. Interest rates were exceedingly high, often 3 or 4 per cent per month, and losses by reason of debt were frequent.

Bernardo, however, seems never to have wavered in his conservative mode of life. He avoided debt. If he suffered from betting on the frequent horse races of his day, there is no record of it. He maintained his hold upon his lands, increased his herds and carried on his farming. He was content to remain upon his rancho, engrossed in its affairs and in the bringing up of his ever-increasing family, to every one of whom he was devoted.

There is a tradition among his descendants of today, that Don Bernardo, while exerting to the fullest his authority as head of the family, held the profound reverence and affection of his children, from the youngest to the eldest. It is said that each morning, Don Bernardo took a seat upon the porch of his home, wearing his ever-present skull-cap, and there received one by one, each of his children, accepting their loving greetings and returning them with affectionate advice and instructions for the day.

According to Mrs. Bess Adams Garner's "Windows in an Old Adobe," Don Bernardo was so closely attached to his home, that he would not remain away for a night. If business called him to Los Angeles, he started early by horseback, transacted his business and returned the same day.

As the elder children grew to manhood and womanhood and were married, Don Bernardo established each upon a piece of land, where a separate adobe house was built and lands arranged for cultivation. Each, also, was given a start in the stock business. Each had his own brand, yet the title seemed always to remain with Bernardo. The children accepted their father's arrangements in the greatest of faith in his fairness.

When the time came for the writing of his will, and for the distribution of his property, Bernardo gave to his children the property that they had settled upon, and specifically he referred to the cattle and horses that bore their brands.

When he was 20 or 21 years of age, Bernardo married María de Jesús Alvarado, daughter of Francisco Xavier Alvarado, retired sergeant of San Diego. From this union there were four children; three grew to maturity, and one, María Dolores Francisca, died young. First born was Raymundo, baptised at San Juan Capistrano November 25, 1825, as José Ramon de los Dolores Yorba, "hijo legitimo del ranchero Bernardo Yorva and Sra. María de Jesús Alvarado." Teodocio was godfather and Magdalena, daughter of José Antonio Yorva and María Ant. Verdugo, was godmother. Raymundo, a favorite of his father, lived for years at Prado, his adobe being located near where the present Excelsior barns are located. In the last years of his life he lived at

Tustin. A son, Raymundo, lives in Santa Ana today. Inez, Bernardo's first daughter, in 1847 became the wife of Don Leonardo Cota, an outstanding leader among Mexicans, and to her Bernardo, in 1849, gave a deed to a part of Rancho Rincón, a deed that is now in the possession of the Southwest Museum. The Cota adobe, once the scene of many festivities and one of the best known of early adobes, was recently acquired by Orange county as a part of the area needed at Prado for storm water storage. The place is in ruins, and cannot long survive even as ruins. The baptismal record at Mission San Juan Capistrano shows Inez's baptism as María Inez Dolores Yorba in 1827 with Pio Pico as her godfather.

The fourth child of the first marriage was Ramona, who in 1844 became the wife of B. D. Wilson, known as Don Benito Wilson, one of the best known Americans of the Mexican period. Mount Wilson bears his name. Ramona was born, April 22, 1828, two days before her mother's death, and died in 1849.

Don Bernardo's second wife was Felipa Domínguez de Yorba, who bore him twelve children, all of whom were living when Bernardo died. Felipa was the daughter of Mariano and Juana Domínguez.

María de Jesús Yorba, born 1831, whose first husband was Anastacio Botiller, and whose second husband was Thomas J. Scully, Irish schoolmaster, some of whose descendants are residents of Prado today, was the first born. Those who have known the delightful Miss Mary Scully, now confined to her home with paralysis, will remember her always as an example of the charm and hospitality of early days.

Prudencio, José de Jesús, Marcos, Andrés, sons, and Leonor, daughter, were the elder children. Trinidad, Vicente, Tomás, Teodocio, and Felipe, sons, and Senobia, daughter, were still minors at the time of their father's death. Felipe was born in Los Angeles the day of his mother's death.

Of these, Prudencio, Vicente, Marcos and Trinidad long remained as leading landowners in the Yorba district, while death took some of the others, and changes in residence carried some of them away from the old rancho.

In the early '50's, Leonor married John Rowland, and some years afterward, her sister Senobia married John's brother, Thomas. These Rowlands were long prominent residents of Puente.

Soon after Doña Felipa's death, Bernardo married Andrea Elisalde, and four sons were born of this marriage, the first being given his father's name, Bernardo; the second, Gregorio, who died in infancy; the third, Javier, sometimes spelled Xavier; the fourth, who died in infancy. In proceedings in court in 1896, Andrea's age was given at that time as 60. That would have fixed her birth as 1836 and her age at marriage to Bernardo as about 16. However, in the Mexican census for Los Angeles in 1836, Andrea's age is given as 6, the daughter of Nicolas Elisalde and Juana de Ds. Rondon de Elisalde. Since this census record is the record for the Andrea who married Bernardo, she was 22 when she became Bernardo's wife a few years before his death.

One of the cherished stories having to do with Bernardo is the one concerned with his marriage, by proxy, to Andrea. This story has been well told in Mrs. Garner's "Windows in an Old Adobe." While Bernardo remained upon his rancho, the ceremony was performed at the Plaza church in Los Angeles with a friend taking the vows at the altar for the absent bridegroom. The story as told by granddaughters of Bernardo today, is that as the hour approached when Bernardo could expect his new wife to arrive from Los Angeles, he took a seat upon his veranda, two of his youngest children beside him. Soon, on el camino real from Los Angeles, came a carriage, bearing Andrea and others of her party. As it came to a stop at the front gate, Bernardo stepped from the yard, leading one child, Senobia, by the hand, carrying the other, Felipe, in his arms. Embracing his wife Bernardo placed the babe in her arms and turning, with Senobia between them, entered the gate and walked into the home.

Among Bernardo's grandchildren living today who heard the story of the proxy marriage from Andrea herself are Miss Mary Scully and Mrs. Martina Pelaconi.

"Soon after the death of Doña Felipa," said Miss Scully, "there was a fiesta at the home of Ramon Vejar in Pomona. The fiesta was for a christening, which in those days was often occasion for a celebration by friends and relatives from far and near. One of the men, jokingly perhaps, said that since Don Bernardo was a widower and very rich, some señorita might well marry him.

" 'And right here with us is the very girl who should marry him,' said he. 'She shall be our candidate for marriage to Don Bernardo. I mean Señorita Andrea Elisalde.'

"The suggestion met with great acclaim from everyone excepting Andrea.

" 'What!' she exclaimed, "I marry that old man with all those children? No, no!'

"But the suggestion spread, and was especially encouraged by Andrea's aunt. It reached the ears of Don Bernardo, and he was interested. Efforts were made to have the two meet in Los Angeles, but the young lady artfully set them aside, until one day a carriage drove to the front of her home, and Andrea's aunt directed her to take a pitcher of cool water out for the visitors to drink. That she did, and among the visitors was Don Bernardo, who instantly approved of her.

"Thereafter, as was often the custom in those days, negotiations for the marriage were carried on by friends and relatives of both parties, and eventually the wedding was arranged. Since Don Bernardo would not leave his beloved rancho, Don Leonardo Cota appeared for the wedding in his stead, and it was Don Leonardo who drove the carriage with the bride to the Rancho San Antonio and delivered her to my grandfather, Don Bernardo."

Following Bernardo's death, came Andrea's marriage to Pioquinto Davila. Their only daughter, Amelia, married José Francisco Velasco, in 1897. Velasco, son of a Spanish newspaper publisher in Tuscon, Arizona, ran a store at Yorba for years.

One of the most interesting of all the stories having to do with the Yorbas, is the story of the image of Saint Anthony that has been a prized and sacred possession of the family for more than eighty years, perhaps even a hundred years. Today it is the central figure in a shrine at the home of Mrs. Herbert Locke, a Yorba, in Los Angeles. This story is one of deep significance, for it brings down from Bernardo himself a great faith in spiritual things.

It seems that at one time, starvation faced the Indians around San Juan Capistrano, who, in spite of secularization, were still zealously looked after by the padres. At that time of great need came Bernardo Yorba with a herd of his cattle that were turned over by him to the padres as a gift for their people.

Seeking in their minds for an expression of gratitude, the padres were reminded of the fact that Antonio was a name greatly beloved by the Yorbas, that, in fact, Bernardo had named his rancho San Antonio. In the old mission church was a sacred image of San Antonio. In humility and thankfulness, this image, with the blessings of the padres, was presented to Bernardo, and was taken by him to his rancho. There it remained throughout Bernardo's lifetime, and on through scores of years, always carefully guarded and revered.

Many are the stories that have to do with the miracles of healing that have been brought about by prayers uttered at the foot of this Saint Anthony. Resting in his arms, and attached to a sash that has been draped about him, are scores of gold and silver ornaments, representing portions of bodies that have been made well.

Years ago, Father O'Sullivan, the greatly loved restorer of Mission San Juan Capistrano, learned in the records of the mission that the image of Saint Anthony had been given to Don Bernardo, and, having located it, he suggested that it be returned to the mission whence it came. This suggestion, however, bore no fruit, for among the Yorbas, it was devoutly believed that the image should remain in the possession of Bernardo's people.

MEXICAN WAR PERIOD

LITTLE is known concerning the parts played in the Mexican War by any of the Yorbas. By the time Bancroft in the '70's was collecting his historical data, all of the second generation of Yorbas were dead. There was none left to tell their story. Teodocio, as previously outlined in this record, gave aid to Pio Pico when Pico was fleeing from the country. In no available record of war activity, does Don Bernardo's name appear. It may be taken for granted that his sympathies were with the Californians, but his good sense may have persuaded him to keep to his beloved rancho, waiting for the storm to pass. The fact that one of his daughters, Ramona, was married to D. B. Wilson, whose activities with the Americans and his capture by the Californians at the Chino Rancho are well known in the history of the period, may have had some bearing upon Bernardo's attitude during the conquest. It seems entirely possible that Wilson advised Bernardo to take no part in the war. One's conjecture, however, might well be influenced in the opposite direction by the fact that Don Leonardo Cota, who fought with General Andrés Pico at the bloody battle of San Pasqual and who probably campaigned with the Californians down to the time of their surrender to the Americans at Cahuenga, was a close friend of Bernardo and in 1847 became Bernardo's son-in-law.

What we do know is that Don Bernardo had relatives on both sides, that his rancho was in the midst of war movements, yet seemingly apart.

The rancho was somewhat off the main travelled roads at all times. El Camino Real of the missions crossed the Santa Ana Valley from San Juan Capistrano to Olive and at Olive turned toward Los Angeles, leaving Rancho San Antonio a few miles to the northeast. Comparatively few travellers, unless on business or for a fiesta or visit, saw the hacienda in the Santa Ana canyon.

One of Bernardo's ranchos in the section we know now as Prado was the Rancho Sierra, located in the Corona-Temescal area, and the other was Rancho Rincón, north of Rancho Sierra. Across these two ranchos came wagon trains that made their way to California by way of Warner's Hot Springs, Lake Elsinore and Chino, during the '40's, '50's and '60's. Over that road went the famous Butterfield stages of the early '60's.

However, while crossing two of Bernardo's ranchos few of those who travelled that emigrant road, turned down the Santa Ana canyon to Rancho San Antonio. The canyon road was one to be avoided, for the crossings were frequent, oftentimes made difficult by high water and quicksands. Floods cut out the fords, and changes of route in the sandy bottom of the canyon were difficult.

The rancho was off the main avenue of travel, but according to family traditions, great numbers of travellers on their way to the mines stopped there, and were always fed at the bounteous table of Don Bernardo. As the story goes, whole beeves were roasting over the fire most of the time during the days of the gold rush, and for years afterward.

BEFORE U. S. LAND COMMISSION

WHEN Bernardo Yorba sought a land grant in 1834, he seems to have used the name Cañon de Santa Ana. As the years went by, the don designated his home as San Antonio. Possibly at first the name San Antonio was not meant for the entire rancho. However, it was not long until the favorite name became attached to the three-league domain. Most of the maps and descriptions of the Santa Ana river area of the '40's and '50's use the name of Saint Anthony, and it was not until Bernardo made application to the United States Land Commission that the authorities swung back to the old name of Rancho Cañon de Santa Ana. Even then, however, appears a deflection in the name, for the map filed by George Fisher, secretary of the commission, Oct. 9, 1850, gives the name as "Cañon de Sta. Anita."

The name Santa Anita must have had an appeal for Don Bernardo. When and why he used it is now a matter of surmise. In comparison with other ranchos, Bernardo's three-league rancho was undersized. That may have been the reason for calling it Little Santa Ana. Most likely he sought a distinction from Santa Ana, the Olive-Peralta settlement of the Yorbas, and Santa Ana Abajo, the West Orange settlement.

When it came to writing his will a few days before his death in 1858, Don Bernardo used the name of the rancho a number of times, and always it was "Cajón de Santa Anita ó San Antonio." However, the name was down on the records of the land commission as Rancho Cañon de Santa Ana, and it was by that name that the property was finally patented by the federal government.

The fact that Bernardo himself, seems to have used the word "Cajon" instead of "Cañon," is interesting. "A cajón" is usually a certain kind of a "cañon", or as we spell it, "canyon." It is a spreading valley boxed in by hills or mountains, while a "cañon" may more properly be a narrow valley with high walls. Thus, the lower part of the rancho might have been technically in a "cajón." with the upper part in a "cañon." The rancho west of the Rancho Cañon de Santa Ana went down on the records using the word "cajón," it being Rancho San Juan Cajón de Santa Ana, on which today Anaheim, Fullerton and Placentia are located.

In this connection it is interesting indeed to note that in 1882 in a court action, George Hansen, founder of Anaheim, testified that "the Santa Ana river where it comes out near Bernardo Yorba's is called Cajón de Santa Ana because it is a narrow place and widens out from Bernardo Yorba's and the valley becomes wider. In the upper part of the rancho the bed is perhaps 400 or 500 yards wide, and further down from 600 to 800. Down below Burruel's (Olive) it is perhaps 1,000 yards wide."

The hearing on the Yorba petition before the land commission was noteworthy for its simplicity and accuracy. First, the Mexican records were produced. It was shown that following the grant, Abel Stearns was appointed to make a survey of the rancho and to give judicial possession, a formality that was quite necessary under Mexican law.

Called as a witness for the applicant, Stearns said that he had been in California since 1829.

"I am acquainted with the Rancho Cañon de Santa Ana," said he. "It is situated on the northwest side of the River Santa Ana and is bounded by the river.

"At the time of giving judicial possession, Dec. 11, 1834," continued Stearns, "Yorba had a house on the land, in which he lived with his family. He had a stock of cattle and horses. He has resided there ever since. He has always been one of the most extensive cultivators of the land in this section of the county. He has two vineyards and at this time has not less than 8,000 head of cattle, with numbers of horses and sheep."

Perhaps a quotation or two from the decision of the land commission will be interesting:

"This is one of the very few cases which have come under the observation of the board in which the requisitions of the Mexican Colonization law of August, 1824, and the regulations of Nov. 21, 1828, appear to have been strictly and literally complied with.

"So far as appears from the records in this case, this may be considered as perfect title under the Mexican laws, investing the grantee with the full legal estate in the premises granted.

"Upon a view of the whole case we consider it one of the best cultivated claims which has been submitted to us for adjudication. A decree of confirmation will accordingly be entered."

LAND TRANSACTIONS

WHEN California came under the American Flag, by treaty, the United States agreed to accept Mexican titles. Many years passed, however, before titles were put into orderly shape. It was several years before the United States Land Commission began its painstaking investigations, and years more before the judges had settled some of the appeals that went into the federal courts. In some instances, when representations were made before the commission compromises between adjoining claimants were necessary. Sometimes it was found that a ranchero had more land than he thought he had, sometimes his domain was whittled down. Sometimes claims were flatly rejected. As to Bernardo, there was no question raised as to boundaries, yet it seems clear that at an earlier date, he had thought his rancho larger than it eventually turned out to be.

There are on record in Los Angeles county, copied also into the records of the Orange County Title Co., two documents of interest in that regard.

If one may guess as to what was back of these documents, the guess would be that Bernardo Yorba and Isaac Williams, owner of the Rancho Santa Ana del Chino, decided to trade lands, Williams to give

The old adobe San Antonio in 1925, not long before it was torn down.

The old San Antonio adobe in 1905. Picture from C. C. Pierce Collection.

(Title Insurance and Trust Company)

to Bernardo the Rancho Rincón, and Bernardo to give Williams all of the northwest portion of Rancho Cañon de Santa Ana. Evidently, at that time Bernardo, by common consent, was believed to be the owner of what we now know as Telegraph, Soquel and Carbon Canyons, up to the top of the ridge, between Brea and Carbon canyons. This would have put his line four or five miles further to the northwest than it was finally fixed by the Land Commission in 1856 and in subsequent patents.

In the negotiations for the trade, it would seem that Williams wanted a strip along the bottom of Brea canyon, recognized as a part of Rancho San Juan Cajón de Santa Ana, owned by Don Juan Pacífico Ontiveras, who lived in his adobe, located today as not over a half mile southeast of the Santa Fe depot at Placentia. A few rooms of that old adobe still stand on the Pioneer ranch, once the home of Daniel Kraemer, one of the first American settlers in that section.

Perhaps the only evidence we now have as to why Williams wanted the Brea strip is found in Judge Benjamin Hayes's dairy for 1850, in which Hayes, speaking of Williams wrote: "I understand he has lately exchanged one of his ranchos (Rincón) for another near here in which he supposes there are inexhaustible beds of coal."

The first document that appears in the consummation of this trade, is a deed dated Sept. 21, 1849, from Ontiveras and his wife to Bernardo Yorba with a description that today seems exceedingly vague. For "$400 in silver coin" Ontiveras deeded to Yorba, land in Cañada la Brea "commencing from some redwood oaks on the summit of the hills which designate the boundary of his ranchos to a distance of 100 varas outside of where said Cañada commences, and the said 100 varas shall run from the mouth of said Cañada skirting along the hills up to a point parallel with a lone elderberry tree situated at the foot of said hills, thence to the boundary line of Bernardo Yorba, on the condition that neither the grantor nor his heirs shall be deprived of the use and benefits of any and all timber which may be growing thereon, be the same dry or live timber, nor shall they be prevented from pasturing stock upon the aforesaid place."

There is concrete evidence that this particular piece of land became of real interest in 1888 when it passed into the hands of the Los Angeles Gas Co. In the Los Angeles records is an old map, a copy of which is in the files of the Orange County Title Co., that shows the vaguely described land deeded by Ontiveras in 1849 as an accurately surveyed property, showing canyon and hills, cornerstones and exact boundaries. The title is: "Map of a part of Rancho San Juan de Santa Ana, Los Angeles County, Calif. Pointed out by Raymundo Yorba and Tomás as the land described in a deed from Juan Pacífico Ontiveras to Bernardo Yorba of date Sept. 25, 1849, and recorded in Book A, p. 753 of Deeds in the Recorder's Office of Los Angeles County, Cal. Surveyed at the request of the Los Angeles Gas Co. August 1888. by Hanson and Solano." And in the center of the map are these words, "Juan Pacíficio Ontiveras to Bernardo Yorba Sept. 25, 1849, containing 1290.55 acres."

The second pertinent document bears date of Sept. 25, 1849, just four days after the deed from Ontiveras was made. It was signed by Bernardo Yorba and Julian Williams, (oftentimes Isaac Williams used the name Julian instead of Isaac). By that transaction Williams received the land transferred on Sept. 21, from Ontiveras to Yorba, and Yorba also conveyed Cañada del Sausal, "situated in his rancho, fixing as a landmark from the elderberry tree which is boundary of lands sold by Ontiveras and running along the foot of the hills in a direct line to a high hill situated at the mouth of said cañada, hence along the road which crosses the ridge towards Ro. del Chino, taking in all the valley up to the said road where said valley concludes."

When Bernardo Yorba made his claim before the Land Commission Cañada del Sausal was not shown to have been a part of his original grant. In fact, it appears to have been in a wide strip of land eventually declared to be public lands lying between Bernardo's Rancho Cañon de Santa Ana and Ontiveras' Rancho San Juan Cajón de Santa Ana.

The name Sausal does not appear on Orange County maps. It is conjectured that the name has been distorted into Soquel. Probably as originally used the name meant elderberry thickets or willow thickets. The name with varying spelling appears in a number of deeds given by Yorbas during the '60's, sometimes applied to the canyon, sometimes to the hills.

During his lifetime, Bernardo kept the old rancho intact excepting for that one trade with Williams in which Cañada del Sausal passed from Bernardo's ownership, excepting also a right of way for a ditch given just before his death to the founders of Anaheim and excepting also a conveyance dated March 23, 1847, in which Juan Pablo Peralta, son of the first co-owner of Rancho Santiago de Santa Ana, was concerned.

The second of these conveyances will be given attention later. The third, which in point of date, comes first, is of such an unusual nature that it deserves presentation here.

It came during a time when the sons and daughters of the two original grantees of Rancho Santiago de Santa Ana were trying to reach a mutual agreement as to the division of the great rancho. Strips were laid off across the rancho that reached from Peralta to the sea, and an effort was made to get unanimous consent to the allotments. One heir, Ramón Yorba, refused to have anything to do with the effort, and probably his attitude was the chief factor that delayed the division until the courts made it in 1868.

Two of the heirs, however, Bernardo Yorba and Juan Pablo Peralta, must have recognized the strips as legitimate units, for on March 23, 1847, Juan Pablo traded his portion to Bernardo and Bernardo conveyed to Juan Peralta land within the boundaries of Rancho Cañon de Santa Ana. The document shows the terms of trade thus:

First, Bernardo agrees to convey and does convey to Juan Pablo "the orchard on his ranch known as the orchard of Julian Manríquez, which is his (meaning Bernardo's) property and fronts on the public road leading to his ranch, said vineyard containing 3,000 vines more or less and 50 fruit trees, part of them bearing. He will also convey three fields of land adjoining said orchard and which were also occupied by said Manríquez for farming purposes. These lands are divided into three fields or parcels which together have an extension of 800 varas or more."

Second, Juan Pablo conveys "one-half league (approximately 1.5 miles) extending from north to south and whatever width it may have from east to west adjoining the lands of Bernardo Yorba and bounded on the north by a valley known as Timber

Valley, running thence along the bank of the river one-half league, and in length from the bank of the river easterly to the boundary of the Ro. Santiago, the property of Teodocio Yorba."

Juan Pablo agrees that he will not sell the Manríquez property to anyone excepting Bernardo or to Bernardo's heirs.

Bernardo retained the interest in Rancho Santiago de Santa Ana that he acquired from Juan Pablo, and his heirs were accorded that interest in the rancho's division in 1868.

Juan Pablo, however, kept his title to his described lands in Rancho Cañon de Santa Ana for just four days over a year, because on March 27, 1848, he signed away that interest to Bernardo. The deed was brief. It was attached to the agreement of March 23, 1847, and set forth that Juan Peralta "deeming it to his best interests to sell to Bernardo Yorba the property described in the preceeding indenture do now make a formal sale for 200 dollars, being the value of five barrels of grape brandy, the receipt of which is hereby acknowledged."

Thus, Bernardo goes forward with his rancho intact.

The mention of Julian Manríquez's name in this connection is interesting. Manríquez was probably a tenant, possibly a majordomo for Bernardo. In the census report for 1836, printed in the Quarterly of the Historical Society of Southern California for

September-December, 1936, he is shown as a resident of Rancho San Antonio (Cañon de Santa Ana,) aged 35, native of San Miguel, married to María Trinidad Domínquez, aged 30, native of San Juan Capistrano. He is listed in that census as a proprietor of land. The number of years he was connected with the rancho does not appear. In his will Bernardo had occasion to describe the house he was leaving to his son, José de Jesús, as located southwest of the Yorba home, "at that place which of old has been known and designated as, and is more particularly described as la casa de Julian Manríquez." Manríquez received a grant to Rancho Laguna, three leagues, in San Diego County in 1844, and may have occupied that property at that time. He was also a claimant for Rancho Temecula in San Diego County, but seems to have failed to sustain his claim before the Land Commission.

THE CHAPEL AND THE CEMETERY

REALIZING that death was not far distant, Don Bernardo early in November, 1858, made prepartion for the disposition of his ranchos and his herds.

First, however, he deeded to Bishop Tadeo Amat of the Catholic Church, plats of ground upon which were located a priest's house and an unfinished adobe chapel, a garden and a cemetery. It is tradition among the Yorba heirs of today that always Don Bernardo maintained a chapel in the big adobe. It is believed that at one time this chapel occupied the southwest corner of the upper floor of the main structure.

There came a time, however, when a public structure seemed advisable. The story of the beginnings of that chapel, known today as Chapel San Antonio, is told in the deed to Bishop Amat, given by Don Bernardo Yorba and his wife on November 6, two weeks before his death. This deed sets forth the fact that previously a meeting of residents of the Santa Ana and San Antonio ranchos had been held, at which meeting Don Bernardo was president, for the purpose of taking steps to erect a church and priest's house and to establish a garden plat for the priest and to locate a cemetery.

The deed declares that "the church is under construction at the expense of several individuals." The matter of title to the properties desired by the residents who had previously held their community meeting is forthwith settled by the deed which transfers to Bishop Amat three pieces of property:

First, a piece of ground 123 feet 6 inches by 47 feet 8 inches, whereon the church and priest's room are being built.

Second, 100 feet square for a cemetery, the plat selected being "on the hill where are the corrals, called La Mesita."

Third, a garden plat of 50 feet square near the vineyard.

When the time came for making his will, Don Bernardo decided that there need be no further contributions toward the construction of the church. He, through his estate, assumed that responsibility, in a paragraph in his will reading as follows:

"Tenth item: I order and direct that out of my estate sufficient funds be set aside for the completion of the building intended for a chapel which is being erected upon my rancho known as Cajón de Santa Anita ó San Antonio."

Executors of Bernardo's will carried out these instructions. For many years the adobe chapel served the community, as a station of the Catholic Church at Anaheim. The chapel records are held today by the priest at Anaheim. Like other adobes of the neighborhood, the chapel gradually disintegrated, and some forty-five or fifty years ago, it was replaced by the wooden church of today, built a few yards west of the chapel started during Bernardo's last days on earth. Today some mounds of earth, grown over with weeds, and bits of wall remain to mark the earlier chapel.

When death came to rancheros along the Santa Ana river or to members of their families during the half century preceeding the establishment of the new cemetery "upon the hills where are the corrals called La Mesita," burial took place at Mission San Juan Capistrano, at Mission San Gabriel or in Calvary Cemetery in Los Angeles. Indians and Mexicans and others were buried in small cemeteries, the locations of which seem to have been lost, with graves unmarked. A cemetery of that kind was found in the excavations for Prado dam.

With the new Yorba cemetery, the long journeys to far-away cemeteries were no longer necessary.

Bernardo, however, was buried in Calvary cemetery in Los Angeles. Tradition has it that he was carried in his fine coffin by grief-stricken Indian and Mexican retainers, changing pallbearers as they went along. In front was led the don's fine white riding horse, bridled and saddled, but riderless.

In 1923, the march of progress in Los Angeles made necessary the removal of the remains of those who had been buried in Calvary cemetery. Arrangements were made with members of the Yorba family, and with reverence, sixty-five years after his death, the remains of Don Bernardo were brought back to the little cemetery upon the hill, and there, in a spot overlooking the valley, a quarter of a mile from the levelled site of the adobe San Antonio, wherein Don Bernardo lived from 1834 to his death in 1858, is the don's last resting place.

Upon the huge granite monument is a bronze plate giving the names of those whose "remains were removed April 24, 1923, from Old Calvary Cemetery, Los Angeles, Calif." as follows:

BERNARDO YORBA
Son of Jose Antonio Yorba-Josefa Grijalva de Yorba
FELIPA DOMINGUEZ
His Wife

FRANCISCA DOMINGUEZ DE YORBA   **JESUS LUGO DE YORBA**
JOSE ANTONIO YORBA   **FRANCISCA YORBA**
RAMONA YORBA DE WILSON   **JOHN WILSON**
AURELIA ROWLAND   **CAROLINA ROWLAND**

Cut into the granite are four inscriptions in Spanish:

"Aqui reposa El Finado Bernardo Yorva que nacio el dia 4 de Agosto de 1801 y fallacio el dia 20 de November 1858."

"Aqui reposa La Finada Felipa Dominguez y Yorva que fallacio el dia 8 de Septiembre del año 1851 de 37 años de edad."

"Aqui reposa La Finada Ramona Yorva esposa de B. D. Wilson que fallacio el 21 de Mayo de 1849 de 21 años de edad."

"Aqui reposa La Finada Francisca Dominguez esposa de Raymundo Yorva que fallacio el 12 de Sept. de 1850 de 21 años de edad."

The inscriptions do not show which of the numerous José Antonio Yorbas is the one whose remains were brought from Los Angeles.

In this old cemetery, now increased in size to several times the original 100 square feet set apart by Bernardo in his deed of 1858, and still owned by the Catholic church, are buried scores of members of the Yorba and Peralta families. Practically all of the names on the headstones are Spanish, among them: Yorba, Peralta, Domínguez, Carrillo, Botiller, Sanchez, De los Reyes and Ruiz. There are hardly a half-dozen English names there.

Of the children of José Antonio, the first Yorba, Bernardo only is there. Of Bernardo's twenty children, gravestones are there for the following: Ramona Yorba de Wilson, born 1828, died 1849; Raymundo Yorba, 1826-1891; Trinidad Yorba, 1841-1881; Vicente Yorba 1844-1903, beside his wife, Erolinda Cota de Yorba, 1854-1933; Prudencio Yorba, 1832-1885, beside his wife, Dolores Ontiveras de Yorba, 1833-1894; Tomás Yorba, 1835-1896; Marcos Yorba, 1836-1892, and there too, is Ramona Yorba, his cousin and wife, daughter of Tomás Yorba and Vicenta Sepúlveda de Yorba, who as the widow of Marcos, married Juan de la Guerra in 1869 and died in 1911. In an unmarked grave lies Doña Andrea Elisalde de Yorba de Davila. Death came to her about 1908, some years after Don Pioquinto Davila had passed away.

In this cemetery lie Rafael E. Peralta, 1817-1894, and his wife, Catalina M. de Peralta, 1822-1886. Rafael was a son of the Juan Pablo Peralta, who with José Antonio Yorba, was joint owner of the old Spanish land grant, Rancho Santiago de Santa Ana. There, too, is the grave of Andrea, 1835-1922, daughter of Teodocio Yorba, brother of Bernardo. Andrea married her cousin Andrés, son of Bernardo.

Broken crosses, on which inscriptions have long since been obliterated, and unmarked graves are scattered over much of the old cemetery. Here and there pepper trees are slowly spreading their graceful foliage over the graves of Spanish Californians of older generations.

THE WILL IS WRITTEN

PROBABLY no will ever written within the confines of what is now Orange County has figured so largely in after events in court as has the will of Don Bernardo Yorba. It has been pointed out as an example of painstaking attention to detail in making known the wishes of the maker of the will. Historians have found in it many items portraying the way in which Don Bernardo had managed the affairs of his family, many items that picturesquely set forth bits of rancho life as it existed in the '50's.

It may be assumed with reasonable certainty, that the will, written in Spanish, was drawn up under the guidance of Ygnacio Del Valle. In the taking of testimony at the time the will was accepted for probate, Del Valle said that he had read the will to Bernardo before it was ready for signing. The document was executed at the rancho on November 14, 1858. At that time, Del Valle, on instructions from Don Bernardo, made several interlineations, among them being one that directed that the widow, Andrea, should have her own trunks and their contents. The witnesses to the will were Del Valle, Dr. John S. Griffin, and Manuel Domínguez, who testified that Bernardo had sent for him at San Pedro to serve in that capacity.

Dr. Griffin's name is one well known in California history. He came west with General Kearney, took a surgeon's part in the battle of San Pasqual, and in the march of Commodore Stockton's army to Los Angeles. For many years he was Los Angeles' leading physician. At the time of entering Bernardo's will to probate, Dr. Griffin testified that he was the attending physician and that Don Bernardo's mind was clear and unimpaired. Dysentery was the cause of his death.

Very plainly the signature of the don appears on the will, with an upward swing and flourish from the letter d in Bernardo, and with a rubric, such as most early Californians used religiously. Bernardo's resembled a flourishing letter z upon its back. The Domínguez signature carries a rubric, Dr. Griffin and Del Valle none.

It is of more than passing interest that Don Bernardo's signature is Yorva, not Yorba. The will throughout used the letter v. Yet all the probate proceedings used the letter b. In earlier years Bernardo used b as often as v.

The will today rests in the files of the County Clerk's office in Los Angeles. Scarcely dimmed by time, the old document has well withstood the many scores of times that it has been unfolded, examined, copied and translated, for use in court actions, many times in recent years by historians. Its pages are bound together by a thin green ribbon, which also is undimmed by the more than eighty years that have passed since the signing. The binding is sealed with hard red wax at front and back, the front bearing the print of the thumb that affixed it.

The will set aside $500 to be used for the expenses of the funeral and for "the alms for masses which shall be said for the good of my soul."

To his wife, Andrea E. de Yorba, Bernardo left all of the unbroken horses bearing her brand, and "twenty horses of which seven are broken to bridle and spur, two carriage horses, both of them palomino in color, and eleven unbroken colts, all the sheep bearing her brand; two carriages with their proper harness, as follows: That one which is considered as the private property of my said wife and the other one which is known as the largest among them;" two carretas, one with "ruedas de razo" (wheels with spokes) and the other with "ruedas del pais", (home made wheels); half of the furniture, kitchen utensils and dishes, the stove, the nuptial bed with all of its furnishings, a wooden bedstead, and all the trunks considered as the property of his wife with everything contained therein.

This señora was given a half-interest in the grist mill, together with the right to use the "impounded water" and rights in the ditch. The other half of the mill was willed to Prudencio, who, a year later paid his stepmother $2500 for her interest.

"All of this property," says the will, "she, my said wife, shall receive and accept by way of gift and in virtue of her widowhood."

The third item left the widow and two sons, Bernardo and Javier, one square league, half to go to the widow, a quarter to each son.

By the terms of the fourth item, the reader of today can see that Don Bernardo, while directing the disposition of tens of thousands of acres and not less than 13,000 head of stock was making known his wishes in many minute details. To Bernardo and Javier, each is given the trunk containing his own clothes, a wooden bedstead, a mattress and "all the necessary bedclothes," and a riding saddle. Javier was given the best of it, it would seem, for he also was given the trunk containing Bernardo's clothes, with all articles of personal use found therein, and also the don's "own wooden bedstead."

The daughter, Senobia, who in later years became Mrs. Thomas Rowland, was given "everything that is recognized as her individual property, in the house occupied by the family." (The name Senobia is spelled at times Cenobia, sometimes Zenobia.).

Of the broken horses that are considered as theirs, Prudencio, Trinidad and Vicente shall take all. From broken horses considered as theirs, José de Jesús, Andrés and Marcos shall be allowed to select twenty each, and no more.

Prudencio is to be given the piece of ground he has fenced and put in vineyard and cultivated and the lot on which his house is situated. Raymundo is to have the property he has fenced and occupied for cultivation. Daughter Inez Yorba de Cota is to have the fenced and cultivated land and her house at Rincón. Daughter María de Jesús Yorba de Scully is to have the vineyard she has fenced and the lot where her house is. Marcos is to have the fenced and cultivated land he has cared for. José de Jesús is to have a lot and home near the family home known as "la casa de Julian Manríquez," together with lumber that Prudencio owes his father, which lumber shall be used to restore the Manríquez house. An adjoining adobe now being built is to go to Andrés, the house having a living room, two other rooms and a backyard. José de Jesús and Andrés are to have land they have fenced for cultivation, but if any of it lies within the league given Andrea and the two youngest sons, that portion shall not go to José de Jesús and Andrés.

To seven sons, Trinidad, Vicente, Teodocio, Felipe, Tomás, Bernardo and Javier, all minors, and to two daughters, Leonor Yorba de Rowland and Senobia Yorba, a minor, in equal shares the big adobe home is willed that they "may possess, enjoy and use the same forever."

But one bequest was made to anyone not a blood relative, and that read: "I give and bequeath unto the young lady, Miss Susana Domínguez, the trunk containing her clothing, a wooden bedstead and a mattress, with all necessary bed clothing which has been assigned for her personal use, from the time that she has been living with my family until the present."

In the closing paragraphs of his will, Bernardo provided for the completion of the chapel, pointed out that his son, Raymundo, had already been given a number of tame and unbroken horses and therefore no other horses are to be given him; that he had loaned Anastacio Botiller, first husband of his daughter María de Jesús Yorba de Scully, ninety-five female beeves that he might start raising cattle, that the beeves had never been returned, that they are now to be turned over to María Scully; that his sons, Prudencio and Raymundo Yorba, and his son-in-law, Leonardo Cota, are to be executors of the will and guardians of the estates of the minors, the latter estates to be held for each, until the minor is married or of age, that the remainder of the estate is to go in equal parts to Bernardo's twelve sons and four daughters, one of them, Ramona Wilson, being dead, to be represented in the distribution by her son, Juan, and her daughter, María Jesús, who afterward became Mrs. Shorb; that all of them shall "take, enjoy and possess the said property forever, with the blessings of God and my own."

DISTRIBUTION OF ESTATE

THE three executors found the distribution a long and at times, a trying duty. Fifteen years passed before they thought they had finished their work. So far as can be learned, the division of the stock was first undertaken. After the designated selections had been made, the remainder was evidently divided into sixteen parts, with each son and daughter, no doubt, putting his or her separate brand upon the horses, cattle, sheep and burros given to them in the family round-up.

Months went by, then years, and still the tens of thousands of acres of the rancho remained intact. Members of the family seem to have continued to live in their own adobes, if they had adobes, with the big house continuing as the home of the younger children.

Those who had specific lots named in the will, by common consent, in 1862 occupied the places designated. That is, each laid claim to what he thought was his, and continued in possession. The younger sons and the daughter, Senobia, however, had no places they could call their own. Definite lines had never been laid out for the one square league given to the widow and her two children.

During the probate of the will, some of the heirs

gave deeds to plats in which they had an interest, some even deeding away their interest in the rancho. Andrés sold his entire interest in the estate, including his adobe, to Pioquinto Davila, for a consideration noted in the deed as $200. Most of them, however, continued to hold their interest in common. The executors might have sold the rancho, and divided the proceeds among the heirs. It seems likely, however, that no advantageous sale was possible, for here and there over the rancho were pieces of land, including the vineyards and the mill, together with ditch rights, that could not be delivered by the executors. Moreover, most of the Yorbas planned to continue living on the old rancho.

While there was a general understanding as to the location of the square league of land that had been left to Doña Andrea and her two sons, there had been no accepted survey, if any at all, establishing the lines, and there had been no division of the league between Andrea and her sons.

No doubt there was some friction between some of the Yorbas and their stepmother. Part of it may have arisen because Doña Andrea had refused to part with $7,000 that was believed to have been in her trunk at the time of Bernardo's death. She may have rightly contended that she was left the contents of the trunk under the will, and that the money belonged to her. It was never mentioned in the inventory, and may never have existed, yet years later Vicente Yorba in a court action, testified that she had kept this $7,000.

That some action to partition the rancho among the heirs was necessary, must have been evident for years. Finally, the widow for herself and her two minor sons, through their guardian, F.P.F.Temple, brought suit in Los Angeles against the other heirs and against persons who had bought interests of heirs.

There was evidently no opposition to the proceedings on the part of the defendants, for they, too, were anxious for a division. So, on May 2, 1873, an interlocutory decree was signed setting forth the partition interests of all concerned.

With this decree as a basis for procedure, the court appointed a commission of three men, J. D. Bicknell, J. J. Warner and George Hansen, who went to work with George C. Knox as surveyor to set definite lines and descriptions of various allotments selected by them. On the face of it, the task must have been difficult, but they proceeded without any particular trouble. Most of the work of the commission seems to have been done by Bicknell, who eventually was paid $250 for his services while Warner and Hansen were paid $150 each, Knox $750, with $100 being awarded for some extra compensation. Warner's name is one of the best known in Southern California history. He was one of the men who had successfully completed the partition of the Rancho

Santiago de Santa Ana, a half dozen years previously, and was probably as well informed concerning the ramifications of Yorba heirships as was any man available for partition duties.

The first duty of the commission was to get surveys for the particular bequests made under the will. When that was done, it was necessary to partition the remainder fairly and satisfactorily. To that end, the commissioners divided the entire rancho into three classes of land. First class land was that portion clearly suited for agricultural development. The survey showed 467.78 acres in that class. In the second class came grazing land, of which there were 6,686.81 acres. In the third class, 1,673.83 acres, were placed river bottom and land that appeared to be neither good grazing land nor good agricultural land.

It is of more than passing interest and illustrative of the change that has taken place in values and land usage since the commissioners made their survey, for one to note that much of the land designated by the commissioners as third class land is today set to first class citrus orchards. That is true not only on the Bryant property, but also further down the canyon.

The final decree of partition was signed by Judge Sepúlveda on February 3, 1874. That decree of partition will remain forever as one of the most important documents among those that have brought the rancho title down from mission days to the present.

While the estate was in probate, the flood of 1862 washed out all of the Bernardo ditches, including the mill ditch, which was never rebuilt. Here and there along the north bank of the river, the torrent took away pieces of farming land. Part of the old walled vineyard at the foot of the mesa a few rods from the Bernardo home and southeast of the chapel was taken. A piece of land, some fifteen acres, above Aliso canyon that José de Jesús Yorba had farmed, was nearly all washed away.

Executors of the estate in listing assets, showed various sums to have been due Bernardo at his death. Eventually many of these sums were reported unpaid, either because they were outlawed, because there was no evidence of debt or because the creditor could not pay. Among those charged off were the following items: Andrés Pico, $1400; Pio Pico, $400; Teodocio Yorba, $4772; Augustin Olvera, $472; Anastacio Botiller, $2830; Ramón Yorba, $700. The total deduction was $12,213.

After the executors had reported the estate settled, a number of pieces of personal property were reported to the court as discovered, having been overlooked earlier. These articles were four gentle horses that had been received in a trade for a buggy, a copper still, a copper boiler, an iron boiler and an anvil. Offered for sale by the court, the lot was sold to Thomas J. Scully for $200.

In the Yorba estate papers are a number of documents that as a study in values are of interest at this late date. Perhaps the most surprising figures are those found in the appraisements made by Narciso Botello, Francisco Ocampo and A. F. Coronel, all well known Mexican Californians of the middle of the century, surprising for the fact that land values were so low.

As a result of the appraiser reports, the executors charged themselves with cattle, $130,500; horses, $15,633; sheep, $4,971; real estate, $30,625; total $241,399.

The inventory on one occasion listed the real estate as follows: Rancho Cajón de San Antonio, three leagues, $6,000. House, "del uso de la familia," $10,000. Rancho La Sierrita, three and one-half leagues, $4,250. Rancho El Rincón, one league, $2000. Una accion Ro. Santa Ana (meaning one share in the old Rancho Santiago de Santa Ana) $1,000. Una accion Ro. Santa Ana bought from Juan Pablo Peralta (meaning the interest of this Peralta bought by Bernardo in 1847), $1,000; orchards and vineyards, $2,550; an old adobe used for habitation located near the principal house, $100; three houses more, $825; one small house of adobe, evidently on Rancho Sierrita, $100. (A Spanish league is 5,000 varas or 2.63 miles; a square league is about 4,000 acres).

As a matter of comparison in values of adobe

houses, it can be pointed out that in 1857 when Vicenta Sepúlveda de Yorba de Carrillo sought a settlement in the estate of Tómas Yorba, her first husband, she stated that adobe walls around two vineyards at Santa Ana (Olive today) had cost $500 and that the house had cost $3,250.

A count of livestock was reported in Spanish to the court. That list, with a translation, follows: Ganada de todo clase, (stock of all kinds), 10,875. Caballos manzas, (gelding horses broken), 148. Yeguas manzas, (mares broken), 10. Yeguas broncos, (mares unbroken), 358. Potros de dos años arriba, (colts over two years old), 118. Potros de un año, (colts yearling), 48. Mulares de un año arriba, (mules over one year old), 32. Mulares de herradero, (mules branded), 16. Potrillas de herradero, (mare colts branded), 128. Potrancas de un año, (mare colts yearlings), 32. Burras y burros, (jennies and jacks), 17. Boregas de toda clase, (sheep of all kinds), 1657. Mulares manzas, (mules broken), 5.

On one occasion a special appraisement gave the value of 7,000 head of cattle as $12 per head.

On another occasion values reported were: Caballos manzas, $30 per head. Yeguas manzas, $25. Mulares, $35. Garañones de manada, (breeding jacks), $30; burros manderos, (burros for burden), breeding male, $50; burros chicos, (burros small), $7; burros chiquitos (burros sucking), $7; boregas (ewes), $3; boregitas, (ewe lambs), $1.

ANAHEIM AND WATER

ON September 1, 1857, Bernardo Yorba and his wife Andrea set their names to a deed that in later years became a document of supreme importance. The money consideration was $200, which at the time may have seemed sufficient compensation for what no doubt was looked upon by Bernardo as an act of no particular significance. However, that deed was the first in a series of deeds that gave title to Anaheim as the Mother Colony of the Santa Ana valley. It was a factor in the establishment of water rights that today are represented by the Anaheim Union Water Company, which supplies water to many thousands of acres in and around Anaheim, Fullerton and Placentia. This deed figured in the most important irrigation case this area has experienced.

It was the first deed given anywhere in what is now Orange County for a strip of land for the construction of an irrigation ditch.

That document may be pointed out as one that marks the passing of the domination of the Yorba ranchos over the immediate Santa Ana valley. It marks the closing of the old, romantic days of the Mexican dons. It marks the beginning of the breaking up of the ranchos, the beginning of the period of modern settlement, of the founding of villages and towns.

This story might best begin in 1856, with gatherings of a group of Germans who lived in San Francisco. They planned to establish a colony in the south end of the state where they could carry on the business of wine-making. Their plan was to grow their own grapes. They formed the Los Angeles Vineyard Society, a corporation.

Eventually, George Hansen, a Los Angeles engineer, was employed as their agent. In conjunction with John Frohling, of the society, Hansen selected the 1165 acres that became Anaheim, surveying the center of the property into town lots and the remainder into 20-acre vineyard lots. This was in 1857.

At that time, Bernardo Yorba occupied his Rancho Cañon de Santa Ana, which had just been confirmed to him by the United States Land Commission, by later surveys determined to contain 13,328 acres. Just to the west of him, reaching from south to north from the old bed of the Santa Ana river a mile north of the County Hospital of today, to the upper portion of Brea canyon was Rancho San Juan Cajón de Santa Ana, later determined to have an acreage of 35,970, owned by Don Juan Pacífico Ontiveras. Between the two was a triangular strip of public lands, with the south point on the river, reaching to a wide area of public lands east of Brea canyon and north of Rancho Cañon de Santa Ana.

For many years, Ontiveras had been taking water from the Santa Ana river on the west side of the bend in the river, east of Anaheim, and conveying it by ditch to some fields in what is today the eastern part of Anaheim. There Ontiveras had done some occasional farming.

When Hansen looked over the situation, he found that the old Ontiveras ditch would not supply sufficient water for the new colony. He would have to take the water out further up the river. The point selected was a few rods south of the Yorba bridge of today. A ditch from that point to Anaheim would cross Bernardo Yorba lands, then public lands and then Ontiveras lands to Anaheim. It seems certain that at the time the deed was given the purchasers did not know that the ditch would cross public lands. Title was secured later through the use of scrip.

It was arranged that Bernardo should deed to Ontiveras the strip needed from him. That transfer was signed Sept. 1, 1857. The document is indeed worthy of examination, for in after-years Anaheim colonists claimed that by it Bernardo had given them the right to keep their ditch full of water at all times, and that all of the Yorbas and Peraltas and men who had bought interests from Yorba and Peralta heirs on both sides of the river, had admitted that right because over many years no protest was made over the fact that the Anaheim people did keep their ditch full.

Briefly, this deed provided that Bernardo and his wife granted to Ontiveras a strip of land "commencing at a point 100 varas below a dam in said river, and running in a westerly direction to the boundary line of said Rancho Cajón de Santa Ana, the said strip of land herein spoken of to be sufficiently wide for the construction of a water ditch of capacity to hold and convey water sufficient for irrigating 1200 acres of land, and for the passage of a man on horseback on either side of said ditch for the purpose of inspecting and keeping in order the same, and said strip of land not exceeding twelve varas in width; and the parties of the first part shall not be liable for any damage which may be done by reason of cattle, horses or other stock passing there over, and also the right to construct a sufficient dam at the before mentioned point in the said river in order to supply the said ditch with water for the uses and purposes above mentioned."

This deed was followed on September 12 by a deed from Ontiveras and his wife, Martina Osuna de Ontiveras, to John Frohling and George Hansen. The consideration was $2,330. The colony tract of 1165 acres was transferred, together with a strip of land for a ditch from the east Ontiveras line to Anaheim, together "with the privilege of using so much of the water from the Santa Ana river as appertains to their said rancho." On that same day, for $10,

Ontiveras and his wife deeded to Frohling and Hansen all of the rights that Bernardo had deeded away on September 1.

To complete these transactions, Frohling and Hansen had used their own money. Soon afterward, the vineyard society members sent their money down and on October 5, the lands and ditches were made over to the trustees of the Los Angeles Vineyard Society.

"I was authorized to buy land and plant a vineyard," said Hansen years after, "the idea being that I was to remain in charge about three years and do all the work that could be done on the general plan. The division was made before the end of three years as they were desirous of getting possession in time to build their houses and before the maturity of the small crop which we expected, so they divided in the latter part of 1859. In 1860 they came, and in the spring of that year took possession.

"I commenced constructing the ditch in Sept., 1857, with about 20 men. The ditch was five or six miles long, eight feet wide at the top, six feet wide at the bottom and two feet deep.

"When I bought, Ontiveras had three or four acres at his house fenced with poplar trees and willows and he plowed around it and sowed barley.

"The place where I built the dam in 1857 was a few hundred yards below Yorba's house, between the houses of Scully and Prudencio Yorba."

So Anaheim was started. It prospered. For years it was known far and wide as an ideal, successful colony.

A decade went by, and before its end the great Rancho Santiago de Santa Ana on the south and east side of the river was broken up by a court decree of 1868. While some of the Yorba and Peralta heirs held their shares, most of the rancho allotments went to men who had bought the interests of heirs. About 1870, Santa Ana, Orange, and Tustin were founded, and American ranchers were busy developing lands all about those brave pioneer villages. The old ditches that had been used by the Peraltas and the Yorbas for perhaps more than half a century were carrying water to full capacity. A. B. Chapman and Andrew Glassell, Los Angeles lawyers, had several tracts of land, some of which they were selling. They founded Orange, and gave their names to the principal streets. Eventually, they organized the Semi-Tropic Water Company, which supplied water from the river to both new and old land owners, using ditches, in places, that dated back to Spanish and Mexican days.

For a few years there seemed to be water enough for all, but in 1877 came a dry year. The Semi-Tropic ditch was taking water on the south side of the river far above the old Anaheim intake, and claimed to be diverting only half of the surface flow. The other half sank into the sand, and there was none going into the Anaheim ditch, which after 1860 was operated as the Anaheim Water Co., and which was supplying not only Anaheim but also 600 to 800 acres just outside Anaheim.

Anaheim's orchards and vineyards were dying for lack of water. No wonder there was consternation. No wonder there was a lawsuit.

Eventually that court action, famed in the annals of California, was under way. No wonder there was now consternation on the south and east side of the river, for the Anaheim Water Co. went into court and proclaimed that it had the right to have its ditch full of water at all times. As against the successors to Bernardo and as against those who had settled on the other side of the river, it asserted that when the Bernardo deed was given in 1857 it was well known that the buyers had the right to keep the ditch full, and that this right was recognized by all of the Yorbas and all of the Peraltas on both sides of the river down through the years, and that that right had become established by long usage.

Interesting as it is, there is no need in this study to go into great detail concerning the trial. At that time Anaheim claimed its population to be 1300, and its valuation $500,000. Orange was a village of 300 and Tustin 250, Santa Ana between 2000 and 3000. A. B. Chapman estimated that the total population south and west of the river was 5,000. Anaheim set forth the fact that $70,000 had been spent in developing its irrigation system.

Early in the trial, the defendants, including Prudencio, Trinidad, Marcós and Vicente Yorba and Ynez Yorba de Cota, owners of land inherited from Bernardo, north of the river, and the Semi-Tropic Water Co., southeast of the river, asserted riparian rights in the river, and by witness after witness emphasized the fact that water had been taken from the river many, many years before Anaheim was organized and that the river's usage for irrigation had never been given up but had in fact continued unbroken from years before 1825 down to the time of the trial.

There is nowhere any record historically so valuable to students of Orange County history, and none so rich in color as is the record of that trial. Details concerning the lives of the Yorbas and Peraltas, first settlers along the river are found there from the lips of a dozen men who lived in the Santa Ana valley in the '30's and '40's and even back in the '20's. The story of the founding of Anaheim is told by George Hansen and others who were among the founders. Experiences of early days are given by the first American settlers of Orange and Olive.

Judgment in the case was entered by Judge W. T. McNealey on April 14, 1882. It was a victory for Anaheim, a terrible blow to those hundreds of men who had settled on the other side of the river. The Judge issued an injunction prohibiting the Semi-

Tropic Water Co., from taking water from the river when taking it would deprive the Anaheim Water Co., of a full ditch. The action had been previously dismissed as against the successors of Bernardo Yorba.

There was no doubt about the meaning of the decree for it said that the plaintiffs, the Anaheim Water Co.,and the Anaheim property owners,"have a good, perfect and lawful right and title," as against the Semi-Tropic Water Co., to divert from the Santa Ana river "waters enough to keep the said Anaheim Water Company's ditch flowing full at all times and seasons of the year to its utmost capacity of six feet wide at the bottom, eight feet wide at the top and two feet deep, for and during all time to come."

Immediately came an appeal to the Supreme Court. Thereafter came seventeen trying, anxious months of waiting. The landowners under the Semi-Tropic Co., merged by that time into the Santa Ana Valley Irrigation Co., knew full well that the decision if sustained, spelled doom for their orchards. In all dry years and many semi-dry years there would not be a drop of water for them.

It was a reversal, a complete history-making reversal, written by Justice Ross, proclaimed Sept. 27, 1883.

Justice Ross set forth that the Anaheim case and the judgment of Judge McNealey were based on four rights: First, by actual deed from Bernardo Yorba; second, by prescription, because of noninterference; third, by prior appropriation on the claim that when Anaheim took out water there were no others using the water; fourth, by estoppel *in pais*.

As to the first contention, the decision set forth that Bernardo's deed to Ontiveras for the ditch was a deed for a strip of land and not for water; and that, although a part owner in Rancho Santiago de Santa Ana, Bernardo gave no rights as against that rancho; that the only riparian rights transferred to the Anaheim colony were those Ontiveras deeded as owner of the Rancho San Juan Cajón de Santa Ana, which had a footage on the river.

The matter of prescription was settled by the upper court by its finding that there had been plenty of water for both sides of the river until 1877, and the fact that the south and east sides had not protested Anaheim's usage was of no force for the reason that at no time had there been an invasion of their rights. In the third contention, the court found that both sides of the river had used water from the river many years before 1857, and had used it constantly without abandonment. The fourth contention was ruled against because there was no fraud and no turpitude whatever shown; the contention therefore was without merit. In sending the case back to the lower court, the Supreme Court had these words to say: "We think it not improper to suggest, in view of the value of the water in dispute and the large interest at stake, whether it is not advisable for the parties to the controversy to divide the water upon an equitable basis, and devote the money that may otherwise be expended in litigation in the proper development and judicious use of it."

The decision of the Supreme Court did bring an end to litigation, for its suggestion was followed out. A diversion dam was instituted at Bedrock Canyon, where the flow of the river is brought to the surface by bedrock. Connecting ditches having been established, half of the flow went to the south and east side of the river and the other half to the north and west side of the river. That arrangement has been made perpetual. While the Anaheim case had been dismissed as against the owners located on Rancho Cañon de Santa Ana, the principle of riparian rights was settled.

At the time of the decision, there were four companies representing land-owners north and west of the Santa Ana river. While the Anaheim Water Co. had been in the forefront of the battle, the other companies were equally interested in the right to take surface water from the river. One of these was the Cajon Irrigation Co., organized in 1877 to supply water to new ranches on what is now Fullerton and Placentia areas and to some of the Yorbas and to John W. Bixby. Others were the North Anaheim

Canal Co., and the Farmers Ditch Co. A successful effort was made to get all of the interested irrigators into one company. That company in 1884 became the Anaheim Union Water Co., which from that time on has supplied 12,000 acres with water. It uses not only half of the gravity water of the river but also the water from its pumping plants. Water stock goes with the land and cannot be separated from it.

South and east of the river all water rights were incorporated in 1877 in the Santa Ana Valley Irrigation Co., which supplies water for approximately 17,400 acres, all within the boundaries of the old Rancho Santiago de Santa Ana. Like its sister company across the river, the Santa Ana Valley Irrigation Co. water stock goes with the land.

Water is the very life of the widespread valley, the very life of its orchards and its cities. Title to water is even more important than title to land. In the Santa Ana valley, title to both land and water go back directly to those Spanish and Mexican grants of long ago, back to the times when dons rode their horses to the edge of the river and said to their majordomos and their Indian laborers, "Here we make the toma."

GOING BACK A CENTURY

HISTORICAL source material in relation to the Santa Ana valley of a century ago and earlier is limited. True, we have colorful accounts of their visits to Yorba ranchos by Alfred Robinson, William Heath Davis and the artist Visscher, but those accounts are brief indeed. Concerning the Yorbas there is much interesting information to be found in the record of testimony given during the trial of the historic Anaheim water case. That record takes us back to the '20's, '30's and later years. It deals largely with irrigation and farming, and it is far too voluminous for more than a passing glance in this book.

Among the witnesses was Rafael Peralta, son of Juan Pablo Peralta, who with José Antonio Yorba, held the Spanish grant to the Rancho Santiago de Santa Ana.

"I was not born on the Rancho Santa Ana but was weaned there," he said. "I am 64 years old. My father irrigated on that ranch as far back as 1825. He was a partner of the rich Yorba. They used to farm a great deal more than they do now. Antonio Yorba and Juan Peralta were partners in taking out one long ditch. (He referred to the first Yorba.)

"Tomás used to have a vineyard and used to occupy himself in taking care of it and his crops, and his vaqueros used to look after his stock. He cultivated and irrigated corn, beans and wheat. Tomás and Teodocio lived together but they were not partners.

"José Yorba had a large number of servants employed. He cultivated land west of Orange, about a mile long and 500 yards wide. He raised corn, wheat, watermelons, pumpkins and a small variety of beans." (This was José Antonio, 2nd.)

José Dolores Sepúlveda lived on the Santa Ana rancho (at Olive) from 1835 to 1841, after which he was a year in Los Angeles at school.

"Tomás Yorba had a merchandise store and cultivated land," said Sepúlveda. "He had twenty or thirty servants. He used to employ them by the year and pay them at the end of the year. In those years we did not know anything about acres, but it is my opinion that Tomás cultivated about 150 acres to wheat, corn and lentils. Don Tomás was a very energetic man, there was not a man in the country like him. He died in 1845, and when he died this industry did not continue as it had during his lifetime. I left in 1848, and a great many people left with me at the time of the gold excitement. The price of cattle went up. The rancheros did not cultivate as much land in these years because the price of cattle was so high.

"I used to visit Rancho Cañon de Santa Ana in

1835 when Don Tomás would send me on some errand. Bernardo Yorba irrigated considerable quantity of land in the Cañon Rancho. During these years he had a vineyard and corn and beans and wheat, and had a great many servants engaged in cultivation. They worked Indians in those days, a great many of them. They used to pay them by the year at $3 a month. Bernardo Yorba had to maintain all these Indian servants. He used to allow a married Indian about 14 pounds of corn.

"José Yorba had a vineyard, some trees and corn and beans. I used to pass by there frequently going after horses. He had a great many servants."

One of the most interesting stories of the ranchos of a hundred years ago was told by Ramón Aguilar, 79 years of age in 1882, then living at Anaheim.

"In 1835 I commenced living on the Rancho Cañon de Santa Ana, and thereafter for about 14 years I was part of the time with Tomás Yorba and part of the time with Bernardo Yorba. I went to Anaheim in 1866. I was a soapmaker and shoemaker. Also I made saddletrees for vaqueros.

"When I went to work for Don Bernardo he had possession of the Rancho Cañon de Santa Ana, and for the first time opened a ditch there, taking out water from the Santa Ana river. The ditch was quite large, six or seven feet at the bottom.

"On the Santiago de Santa Ana side there were three or four ditches, and José, Tomás and Teodocio Yorba and the Peraltas irrigated. I became familiar with those irrigations in 1834. In 1840 they took out another ditch which ran by the point of the hill, and Teodocio by that means cultivated extra land and sowed wheat and corn.

"The Bernardo Yorba ditch was kept full of water until it was swept away in 1862. Bernardo had a zanja that was used for a mill in 1857 and 1858. The mill ground wheat and corn.

"There was another ditch constructed by Bernardo above the mill. In 1848 Bernardo harvested about 2,000 bushels of corn, beans and wheat that he had irrigated from this upper ditch.

"Bernardo Yorba's ranch was a sort of public place. At the house of Bernardo Yorba there was a barroom where wine and aguardiente were kept for sale. They were sold to travellers."

Trinidad, Prudencio and Marcós, sons of Bernardo, were called as witnesses, and gave detailed testimony concerning ditch operations and crop growing on their father's rancho in the '50's and '60's.

"There were quite a number of Sonorians on the ranch," said Trinidad, "and 25 or 30 families of Indians, all of whom cultivated and irrigated." Another witness pointed out that while Tomás and Teodocio rented out a good deal of land, mostly to Sonorians, Bernardo cultivated his own ground.

Other witnesses included Thomas J. Scully, Pioquinto Davila, and John J. Warner.

F. A. Korn, Theodore Reiser, John Fischer, John P. Zeyn, Benjamin Dreyfus and several other well known Anaheim settlers testified, as did F. C. Hazen, A. B. Clark, E. R. Squires, Henry Watson, Jonathan Watson, Patterson Bowers, Joel Parker and other early-day settlers of Orange and Olive.

The story of the Semi-Tropic Water Co., was told in detail by A. B. Chapman, one of the founders of Orange, making page after page of interesting reading. One bit of testimony was of particular interest in view of the fact that a number of orange trees at San Gabriel are generally conceded to be the oldest orange trees in California.

"Right at Burruel's Point (Olive) is what they call the Tomás Yorba place, subsequently called the Carrillo place, and now called the Watson place. It is a matter of tradition that the oldest orange tree in the state is on that tract. The fruit trees are the largest I have seen."

Following this lead, recently the writer talked to E. C. Conger, who bought land at the point of the hill at Olive in 1889. Where his house now stands were remains of old parts of adobe construction, no doubt part of the Tomás and Teodocio adobes of the '30's, 40's, '50's and early '60's. A few rods north of Conger's house, when he built it in 1889, were the ruins of the old Teodocio Yorba home, a one-story structure, at that time fast going down, surrounded by weeds and disorder.

"When I came here in 1889," said Conger, "there were some old Australian navel trees between where my house now stands and the railroad tracks. I have no knowledge of any old orange trees such as you describe."

So we must pass from the story of the old water suit, its far-reaching decision leaving no question but what the old ranches touching the river had riparian rights that had not been disturbed by the old deeds given by Bernardo Yorba and Juan Pacífico Ontiveras back in the late '50's.

PURCHASES BY J. W. BIXBY

SOON after the decree of partition was entered in the Los Angeles courts, John W. Bixby began negotiations for the purchase of the league of land that had been left by Bernardo's will to his widow and two youngest children. Possibly, and quite likely, the negotiations had been underway for some time. The records indicate plainly that the purchases were furthered jointly, for the deed to the widow's allotment followed the court deed to the minors' allotment by a day.

F. P. F. Temple, guardian of Bernardo and Javier, petitioned the court for permission to sell the 2155.9 acres that stood in the name of the two boys, it being the eastern portion of the Bryant ranch as it stands today. Duly advertised and with bids received the sale was made to F. M. Slaughter for $6,780. The order of court was signed June 1, 1875, by Judge K. S. O'Melveny. The deed was recorded June 24, 1875.

The same day and for the same amount, $6,780, the property was deeded by Slaughter to John W. Bixby. No doubt Slaughter had appeared in the court proceedings as an agent for Mr. Bixby.

On that same day, Mr. Bixby recorded a deed for 3,000.30 acres from Andrea E. de Davila, the widow of Bernardo. According to the deed, the price paid was $9,000.93, by which it may be concluded that the price paid was on a basis of $3 an acre, approximately what had been paid for the 2,155.99 acres taken over from the minors.

That the price was not out of line with other sales made during the period can very well be shown. While romantic historians often look back upon the acquisition of ranch properties from old California families with the idea that the Californians were dealt with unfairly, records show that sales made by Californians were generally at prices comparable with sales being made by Americans to Americans.

It is of interest to point out that the price paid by Mr. Bixby was just about the same as that paid by James Irvine, who came to California in '49, when he bought out his partners as shown by a deed of September 27, 1876. The partners, Llewellyn Bixby and Frank Flint, were paid $150,000 for their half-interest in approximately 108,000 acres.

By the terms of Don Bernardo's will, a sycamore tree became the starting point for the surveys that later established the lines of the present day Rancho Santa Ana. It seems fitting that a native tree of California should have had an important part in an early survey of the property on which today the Rancho Santa Ana Botanic Garden of the Native Plants of California is located.

The third item of Bernardo's will, translated, reads as follows:

"I give and bequeath unto my said wife, Andrea Elisalde de Yorba, and to our two minor sons, Bernardo Yorba and Javier Yorba, one square league of land in that property known as Ro. Cajón de Santa Anita ó de San Antonio. The survey of said league shall begin at an aliso grande (large sycamore) which shall serve as one of the monuments, and is to be found near the river known as Rio de Santa Ana on the camino real (highway) leading from the San Antonio house to the Rincón."

When the Rancho Cañon de Santa Ana was partitioned by the Los Angeles courts, the surveyor, George Hansen, started his survey at a large sycamore tree that he said was pointed out to him by the Yorbas as the tree indicated by Don Bernardo. This tree was located, said Hansen, on the bank of the Santa Ana river, opposite the mouth of Aliso canyon. That canyon, by the way, today bears that same name. It is a name that has been used as designating that canyon for nearly a century, possibly much longer. The crude map filed by Bernardo Yorba when he recorded his petition with the United States Land Commission in 1852, designated the canyon as "Cañada de los Alisos."

In his testimony in the partition case, Hansen was called on to give a detailed description of this important sycamore. He said that it had two "prongs", one measuring three and a half feet in diameter, rising perpendicular from the ground, and the other three feet in diameter, inclined toward the east, forming with the ground an angle of about 45 degrees, and from this sycamore "bears" a cottonwood tree three feet in diameter n. 85 degrees west, 50 links distant.

It was brought out that the location of el camino real in the canyon had been changed by reason of a flood. E. G. Johnson, superintendent of Rancho Santa Ana today, says that he has no knowledge of this tree and believes that it must have been destroyed many years ago.

After his purchases in 1876 from the widow and her two minor sons, John W. Bixby entered into possession of the property, making use of it for stock growing. A number of years went by before the third purchase was made of the three that went to make up his Santa Ana canyon ranch.

This last purchase was for 501.8 acres, just west of the Davila allotment, bringing the west line of the ranch to the place where it is today, near the Horseshoe Bend railroad station and bringing the ranch to its completed area of about 6,000 acres.

The deed for this 501.8 acres was given to John W. Bixby by Benjamin Dreyfus on August 6, 1881. The consideration shown in the deed was $1,300.

This allotment was one distributed in the partition suit to Wolf Kalisher and Henry Wartenburg, who on April 28, 1871, had secured a deed from José de Jesús Yorba and his wife, Soledad Lugo de

Yorba, for all of Jesús' inheritance in Rancho Cañon de Santa Ana.

A small part of the present Rancho Santa Ana lies in San Bernardino county. During his lifetime, so far as the records for the portion lying in Orange county are concerned, John W. Bixby gave only two conveyances. The first of these was to the Santa Ana Valley Irrigation Company, and was for the right to construct a submerged dam. The date was Oct. 11, 1883.

The second was a deed for a railroad right-of-way across the entire ranch to the Riverside, Santa Ana and Los Angeles Railway, the strip to be 100 feet wide "as may be located." The consideration recited in the deed was "$1 and the advantage of a railroad across my land." It was stipulated that the railway must be located, constructed and operated within two years from the date of the deed.

The old partition decree of Rancho Cañon de Santa Ana carried with it what appeared to be definite water rights on the part of the heirs and those who were successors to heirs, but as years went on developments brought about a situation that caused Mrs. J. W. Bixby, as successor to J. W. Bixby, to go into the Superior Court of Orange County, in a determined fight to protect the water rights of the ranch.

The year was 1896. That same year negotiations with James Irvine resulted in securing a definite compromise line between the Irvine and Bixby properties along the Santa Ana river. As the years passed, it had become necessary to fix boundaries by surveyor posts, instead of depending upon a changeable river bed, such as had been used as a boundary line with ease and comfort during Mexican days. The survey found in Recorder's Maps, Book 1, page 37, was made by Charles T. Healey and Richard Egan, the latter being the well known pioneer resident of San Juan Capistrano.

The court action was against the Anaheim Union Water Co., which long before that time had its main ditch from the present intake, down across the Bixby lands, thence through Yorba and on to the Placentia and Anaheim sections. The Bixby interests were represented by Attorneys Chapman and Henricks. The complaint asserted that the Bixbys had been allowed use of water out of the Anaheim Union ditch without question until about 1894. There was also a ditch that took water from a point on the Bixby property. This ditch, while dating back to the Yorba days, was known as the Bixby ditch. At the time of the controversy this old ditch was clogged and out of use.

The issue concerning water rights was forced into the open when Mrs. Bixby found that the ditch company had refused to allow water to be taken from the ditch for the use of a Frenchman who was running sheep on the lower part of the Bixby ranch.

Testimony in the case went back into the organization of the Cajón water district, the deeding of the rights of that district to the Anaheim Union Water Co., at the time that all the irrigation systems north and northwest of the Santa Ana river were put under that company. The Bixbys established their case successfully, and judgment was in their favor.

Judge J. W. Towner of Santa Ana decreed that the plaintiff held riparian rights in the river, that the Bixbys were entitled to take out through the Bixby ditch a reasonable amount of water to irrigate lands under that ditch susceptible to irrigation, and further that the Anaheim Union Water Co., should deliver water for the irrigation of an acreage under the Anaheim Union Water Co.,

Attorneys Richard Melrose and John D. Pope for the Anaheim Union Water Co., took the case on appeal to the Supreme Court. There the Bixbys won, and the appeal was dismissed February 25, 1901.

This action in court led to a settlement of water rights of the ranch, the action itself seemingly having served to bring the question to an issue and final adjustment.

THE CONTESTS OF 1896 AND 1915

ANOTHER court case developed in the year, 1896. Thirty-eight years had passed since Bernardo Yorba died in his adobe mansion on the banks of the Santa Ana river. His heirs had long since occupied their inheritances. Some had sold their properties. Some had died, and in those instances, old rancho lands had been divided among the younger generation of Yorbas.

Twenty-one years had passed since John W. Bixby had taken deeds to the allotments given to Bernardo's widow and two minor sons. Mr. Bixby had died, and his property in the canyon had passed by inheritance to his wife, son and daughter.

Then in 1896 there appeared August Bila of Santa Ana, claiming that the estate of Don Bernardo had never been settled and that he, as purchaser of the rights of Andrea Elisalde de Yorba de Davila, was entitled to a substantial interest in all of the ranchos that had been owned entirely or in part by Don Bernardo.

As one views the records today, it appears that the claim was a flimsy one, yet it was a claim that had to be met in court. Bila himself was not a man of consequence. His voter's registration for 1896 gave his occupation as a laborer.

Bila based his claim on a number of deeds given to him during the year by the widow, who at that time was living at Yorba. As later produced in court, these deeds were extremely broad and all-inclusive. One of them, for instance, was a deed "to all my interest in Bernardo Yorba's estate." Another was "to all my interest in Rancho Cañon de Santa Ana." Bila was represented by Attorneys McKelvey and Bowes, a well known pioneer law firm of Santa Ana. The action was based upon the contention that the widow had been entitled to one-third of Bernardo's estate, but had never received it.

Whether the woman had been paid a sum for the deeds or whether the proceedings were based on a contract by which she would share in the winnings, if any, does not appear. Two deeds, however, recite a consideration of $2,500. That she had at times held out for payment of money before signing quit claim deeds, was shown in testimony given later by Vicente Yorba, who had sold his Rancho Sierra property, where Corona is now located, to a group of men, spoken of in the deposition as the South Riverside people. Vicente said that the buyers wanted a quit claim deed from Mrs. Davila, and when Vicente approached her on the matter, she wanted $500 for her signature. Vicente said he paid her nothing, and declared that the incident did not show that he recognized that his step-mother had any interest in his father's estate other than that long before given her.

The action in court brought an immediate defense from various property owners, among them Mrs. John W. Bixby, and her son and daughter. Some of the Yorbas went into court to fight the Davila-Bila claim. There, too, appeared a group of Santa Ana pioneer property owners, Noah Palmer, Daniel Halladay, Joseph Yoch, W. H. Spurgeon, James McFadden, Levi Gilmacher and Judge J. W. Towner, who found that the title to lands they had bought in the old Rancho Santiago de Santa Ana was concerned.

All of these defendants contended that the estate had been lawfully distributed by 1873, as shown by the discharge of the executors. On a technical point, Bila contended that there had been no discharge. On that point, Bila lost.

The court determined that the widow had long since received her inheritance provided her in the will of 1858, as shown by the decree of court in the partition suit, and by her deed to John W. Bixby.

The decision in the case came in 1897 and was against Bila. Thereafter years went by without a shadow of doubt being raised concerning the title that had been given under the don's will.

Then, in 1915, just fifty-seven years after Bernardo's death, another action was brought, based upon a claim that Bernardo Yorba, Jr., had never received his share of the estate. This action directly attacked the Bixby title to the eastern portion of

Rancho Santa Ana, that is, the 2,155.99 acres deeded to John W. Bixby by Slaughter in 1875.

The plaintiff in the case was Beatrice Arnaz de Johnson, daughter of Bernardo, Jr. This Bernardo married Julia Dryden in Los Angeles, Sept. 28, 1878, died in 1888, leaving two heirs, Beatrice, daughter, and Arturo, son.

Why Beatrice in 1915 became convinced that she might profit by the suit, does not appear. Possibly, it was thought by her attorneys that some compromise settlement could be worked out. No doubt, the woman herself was perfectly sincere in her suit.

No sooner had Beatrice Arnaz de Johnson brought suit, than another claimant appeared in the person of Javier's daughter, Roberta Yorba de Bailey, who seems at that time to have been living in Los Angeles. When the 1896 action was filed it was shown that she was living in Skagway, Alaska.

Between 1896 and 1915 Roberta had figured in a probate contest in the Orange County Superior Court. That story illustrates graphically the fact that the descendants of the original Californian Yorba, Don José Antonio, even by the turn of the century, were scattered far and wide. Those descendants today number in the thousands.

This probate case is No. 2221. The deceased, Javier Yorba, was known also as Xavier Yorba and Javier Francis Yorba. He had departed from the quiet fields and hills of his father, and at the time of his death, May 11, 1900, he was living at Tuxtepec, Oaxaca, Mexico, his occupation listed as an agricultural engineer and he was still an American citizen. He left there a widow, Angela Romero de Yorba, of Mexican birth, and two sons, Alberto, aged 5, and Luis Rodolfo, aged 1 year and 5 months.

By his will, Javier left his estate to the widow and these two sons. At his death, Javier had an estate in Mexico and interest in real estate left in California, that interest consisting of a one-fifteenth interest in ranch property left by a brother, Tomás Yorba. Tomás had died Feb. 18, 1896, unmarried, leaving his living brothers, Vicente, Teodocio G., Felipe, and Javier, and his living sisters, Ynez Cota, and María Scully, and the children of deceased brothers and sisters as his heirs.

In order to secure administration of Javier's share of Tomás' estate, letters were sought in Orange County, by A. G. Hinckley.

Roberta's claim to an interest in Javier's estate, despite the fact that she had not been recognized in his Tuxtepec will, was based on the fact that she was the daughter of Javier by a California marriage. Her mother was Victorine Alphonsine Yorba, who had divorced Javier in Sacramento. She had married Javier as Victoria Carnahan of Tuscon, Arizona. In Roberta's contest, waged for her by Attorney Homer G. Ames, a compromise was entered into by which Roberta received $223.08, one-sixth of the California estate, the remainder, $1,115.41, going to the Mexican widow.

While Roberta, then Mrs. Bailey, appeared in the contest, brought by Beatrice Arnaz de Johnson in Los Angeles in 1915, no hard fight was made for her. Evidently, her attorneys figured that if Beatrice managed to make a case for herself, Roberta would be in a position to assert equal rights. The real contestant was Beatrice.

Her attorneys took the ground that there had been no real discharge of the administrator of Don Bernardo's estate. For the purposes of the 1896 action, Felipe Yorba had been appointed administrator. It was alleged that the judge in the 1896 case had never signed a judgment, that what he had signed was designated as "opinion-order."

On this point, when the 1915 case was decided by Judge J. C. Rives, the court found that there had been a final settlement of the case, and that there was nothing upon which it could be re-opened. Beatrice's attorneys took the case to the Supreme Court, and there Judge Rives' decision was affirmed, and this, the last attack upon titles that had come down under Don Bernardo's will was brought to an end.

TODAY WHERE BERNARDO LIVED

TODAY from the top of the hill that of old was known as the "hill on which Don Bernardo Yorba sits on horseback," we can look out upon the land that a hundred years ago was the center of Don Bernardo's widespread domain.

Down there the easy years went by. There the great herds wandered. On these hills the cattle grazed. In the heat of the day, sycamores along the Santa Ana river offered them shade in which they could lie and chew their cuds. Brown adobe walls enclosed vineyards and orchards. A glistening ditch carried water from the river to the new grist mill and to fields of corn and beans. A carreta drawn by oxen, and loaded with hides, started to the distant port of San Pedro. Smoke arose from the barbecue pits, where beeves were roasted for daily food for those who lived there in the "cajón", and for visitors who sat at the don's tables. Here, on horseback Bernardo Yorba sat straight in his silver-mounted saddle, astride as fine a horse as there was among all the ranchos, a beautiful, high-stepping animal, one that could travel all day and never tire.

Did he dream of a California that was to be, or was he content with his herds, his fields and his family, enjoying his every-day life in this land of mañana?

Here, tradition has it, he made his plans. Here he looked down upon the place that he had made his home, where he believed his children would grow to manhood and womanhood. Here, roundabout, were the river, the valley and the hills that he had come to love greatly.

There below, upon a bit of high ground overlooking the river stood his adobe house, San Antonio. There in the yard the younger children were at play. Yonder, shouting and swinging their riatas rode his boys, in their teens doing men's work with the cattle and horses. Soon they would be marrying, and he would be establishing them in adobes of their own, with cattle brands of their own, and soon they would have children of their own.

Not on horseback today would we travel to the top of this hill. We would take the narrow road that an oil company has built among its wells scattered over the hills, and within three or four minutes after leaving the paved highways below we would be sitting in an automobile upon the very hill from which the hoofprints of Bernardo's horse were obliterated by rains and winds many years ago.

Down there today streams of automobiles hurry along the highway from Placentia and Fullerton. They are crossing the Yorba bridge. They are joining other streams on the highway between Olive and Corona. There upon this modern el camino real more thousands of people are rushing by every hour of a busy day perhaps than ever set foot on Don Bernardo's Rancho Cañon de Santa Ana during his entire lifetime. Close below a railway train rolls by on the tracks of the Santa Fe.

On both sides of the river below us are squares and oblongs of dark green orange groves, some of them owned today by members of the Yorba, Peralta, Domínguez, Travis, Kraemer, Reeves and Locke families, all of them of Yorba blood. Yonder, on small mesas are the brown ruins of the adobes built by Prudencio Yorba and Doña María de Jesús Yorba de Scully in the '50's before the death of their father. Each winter's rains wear the old walls away. To the left afar is the ridge of the brush-covered Santa Ana mountains. Straight across against the sky is the outline of grassy hills unchanged by a hundred years. Unchanged? Not entirely so, for against the skyline off to the right are raised the silver towers of a power line.

We leave this entrancing spot and quickly pass down by the oil wells. There are no cattle, no horses, no burros along the way. We come to the old cemetery. Half a dozen swarthy boys with hoes are at work among the graves clearing away the winter's growth of grass and weeds. During the wet months some of the old crosses have rotted at the base and have fallen. Another ancient wooden fence that surrounded a family plot has gone down. Here in this spot we are reminded of the fact that the long years have been going by, that hereabouts lives have been lived to their end, that here in these sun-warmed hills are sleeping the quiet dead, yet the hum of bees is heard and the laughter and shouts of young boys of Spanish blood ring out, and we are happily aware that even among the graves there is youth and happiness, that the sun still shines upon the cypress and pepper trees.

To the left a little way, a plowman mounted upon a tractor is upturning the earth in a corn field across the place where Don Bernardo's great adobe stood. Too, he upturns squares of floor tile, pieces of black brea and bits of broken china and glassware. Faint ridges mark the lines where the old walls stood.

It is hard to realize that here was the very center of a life in full swing, that here was proudly built the casa of a great don of early California. Still, we can pause for a moment and in imagination see the home as it was long ago. Here, right here, was the spot where Don Bernardo sat each morning to receive the affectionate greetings of his children, one by one. Here, perhaps, the living room; here, the family chapel. Yonder stood the adobe "known of old as la casa de Julian Manríquez."

It is but a quarter of a mile to the present chapel, its white steeple and walls standing high above a mass of weeds and wild shrubs. In the heavy growth, the adobe ruins of the old adobe chapel are hardly visible.

The newer chapel even as a mission of St. Boniface's Catholic church at Anaheim, seems almost to have served out its usefulness. The story is that the local communicants ride by automobile to Anaheim and are worshipping there, and there is now little need for this chapel San Antonio.

We bump over the crude crossing of the Santa Fe, and ride along a lane, with weeds brushing the bottom of the automobile and switching at its sides. A tractor has been run over the grounds close to the church to rid the building of the menace of fire. Windows have been covered with heavy-meshed wire to prevent breakage. A white bit of paper is pinned to the front door. It is a message to children who, it seemed, were to have gathered there that afternoon. The message said that its writer could not get away from the packing-house, and there would be no meeting.

To the rear and east of the church stood the old adobe chapel begun during the year of 1858 and finished under the direction of the executors of Don Bernardo's will. Its walls are nearly all down. Beside the highest corner of the ruined adobe wall treasure hunters have dug a hole four or five feet deep, and beyond the corner are other pits. But a few years can pass before the walls are level with the yard. For many years a most familiar feature of the Chapel San Antonio has been a large white cross planted a few feet north of the church. Photographs taken nearly forty years ago show this white cross gleaming in the sun like a holy light.

It is gone. Where it stood is a pit dug by seekers after treasure.

So, here in this land of yesterday, even the white cross has vanished. Though that be true, yet through all this valley, over its hills and along its by-ways and highways, among the guatamotes and willows and sycamores of the river bottom, upon the mesas and in the cañadas, up there where stood the old adobe and yonder on "la mesita where were the corrals" and where now rest the remains of Don Bernardo, everywhere lingering like a breath of incense is an atmosphere of romance and gaiety and happiness from old California.

THE CHICANO HERITAGE

An Arno Press Collection

Adams, Emma H. **To and Fro in Southern California.** 1887

Anderson, Henry P. **The Bracero Program in California.** 1961

Aviña, Rose Hollenbaugh. **Spanish and Mexican Land Grants in California.** 1976

Barker, Ruth Laughlin. **Caballeros.** 1932

Bell, Horace. **On the Old West Coast.** 1930

Biberman, Herbert. **Salt of the Earth.** 1965

Casteñeda, Carlos E., trans. **The Mexican Side of the Texas Revolution (1836).** 1928

Casteñeda, Carlos E. **Our Catholic Heritage in Texas, 1519-1936.** Seven volumes. 1936-1958

Colton, Walter. **Three Years in California.** 1850

Cooke, Philip St. George. **The Conquest of New Mexico and California.** 1878

Cue Canovas, Agustin. **Los Estados Unidos Y El Mexico Olvidado.** 1970

Curtin, L. S. M. **Healing Herbs of the Upper Rio Grande.** 1947

Fergusson, Harvey. **The Blood of the Conquerors.** 1921

Fernandez, Jose. **Cuarenta Años de Legislador:** Biografia del Senador Casimiro Barela. 1911

Francis, Jessie Davies. **An Economic and Social History of Mexican California** (1822-1846). Volume I: Chiefly Economic. Two vols. in one. 1976

Getty, Harry T. **Interethnic Relationships in the Community of Tucson.** 1976

Guzman, Ralph C. **The Political Socialization of the Mexican American People.** 1976

Harding, George L. **Don Agustin V. Zamorano.** 1934

Hayes, Benjamin. **Pioneer Notes from the Diaries of Judge Benjamin Hayes, 1849-1875.** 1929

Herrick, Robert. **Waste.** 1924

Jamieson, Stuart. **Labor Unionism in American Agriculture.** 1945

Landolt, Robert Garland. **The Mexican-American Workers of San Antonio, Texas.** 1976

Lane, Jr., John Hart. **Voluntary Associations Among Mexican Americans in San Antonio, Texas.** 1976

Livermore, Abiel Abbot. **The War with Mexico Reviewed.** 1850

Loyola, Mary. **The American Occupation of New Mexico, 1821-1852.** 1939

Macklin, Barbara June. **Structural Stability and Culture Change in a Mexican-American Community.** 1976

McWilliams, Carey. **Ill Fares the Land: Migrants and Migratory Labor in the United States.** 1942

Murray, Winifred. **A Socio-Cultural Study of 118 Mexican Families Living in a Low-Rent Public Housing Project in San Antonio, Texas.** 1954

Niggli, Josephina. **Mexican Folk Plays.** 1938

Parigi, Sam Frank. **A Case Study of Latin American Unionization in Austin, Texas.** 1976

Poldervaart, Arie W. **Black-Robed Justice.** 1948

Rayburn, John C. and Virginia Kemp Rayburn, eds. **Century of Conflict, 1821-1913. Incidents in the Lives of William Neale and William A. Neale, Early Settlers in South Texas.** 1966

Read, Benjamin. **Illustrated History of New Mexico.** 1912

Rodriguez, Jr., Eugene. **Henry B. Gonzalez.** 1976

Sanchez, Nellie Van de Grift. **Spanish and Indian Place Names of California.** 1930

Sanchez, Nellie Van de Grift. **Spanish Arcadia.** 1929

Shulman, Irving. **The Square Trap.** 1953

Tireman, L. S. **Teaching Spanish-Speaking Children.** 1948

Tireman, L. S. and Mary Watson. **A Community School in a Spanish-Speaking Village.** 1948

Twitchell, Ralph Emerson. **The History of the Military Occupation of the Territory of New Mexico.** 1909

Twitchell, Ralph Emerson. **The Spanish Archives of New Mexico.** Two vols. 1914

U. S. House of Representatives. **California and New Mexico: Message from the President of the United States, January 21, 1850.** 1850

Valdes y Tapia, Daniel. **Hispanos and American Politics.** 1976

West, Stanley A. **The Mexican Aztec Society.** 1976

Woods, Frances Jerome. **Mexican Ethnic Leadership in San Antonio, Texas.** 1949

Aspects of the Mexican American Experience. 1976
Mexicans in California After the U. S. Conquest. 1976
Hispanic Folklore Studies of Arthur L. Campa. 1976
Hispano Culture of New Mexico. 1976
Mexican California. 1976
The Mexican Experience in Arizona. 1976
The Mexican Experience in Texas. 1976
Mexican Migration to the United States. 1976
The United States Conquest of California. 1976
Northern Mexico On the Eve of the United States Invasion:
　　Rare Imprints Concerning California, Arizona, New Mexico, and Texas, 1821-1846. Edited by David J. Weber. 1976